THE GARMENTS OF SALVATION
Orthodox Christian Liturgical Vesture

The Garments of Salvation

Orthodox Christian Liturgical Vesture

Krista M. West

ST VLADIMIR'S SEMINARY PRESS
YONKERS, NEW YORK
2013

LIBRARY OF CONGRESS CONTROL NUMBER 2013940518

Cover image: Portion of mosaic icon from the church of Sant' Apollinare in Classe, Ravenna, Italy, circa 6th century. Photo property of the author.

All photographs and sketches are the property of the author, unless otherwise indicated.

Copyright © 2013 by Krista M. West

ST VLADIMIR'S SEMINARY PRESS
575 Scarsdale Road, Yonkers, NY 10707
1–800–204–2665
www.svspress.com

ISBN 978–0–88141–477–6 (paperback)
ISBN 978–0–88141–478–3 (hardback)
ISBN 978–0–88141–479–0 (digital)

All Rights Reserved

PRINTED IN THE UNITED STATES OF AMERICA

To my own hundredfold:
Alban, Josephine, Honoria, and Georgia

Table of Contents

Acknowledgments		9
Foreword		13
Prologue		15
CHAPTER 1	*Longing for Paradise*	21
CHAPTER 2	*Of Tunics, Togas, and Tradition*	41
CHAPTER 3	*The Garments of Salvation*	79
CHAPTER 4	*The Paraments of Paradise*	127
CHAPTER 5	*A Meadow in Full Bloom*	165
CHAPTER 6	*Woven unto Life*	199
Afterword		243
APPENDIX A	*Care and Laundering of Orthodox Liturgical Vestments and Paraments*	247
APPENDIX B	*Liturgical Color Rubrics*	253
APPENDIX C	*Vesting Prayers*	257
APPENDIX D	*Glossary*	267
APPENDIX E	*Sketches of Fully Vested Clergy*	273
Bibliography		277
Index		287

Acknowledgments

Writing a book is a long exercise in discovering how little you know and how dependent you are on the kindness of others. If one thinks he is an island, he has only to write a book to find otherwise. I would never have written this book if I had not been helped along the way by many kind and generous people. My thanks belong first to Fr Chad Hatfield, Dean of St Vladimir's Orthodox Theological Seminary, who originally approached me about writing a book on vestments following my lectures at the seminary, and to his staff.

Once having begun this rather daunting task, Gretchen Brown's expertise as a librarian and cheerful willingness to discuss the book was invaluable. The staff of the Multnomah County Library system consistently went above and beyond the call of duty, allowing extra lending time on certain books and even shipping reference books to my home so I could study them at length.

To my gracious and insightful proofreaders, Fr Zosimas of Xenophontos Monastery, Nektaria Blalock, Presvytera Dr Eugenia Constantinou, Rev. Dr Chrysostomos Nassis, Prof. Christos Karydis, and Gretchen Brown, I owe many thanks as the book was much stronger for their contributions. Translation work was an especially thorny problem for me as I do not have command of any scholarly languages, so I am grateful to Fr Kilian Sprecher, Rev. Dr Chrysostomos Nassis, Fr Patrick O'Grady, and Fr Alban West for their translations and comments on certain texts.

Dmitry Shkolnik generously advised me on iconography for the cover of the book. I thank Leslie Schaill for setting my feet on the path of ecclesiastical tailoring and for being such a demanding teacher. To my wonderful clients, I thank you for constantly challenging me to become better at my craft and to keep searching for the answers to your questions.

I owe a special debt of gratitude to His Grace, Bishop Anthony (Michaels), with whom I have shared many inspiring conversations over the years about the importance of vestments within the liturgical life of the Church. Dr Warren Woodfin kindly answered my most trivial emails and graciously shared his wide knowledge of the study of Byzantine vestments, Prof. Christos Karydis provided information on the conservation of Orthodox textiles, and Eleni Vlachopoulou provided helpful information about the history of liturgical embroidery as well as reviewed Chapter Four.

My dear friends Nektaria Blalock and Athanasius Blalock cheerfully and enthusiastically reviewed the text and prepared the manuscript. I am also grateful to those who showed me hospitality during my trip to Greece and Italy in September 2012 for research: Dimitris Bales, Gerontissa Theophano and her Sisterhood of the Panagia Odigitria Monastery in Portaria, Greece, the sisters of Holy Trinity (Agios Nektarios) Monastery in Aegina, Greece, the Giagmouris family, and the Nassis family.

For their ongoing encouragement, support, and prayers, I would like to thank Athanasius and Nektaria Blalock, Alexandra Obeid, Gerontissa Efpraxia and her Sisterhood of St John the Forerunner Greek Orthodox Monastery in Goldendale, Washington, Gerontissa Theophano and her Sisterhood of the Panagia Odigitria Monastery in Portaria, Greece, Mother Sergia and her Sisterhood of Presentation of the Virgin Mary Monastery in Marshfield, Missouri, the parishioners of St George Orthodox Church in Portland, Oregon, and my in-laws, Don and Karen West and Gregory and Melanie Nickel. I am especially indebted to the generosity of Karen West and Melanie Nickel who were always willing to help tend my home fires while I was writing. Their constant and unfailing support was an outpouring of their love for me and my children and I am deeply grateful for it. To my three beautiful daughters, Josephine, Honoria, and Georgia, my heart overflows with thankfulness for your ever-cheerful encouragements and your willingness to share your mother with others, even when it meant you had to give of yourselves.

But my deepest and most heartfelt thanks go to my dearest friend and beloved husband of twenty-five years, Fr Alban West, without whose steadfast encouragement, rigorous editing, and ever-willingness to discuss all-things-vestments this book would never have come to fruition.

Khouria Krista M. West

Foreword

Kh. Krista West's book on the origins, history, and theological meaning of Liturgical vestments is both an intellectual and spiritual achievement covering many academic disciplines at once: it is engaging history that traces the civil lineaments of what finally became sacred vestments; it is systematic theology true to holy tradition, teaching you can touch; it is evangelical in that it proclaims the faith in fabrics; it is pastoral, showing how we as members of the clergy are chosen to "put on glorious apparel" as a reflection of Christ Who sits at the right hand of His Father.

    She has structured the text of her book so that the theological outline for vestments in the first chapter permeates and legitimizes the other chapters, grounding her discussion of how clothing developed into garments exclusive to worship in a startlingly spiritual framework. So the reader gains a pious experience from reading these words. We can reverence the beauty of the aesthetics of liturgical clothing and ornamentation and realize, through that reverence, an ascetical dimension to the practice of our own faith. I thought that the external and sanctified clothing we put on our bodies must somehow co-ordinate with the inner man of the soul that St Paul talks about in his letters to the churches. The tempered passions of the soul match the luster of textiles. The luminous things I put on to serve the services are rays of the light that shine out from my heart. Kh. Krista writes: "some of the most ornate and elaborate vestments in use today can be seen in the churches of what is, paradoxically, one of the most austere settings in the world: the monasteries of the Holy Mountain. Such devotion to material beauty by those who have found their calling in a life of liturgy and prayer is surely a further witness to the understanding within Orthodox Christianity that physical matter is not only redeemed, but also has a vital role to play in the salvation of mankind." Asceticism diminishes carnal needs to embellish heavenly goals. The material makes palpable the ethereal.

The craftsman who makes vestments is like the artist who writes or paints icons, as she lyrically describes here. The iconic nature of both tailor and painter displays the picture of His presence everywhere in the Church. After reading this book my perception of priestly ministry expanded. Kh. Krista helped me see offerings everywhere. Now I know that "prosphora," the bringing out or bringing forth, is giving my gifts to Christ to use as He wants, and that "anaphora," the lifting up of myself as an offering of my life to Life Himself, is an essentially priestly vocation that everyone has, since everyone is made in the Image and Likeness of God. All material things, once transformed into both functional use and sacramental meaning by us, have a transcendent destiny, liberating them through art and skill and training, from their earthly settings and giving them wings for an ascent to heavenly places.

Kh. Krista has been my teacher. It is an honor for me to introduce this essential book.

Rt Rev. Bishop ANTHONY (Michaels)

Prologue

I began my career as an ecclesiastical tailor in the winter of 1995, two years after my conversion to the Orthodox Christian Church. I found it a vocation filled with much hard work, but much joy, as I began to understand and recreate the garments that had been part of the Church for almost two millennia. As time went on and I had a wider circle of clients, I found myself fielding all sorts of questions: Which color is the best for Lenten vestments? Where did the exorason come from? Sometimes I knew the answer, but more often than not I had no idea how to answer these inquiries. I began searching for books on Eastern Orthodox Christian vestments, but with the exception of one or two brief surveys, there did not seem to be much available in English on the subject. I cast my net a little wider and began reading anything I could find on vestment history, which led me to works focused almost exclusively on vestments of the Western tradition. Several of these volumes were written in the late nineteenth century by Victorian, self-styled scholars who, while offering panegyrics on the wonders of Western vestments, would also occasionally present a small, poorly researched chapter on Eastern vestments. I found in these works a prevailing presumption that Eastern Orthodox Christian vestments had their origin in Western vestments, when a basic survey of early Church history suggests that it had to be the other way round.

Being a bookworm from childhood, I found that this lack of information rather shook my sure and steady faith in the power of books. So, in desperation, I began at what I thought of as the beginning, searching out books on the garment history of the ancient world. It was here that I found many gems of knowledge, and these books began to inform my study of Orthodox liturgical garments. Before I knew it, I was traipsing through textbooks on natural dyes, travelogues from nineteenth-century Russia, and doctoral dissertations on the Byzantine silk industry. I traveled to Crete to participate in conservation work being done in a local monastery so that I could see very old vestments firsthand, something virtually impossible in America. One fascinating topic seemed to lead to another and I realized that I had the makings of a book on Eastern Orthodox vestments. But, despite my groaning bookshelf and sheaves of notes, I was hesitant to begin. After all, I am just a tailor, someone who spends her days measuring and cutting, buying buttons, and drafting patterns. I do not have any letters after my name and I certainly am not a scholar.

However, simultaneously with my historical research, I was becoming more and more aware of the spiritual significance of vesture. I began to recognize vestments as integral to Orthodox Christian praxis in the same way that an altar faces east or the Pantocrator icon is depicted in the main dome of a church, and integral to Orthodox Christian theological expression in the same way that the veneration of icons manifests our belief in the Incarnation. Vestments are not simply "pretty clothes," they are absolutely essential to our celebration of the Divine Liturgy, one of the ultimate expressions of material theology in the Orthodox Church. On a personal level, my tailoring work was slowly changing my life, bringing me peace of mind and a delight in work that I had never imagined possible. There was something in this work that was beyond my own hands and it compelled and intrigued me.

These two parallel tracks merged into a single road when I met the twentieth-century iconographer, chanter, and Byzantine artistic theorist *par excellence,* Mr Photios Kontoglou. Somewhere between the Victorian vestment writers and the Russian travelogue, I discovered a wonderful little volume of Kontoglou's writings, *Byzantine Sacred Art*, edited by Dr Constantine Cavarnos. With the first paragraph I knew I had found truth:

> Byzantine art is for me the art of arts. I believe in it as I believe in religion. Only this art nourishes my soul, through its deep and mysterious powers; it alone quenches the thirst that I feel in

the midst of the arid desert that surrounds us. In comparison with Byzantine art, all the others appear to me trivial, "troubling themselves about many things, when but one thing is needed."[1]

Reading through Kontoglou's writings was sheer joy. Here I found deep resonance with my own experience of this work—that somehow, these physical things, crafted to ornament and beautify the Church, are vitally important and are, in fact, necessary for our full experience of the Kingdom of Heaven on earth. I found Kontoglou's bold statements particularly refreshing since they are diametrically opposed to the assumption I had encountered all too often that vestments are a sort of liturgical afterthought or an unimportant detail that might be casually modified or updated. My heart cried "amen" as I read:

> Let those who want innovations and who seek secular delight from the Liturgy note what I have just said. They are wrong in thinking that the form of a church and its vessels, the character of its psalmody, its iconography, and the vestments of the priests have only a "nonessential" significance. These things cannot be changed to accord with the conceptions of churchgoers who take as a standard for them the secular spirit of each epoch. They have this idea because—I repeat it—they regard these things as conventional human creations, not as permanent, eternal, and true expressions of the one and only spirit of the Orthodox faith. For them the form of the holy icons, the character of church psalmody, the architectural form of the church, and so on are simply "aesthetic" inventions of the men who created them out of their sensibility and imagination. They do not know that these are truly works of the Divine Spirit, made with the hands and the

---

[1]. Constantine Cavarnos, *Byzantine Sacred Art* (Boston, MA: Institute for Byzantine and Modern Greek Studies, 1985), 17.

sanctified minds of the faithful, truly *spotless archetypes* by means of which the divine essence of the Christian religion becomes apparent and palpable to the senses. . . . They are sentimentalists who want "aesthetic", secular, superficial experiences, and who do not distinguish the *holy* from the secular, *contrition* from aesthetic experience. For them singing and psalmodizing, painting and iconography, literature and hymnography, the theater and the church are one and the same thing.[2]

I began to fear that if we did not endeavor to comprehend the spiritual significance of our vestments, the Orthodox Christian Church could be subjected to a simplification or, worse yet, a rejection of tradition similar to that experienced in the Western communions. Prior to the mid-twentieth century, beautiful vestments were still in use in many Western communities. Fine Italian and English brocades, exquisite embroidery, velvet work: all were considered appropriate and even necessary to the celebration of the Eucharist. However, in the late 1960s Western vestments began to be simplified, which turned out to be quite a slippery slope given that today—not two generations since—the plain, novel or costume-like vestments used in many Western communities could scarcely be recognized as cousins of the wondrous vestments of previous ages.

Having been privileged and blessed to participate in the beautiful, glorious, and heavenly vestment tradition of the Orthodox Christian Church, I felt I had to defend this tradition to the best of my ability. Kontoglou's writings were my clarion call, my reminder that the brocades and silks under my scissors were going on to a life of mystic significance and that anything I could do to further an understanding of their importance was a worthwhile endeavor, despite my own personal shortcomings. After all, it was Kontoglou's own completion of over 5,000 square meters of iconography that had informed his insights into Byzantine art. Inspired by his example, I began to understand that

---

2. Cavarnos, *Byzantine Sacred Art*, 126.

the greatest disadvantage I had in writing a book on vestments, that I am no scholar but a mere tailor, might be the very thing to give at least a small measure of veracity and insight into the world of Orthodox Christian vesture. So I humbly present this volume in the hopes of making better known the sublime beauty of our hieratic vestment tradition.

Thank you, Mr Kontoglou.

Khouria Krista West
Portland, Oregon
2013

Chapter One

Longing for Paradise

Liturgy consists of the various means whereby the church makes it possible for the faithful to experience through their senses the mysteries of religion, that is, the sweetness of the kingdom of God. These means are material: the church building, the vessels, hymnody, psalmody, iconography, the vestments of the priests, and so on. All these things have gradually taken a holy form, on which has been stamped the mystical seal of the Spirit. In other words, they are not works of chance human preference but of mystical activity.

Photios Kontoglou, *Byzantine Sacred Art*[i]

Heavenly Beauty and the Soul

When we enter an Orthodox Christian church, we are entering into the Kingdom of Heaven. To the modern mind this statement might seem a somewhat quaint and naive construct fashioned to provide a sort of spiritual, theatrical backdrop to worship, but the theology of the Orthodox Christian Church makes quite clear that the physical church is really and truly a manifestation of the Kingdom of Heaven and, as such, serves as the intersection between this present, earthly life and the heavenly life to come. Orthodox Christian tradition maintains that the very angels of God surround the altar and fill the church continually and that when we come to celebrate the Divine Liturgy we are not creating something of our own but are entering into a celebration that is already well under way. This conviction that the church building is a true outpost of the Kingdom of Heaven on earth forms the basis for our understanding that vestments, as well as other adornments, serve a divine and holy purpose. They do not exist simply to look pretty or to dress up an otherwise bare church interior, but are in actuality a manifestation of the beauty and glory present in the eternal Kingdom. They are not there simply to remind us of Heaven or, in a more modern construct, to represent Heaven; they are there to participate in the reality of Heaven on earth. As one writer has explained, "The cosmic matter of the sacraments [is] not accidental. The simplest things conform to a very precise destiny. Everything is an image, a likeness, a participation in the economy of salvation; everything is a hymn, a doxology."[ii]

Much of the beauty of an Orthodox Christian church building comes from the layering of adornment found therein. The first layer of this adornment is the church's orientation to the east, manifesting our spiritual orientation to the Morning Star, Christ our Lord and his position as the "comprehensible Sun of righteousness [which] appeared on Earth in those regions of the East where the perceptible sun rises."[iii] The next and most substantial layer is formed by the architecture of the building, a style that dates back to early Christian centuries and, in its purest form, aims to evoke an "outside-in" experience, meaning that,

> The Byzantine architect was more concerned with the decoration of the interior of the church than with that of the exterior. Externally the Byzantine church is relatively plain, free of all superfluity, while inside it has an unsurpassed wealth of decoration. As a Christian church, it "could not be, like the temple of the heathens, a dwelling of a god according to the prototype of the dwellings of men," that is, a mansion built out of marble, but had to become a miniature of the universe, because in it dwells the one and only God.[iv]

Once inside the "miniature universe" of the church, the senses are overwhelmed by layer upon layer of decoration: iconography which adorns the walls, domes, and ceilings with powerful images of the saints, the Mother of God, and events in Christ's life; beautifully carved icon screens, altars, sacrament tables, icon stands and their embroidered coverings; and elaborate marble and tile work. Finally, in chant and liturgical vestments, we find special layers of adornment in that these require a living human presence: chant requires voices and vestments must be worn. These multiple layers of beauty in an Orthodox Christian church work together to create a most compelling and harmonious expression of the Kingdom of Heaven, a mystical and awe-inspiring place, a veritable microcosm of heaven on earth.

Through the beauty of the church the human soul is drawn toward *theosis*, or union with the Holy Trinity. Man, created in God's image, forever experiences a longing for the beauty of his Creator and thus knows a sense of peace and grace when he sojourns within the church, the heavenly dwelling place of the Creator God. While the natural beauty of the world, such as might be found in a restful forest or a rushing waterfall, may also inspire this desire for *theosis*, it is in the beauty of a church that the fullest expression of beauty is to be found. In the traditions of the artistic forms of architecture and adornment that have been handed down for generations are found a stability that nourishes the soul amidst the inconstancies and whims of the current age.

The sublime beauty found within the church is understood to be the pinnacle of beauty because it is physical matter transformed from its earthly state to a heavenly reality, much as bread and wine assume a mystical identity in the celebration of the Eucharist. This spiritual beauty draws the creature to his Creator and inspires man to strive and struggle in spiritual *ascesis* to draw continually closer to his God. Not only an inspiration but also a source of spiritual nourishment, the beauty of the church refreshes and restores the Christian along his journey, and the church, with its requisite beauty and adornment, becomes his fortress, protection, and encouragement as he advances on the path of salvation.

One of the hallmarks of beauty within the Church is its quality of "unending gladness and delight." There is a peaceful quality to the beauty in the Church as expressed in her architecture, chant and adornment that is restful to the *nous*, that part of our being that meets and knows God for who He is—our Creator and Savior. The beauty of the Church is not sentimental or emotive. There are no jarring or discordant melodies or motifs, but rather a sweet gladness, a joyful delight that keeps one coming back for more. The colors are exquisite and compelling, the sounds are prayerful and fascinating, the space is one of purity and harmonious repetition. There is a depth and richness to beauty in the Orthodox Church because her beauty does not originate from the exterior, which is the physical, corruptible world, but rather from the interior, which is the spiritual, incorruptible world.

While the earthly church temple grants man access to the heavenly realm, so also it is in the physical space of a church that Christ incarnate comes to man in the Eucharist. Through the Incarnation and Resurrection of Christ the entire created world experiences redemption and resurrection, no less the very trees, stones and fibers that are the earthly elements of our church buildings. An Orthodox Christian enters a church and sees the priest adorned in glorious apparel and he gives thanks that Christ so raises man up from his sinful state to such glory. He has before him the living proof that he is a son of God by adoption and has been given garments of honor and majesty, despite his ever-present sinfulness. Such awareness of Christ's great love and mercy in turn humbles man and causes him to desire even more to approach the Creator of All. A great, cosmic interchange is opened up between man and God in the physical space of a church that allows the fallen Adam to enter once again into Paradise, the rightful place he was created to inhabit. This truth is best described in a hymn of the *Lenten Triodion* for Forgiveness Sunday:

> O precious Paradise, unsurpassed in beauty, tabernacle built by God, unending gladness and delight, glory of the righteous, joy of the prophets, and dwelling of the saints, with the sound of thy leaves pray to the Maker of all: may He open unto me the gates which I closed by my transgression, and may He count me worthy to partake of the Tree of Life and of the joy which was mine when I dwelt in thee before.[v]

One of the primary qualities of beauty in the Orthodox Church is that it is God-created, not man-made. To fully participate in the return to Paradise through the grace-filled beauty of the Church, we must first and foremost grasp that true beauty is a manifestation of the energies of God. As can be seen in the hymn quoted above, Paradise is surpassingly beautiful and wondrous because it is "built by God" and contains not only visual appeal, but also deep, lasting spiritual joy and gladness. It is in no way artificial or superficial, but rather is entirely and ultimately true and profound. The artisans of our Church—iconographers, chanters, woodcarvers, and tailors—have performed their work throughout the centuries in the full knowledge that they create nothing out of their own fallen and sinful human existence, but rather labor in cooperation with the Divine energies to produce works that are ultimately "built by God."[1]

The Church's artistic traditions have been shaped and formed over many centuries and are not the work of any single person, but rather they incorporate the inspired efforts of a long line of artists and craftsmen, all working as a community within the forms handed down from one generation to another through the grace of the Holy Spirit. Despite the modern misconception that such limitations on individual creativity lead to ossified and stilted artistic forms, working within such bounds has created some of the most sublime and compelling art the world has known. Consider the mosaics at Ravenna with their masterful technique, each tessera set at a precise angle to cause a specific reflection of light, or wonder at the silk brocades of the Byzantine era whose quality and design have never been replicated, or simply contemplate the stunning architectural grandeur of Constantinople's Agia Sophia, and one cannot help but come to the conclusion that something dynamic occurs when an artist works within the confines of tradition. The true craftsman of

---

1. Artistic self-expression is not valued in Orthodox Christian tradition because such human self-expression is considered simply too limited to express the beauty of God. As the eminent Byzantinist Henry Maguire states, "One of the guiding principles of Orthodox church art was that artists did not invent" (Paul Stephenson, ed. *The Byzantine World* [Oxford: Routledge, 2010], p. 322), meaning that Byzantine artists worked within a tradition of highly circumscribed forms, rather than pursuing creative invention for its own sake.

the Church understands that his goal is not to create something from his own limited human imagination but rather to serve and perpetuate an ultimately God-created, not man-made, tradition. Kontoglou makes the following comments regarding iconography, but their meaning can readily be extrapolated to other types of adornment within the Church:

> The works of Eastern iconography attained an hieratic perfection and venerable stability which can be accounted for by the faith which painters had that their work was fearful, like the dogmas of the Church. For this reason, they worked with humility on the archetypes which had been handed down to them by earlier painters, without inopportune and inappropriate changes. To this stability, which we see in their works, contributed the fact that they painted in every church the same forms, century after century. In this way they developed forms which were more and more stable, because through elaboration they were freed from everything superfluous and inconstant.[vi]

Heavenly beauty that nourishes the soul is to be found not in innovation, but in the venerable forms vouchsafed by holy Tradition.

Incarnational Theology and the Beauty of the Church

As we consider those distinctions which make the beauty of an Orthodox church building unique, we discover yet another quality of true beauty in the Orthodox Christian conception: its participation in the Incarnation and Resurrection of Christ. Orthodox Christian theology begins, continues, and ends with the Incarnation and therein finds its understanding of the material world. Metropolitan Kallistos (Ware) emphasizes the importance of matter within the Orthodox Christian theological schema: "It is the human vocation to manifest the spiritual in and through the material. Christians in this sense are the only true materialists."[vii] Through the incarnation of the eternal

Logos, the Creator God takes on the matter of the earthly world in order to save us, His creation. We do not repudiate the world or earthly matter, but rather we recognize that this matter has been redeemed and resurrected for our eternal benefit through the saving death and resurrection of Christ, who took on matter in order to achieve our salvation. This understanding is of vital importance to any study of vesture within the Orthodox Christian Church as it places liturgical vestments in their proper theological category as "images" and demonstrates that vestments (as well as the other images in the Church, such as iconography, architecture, and chant) are not mere physical adornments meant to please the senses, but have as their ultimate purpose the manifestation of grace as a means to salvation. As St Germanos instructs us, "In this way earthly things imitate the heavenly, transcendent, the spiritual order of things...."[viii]

At various times throughout Christian history there have been misguided reactions against the material world, from the iconoclastic heresy of the eighth and ninth centuries, with its rejection of sacred images, to modern-day Protestant sects that consciously eschew any type of vestments, iconography, or physical adornment of their meeting spaces. From such an anti-materialist viewpoint, any kind of thoughtful consideration of the beautification of the church is seen as a shallow pursuit, beneath the notice of the true believer whose mind should be on higher, more ethereal things. This type of deliberate abandonment of imagery or adornment views the material world as superfluous and nonessential and is, at its heart, a sort of Manichaeism, a heresy which rejects the physical body and matter and instead promulgates a hyper-intellectualized spirituality, a faith experienced solely with the mind and having no interaction with the created world. This false teaching has crept into Christendom throughout the ages in various guises. In the eighth century, facing the anti-materialist bias of the iconoclast heretics, St John of Damascus was compelled to explain the Orthodox view of matter by stating:

> I do not worship matter; I worship the Creator
> of matter who became matter for my sake, who
> willed to take His abode in matter; who worked

> out my salvation through matter. Never will I cease honoring the matter which wrought my salvation! I honor it, but not as God.... I salute all remaining matter with reverence, because God has filled it with His grace and power. Through it my salvation has come to me. Was not the thrice-happy and thrice-blessed wood of the cross matter? Was not the holy and exalted mountain of Calvary matter? What of the life-bearing rock, the holy and life-giving tomb, the fountain of our resurrection, was it not matter? Is not the ink in the most holy Gospel-book matter? Is not the life-giving altar made of matter? From it we receive the bread of life! Are not gold and silver matter? From them we make crosses, patens, chalices! And over and above all these things, is not the Body and Blood of our Lord matter? Either do away with the honor and veneration these things deserve, or accept the tradition of the Church and the veneration of images.[ix]

A deeper investigation of historical Orthodox theology reveals yet further refutations of anti-materialism. In the words of one of the Church's foremost theologians, St Athanasius the Great:

> [Christ] has been manifested in a human body for this reason only, out of the love and goodness of His Father, for the salvation of us men. ... for the first fact that you must grasp is this: *the renewal of creation has been wrought by the Self-same Word Who made it in the beginning.* There is thus no inconsistency between creation and salvation; for the One Father has employed the same Agent for both works, effecting the salvation of the world through the same Word Who made it in the beginning.[x]

And:

> God knew the limitation of mankind, you see; and though the grace of being made in His Image was sufficient to give them knowledge of the Word and through Him of the Father, as a safeguard against their neglect of this grace, He provided the works of creation also as means by which the Maker might be known. . . . They could look up into the immensity of heaven, and by pondering the harmony of creation come to know its Ruler, the Word of the Father, Whose all-ruling providence makes known the Father to all.[xi]

And yet again:

> The Saviour of us all, the Word of God, in His great love took to Himself a body and moved as Man among men, meeting their senses, so to speak, halfway. He became Himself an object for the senses, so that those who were seeking God in sensible things might apprehend the Father through the works which He, the Word of God, did in the body.[xii]

It is instructive to note that on Mt Athos, the center of Orthodox Christian monasticism, great care and devotion is given to the adornment of the church buildings and the vesting of the clergy. Some of the most ornate and elaborate vestments in use today can be seen in the churches of what is, paradoxically, one of the most austere settings in the world: the monasteries of the Holy Mountain. Such devotion to material beauty by those who have found their calling in a life of liturgy and prayer is surely a further witness to the understanding within Orthodox Christianity that physical matter is not only redeemed, but also has a vital role to play in the salvation of mankind.

As if the witness of the great Church Fathers were not sufficient to establish the fact that the very cornerstone of our theology is anchored in the material world, some have argued against the beautification of the church building by saying that there is no mention of such adornments in the New Testament. While the specific traditions of how we beautify and adorn the church—such as the artistic expressions of our icons, the style of our liturgical garments or the decorative forms that are employed in woodcarving or ornamentation—are not explicitly mentioned in Scripture, St John of Damascus once again illuminates us on this point:

> The tradition of the Church is not only passed on in written documents, but has also been given in unwritten form. . . . St Basil says, "Among the carefully guarded teachings and doctrines of the Church, there are some teachings we received from written documents, while others we receive secretly, for they have been handed on to us from the apostolic tradition. Both sources have equal power to lead us to righteousness . . . ." What is the origin of the three immersions at baptism, or praying toward the east, or the manner in which we celebrate the eucharist? Therefore the holy apostle Paul says: "So then, brethren, stand firm and hold to the traditions which you were taught by us, either by word of mouth or by letter."[xiii]

Our understanding of beauty in the Church has both its origin and its fulfillment in the Incarnation and the subsequent redemption of the material world, and finds its standardized expression in the traditions of the Church, both written and unwritten. We realize that adornment begins with the material world, but by working within the forms and traditions handed down, and through the grace of the Holy Spirit, "mere" matter is transformed to find its ultimate purpose in manifesting Paradise on earth and drawing man to God. All things are gathered up to God in one great hymn of praise and the entire material world finds its "true destiny, that is, to be blocks in the cosmic temple of God's glory."[xiv]

A Holy Fulfillment: The Old Testament and the Adornment of the Church

Any discussion of the theological importance of liturgical vesture within the Church is not complete without considering the place of the Old Testament Scriptures that specifically refer to garments used in Levitical worship. The primary scriptural references to the priestly garments of the old covenant are found in Exodus 25–36, in which God gives explicit instructions to the Prophet Moses for the outfitting of the Tabernacle as well as the garments to be worn by the priests. Indeed, these instructions read like technical notes, with emphasis given to *how* things are to be made: "The hem shall be interwoven with the rest, to prevent ripping" (Ex 28.27); *what* they are to be made from: "Gold, silver, and bronze; blue, purple, and scarlet cloth; fine spun linen, and female goats' hair, ram skins dyed red and skins dyed blue, and incorruptible wood; oil for the light, and incense for anointing oil and for composition of incense; sardius stones, and stones for the carved work of the breastplate and the full-length robe" (Ex 25.3–7); and *who* is to make them: "Now Bezalel and Aholiab, and every gifted artisan in whom the Lord put wisdom and knowledge to know how to do all manner of work for the service of the holy place, did according to all the Lord commanded" (Ex 36.1).

It is interesting to note that over one quarter of the book of Exodus is devoted to these detailed instructions for the outfitting of the Tabernacle and the garments of the priests of God. The decorations of the tabernacle, ephod, and breastplate are no mere afterthought; indeed, thirty-eight verses are devoted solely to the curtains and the garments of the priests and are quite specific in the colors and symbols that are to be used (gold, blue, purple, and scarlet fabric and pomegranates and bells, respectively). There is a careful and methodical approach to these adornments and in this it is demonstrated that the worship of God must be attended to with order and reverence. Through this meticulous precision we see God teaching mankind that things used for his glory are to be "built by God."

On account of these detailed passages, some authors have argued that Christian vestments have their origin in Levitical dress, but even the most desultory comparison of the garments clearly illustrate that this could not be so (see Chapter Two for more on this topic). But just as the study of Orthodox Christian theology reveals much about the qualities of beauty within the Church, so it is through a reading of these chapters in Exodus that yet another quality of beauty within the Church is revealed: the fulfillment of types. This fulfillment is found in the progression from the Levitical understanding of worship, as outlined in the Old Testament, to the Christ-centered understanding of liturgy as found in the New Testament and the unwritten tradition handed down by the early Church—a rapidly coalescing tradition which led to the standardization of vestments and other adornments of the Church in the first few centuries following Christ's earthly life.

St John of Damascus, writing in response to the iconoclasts who were arguing for a rejection of images based on Old Testament passages such as "You shall not make for yourself a graven image, or any likeness of anything that is in heaven above, or that is in the earth beneath" (Ex 20.4), states:

> It is not I who am speaking, but the Holy Spirit who declares plainly through the holy apostle Paul, "God spoke of old in many various ways to our fathers by the prophets." Note that God spoke in *many and various ways*. A skillful doctor does not prescribe the same for all alike, but each according to his need. . . . In the same way the most excellent physician of souls prescribed correctly for those who were still children and susceptible to the sickness of idolatry, holding idols to be gods, and worshipping them as such, abandoning the worship of God, offering to the creature the glory due the Creator.[xv]

He goes on to further explain this fulfillment of types by quoting from a sermon of St John Chrysostom on the Epistle to the Hebrews:

> How can what comes first be the image of what is to follow, as Melchizedek is of Christ?

Melchizedek is used as an image in the Scriptures in the same way as a silhouette is an outline for a portrait. Because of this, the law is called a shadow, and grace and truth are what is foreshadowed. Consequently, the law personified by Melchizedek is a silhouette of Him whose portrait, when it appears, is grace and truth inscribed in the body. So the Old Testament is a silhouette of things to come in a future age, while the New Testament is the portrait of those things.[xvi]

St John recognized that just as a tiny seed looks nothing like the blooming, flourishing plant, so it is necessary to be mindful that Orthodox Christian worship is not designed to look like Old Testament worship. The fulfillment of the beauty and liturgy of the Church, like the fulfillment of the salvation of mankind, comes in no less a person than Christ himself through his Incarnation, Crucifixion, and Resurrection. The instructions in Exodus lay the groundwork, teaching that adornment of the holy things of God is integral to our worship of Him. But just as Christ took the place of rams sacrificed on stone altars, the adornment of our churches took a new and holy form through Christ's Resurrection, molded by the time and place in history in which the Resurrection took place and by the subsequent establishment of a Christian nation in the Byzantine Empire.

We know that the Fathers of the Church had a deep and thorough knowledge of the Scriptures (after all, St John Chrysostom spent two years memorizing the Scriptures in their entirety) and such an education could not have left them puzzling over how to outfit the churches of their day. Add to this the unwritten tradition which they had inherited and it would be completely illogical to suppose that men so formed by these Scriptures and providentially shaped by a world in which honor and majesty were the cornerstone of political and social hierarchy would have been able to construct liturgies to the Creator of All without glory and beauty. "Bring to the Lord the glory due His name; worship the Lord in His holy court" (Ps 28.2). They knew that "holiness is proper to Your house, O Lord" (Ps 92.5) and that "they shall speak of the magnificence of the glory of Your holiness, and they shall describe Your wonders" (Ps 144.5).

While Exodus teaches that order and reverence are necessary components to the worship of God, the Church Fathers knew that any reading of the Old Testament Scriptures must be undertaken with an understanding that such Scriptures have their fulfillment in the coming of Christ and the traditions of the Church. Majestic and holy worship began with the Old Testament Levitical patterns but did not find its culmination until the Resurrection of Christ and the subsequent redemption of the world. With Christ's coming everything is raised to a higher order, so the Church's worship follows the same essential patterns, yet looks different. As adopted sons of God, we are the inheritors of this holy fulfillment. As the Psalmist prophesies:

> They shall be intoxicated with the fatness of Your house, and You will give them drink from the abundant water of Your delight. For with You is the fountain of life; in Your light shall we see light. (Ps 35.9–10)

In the beauty of the Church's worship we find the fulfillment of the prophetic words and foreshadowing of all the Old Testament Scriptures.

Manifesting the Kingdom of Heaven on Earth: A Call to Beauty

Once we understand that the beauty of the material church temple is integral to the theology of the Church, the adorning of the earthly temple is no longer seen as a "fussy" or "luxurious" pursuit, but becomes a holy and worthy endeavor. The physical church must manifest the reality that we enter into Heaven in the midst of its material environs and that the adornment of this space reflects a spiritual reality. We strive to embrace this "outside-in" paradox in which the physical world becomes the sacramental reality of the heavenly kingdom.

In this undertaking, we join with a community of saints who have had a particular calling to beautify the house of God. One of the most compelling of these holy ones is St Erasmus, whose story is related in the *Prologue of Ochrid*:

> Erasmus was a monk in the Monastery of the Caves in Kiev. He inherited great wealth from his parents and spent all on adorning churches, especially on silver-plating and gilding icons. When he had become impoverished and remained without anything, he was despised by all. The devil whispered to him that he squandered his estate in vain; instead of distributing his wealth among the poor, he gave it for the adornment of churches. Erasmus succumbed to this temptation and believed it for which he despised himself and fell into a state of despair and began to live aimlessly and lawlessly. When the hour of his death approached the brethren assembled around him and discussed his sins which he himself was not conscious of. All at once, he straightened up in bed and said: "Fathers and brothers, it is as you say; I am sinful and unrepentant, but behold St Anthony and St Theodosius appeared to me and after that, the All-Holy Mother of God told me that the Lord gave me more time for repentance." The Mother of God also spoke these encouraging words to him: "The poor you have with you in every place and my churches you do not." Erasmus lived for three more days, repented and fell asleep in the Lord. This teaches us that zeal for the Church and adornment of the churches is a task pleasing to God.[xvii]

It is interesting to note that the devil used St Erasmus' devotion to adorning churches as a weapon to achieve the saint's fall. The last thing the Evil One wants is for the church to be beautiful and so he whispers to St Erasmus that he should have distributed his wealth to the poor, but therein lies another sly deception: the devil does not want the poor to be provided for any more than he wants the church to be beautiful. Yet he targets St Erasmus' great devotion to this "task pleasing to God" because the enemy knows that the beauty of the church reveals the Kingdom of Heaven on earth, and this is something he cannot tolerate. So, he cunningly creates a false dichotomy—either you adorn the church or you give to the poor.

This dichotomy continues to our present day, and if possible, is even more robust due to the anti-materialist religious climate that surrounds us. It can be tempting to view the architecture, icons, woodwork, and vestments as so much "dross," the money spent on which would have been put to better use by giving to those in need. But as Orthodox Christians, we are called to provide for those in need and to manifest the glory of Christ within the church. A tall order? Certainly, but as Christ himself says, "For everyone to whom much is given, from him much will be required; and to whom much has been committed, of him they will ask the more" (Lk 12.48).

Through the witness of such saints as St Erasmus and St John of Damascus, we comprehend that the labors they expended in adorning and defending the physical church were one of the means of their achieving salvation. This work was part of their journey toward theosis, creating not only beautiful churches for the honor and glory of God, but also beautiful souls as well. The churches they built, the chalices they donated, the books they wrote, the icons they gilded, were just as much a part of their salvation as their prayers, fasting, and almsgiving. The holy examples of these saints present another quality of beauty within the church, and this is its ability to be a powerful means of repentance. Beautification of the churches of God is not just a rote task to be checked off a liturgical "to do" list, but rather, a holy work that draws us closer to the source of all beauty, our Heavenly Father.

We live in an age that is replete with assaults upon the senses in the form of frenetic and immoral images, and this, combined with the influence of heresies that repudiate the material world, creates an atmosphere of negative anti-materialism that sours our physical senses and dulls them to the beauty of God. By giving attention to the adornment of our churches, we effectively turn our senses back towards God. In the early Christian mind the physical and the spiritual were intrinsically linked: if the physical sense was defiled, then the spiritual sense was likewise.[2] By beautifying our churches, we open the doors of repentance to our senses and have yet another means to create beautiful souls within ourselves through the grace of the Holy Spirit.

Repentance comes with much work and struggle, and it is an interesting facet of the beauty particular to the Orthodox Christian Church that there is a profound, mystical link between aesthetics, or the sense of beauty, and *ascesis*, the spiritual struggle of the *nous*. Orthodox Christian aesthetics is not a preoccupation with pretty things to engage and delight our senses, but a consciously cultivated awareness that we have left Paradise through our sinful rejection of God and that this situation must be rectified. If we were truly holy, the entire world would still be Paradise. The beauty that delights our eyes in the church does so through a veil of tears, the tears of repentance. Like the prodigal son, we return home, but in the bittersweet knowledge that we have rejected this very abode. We see heaven before us in the Divine Liturgy and we perceive with despair that we are outside the gates. This recognition of our great need for repentance gives a quality of humility to the beauty of the church.

The principle of beauty perfected through humility is intriguingly demonstrated in the iconography and other artwork produced after the fall of Constantinople in 1453. With such social and political upheaval it might be expected that the artwork of the Church would suffer and degrade. However, as the highly skilled craftsmen of Byzantium—the iconographers, woodcarvers, metalworkers, silk weavers, and musicians—were dispersed throughout the medieval world, they took their craft with them and their work was shaped with a new tool, that of personal suffering through the loss of their homeland. Rather than perpetuating rote, ossified forms, this suffering, because it mirrored that quality of aesthetics interwoven with *ascesis*

---

2. In our time there is a pervasive notion that beauty is "uplifting" but ugliness is somehow "neutral" or without effect. In my opinion, nothing could be further from the truth. Ugliness is the opposite of beauty and it has an opposite effect. I do not think it is putting it too strongly to say that ugliness is evil. Case in point: have you ever been inspired to glorify the Creator of All by the tile floor of your local fast food restaurant or the vast asphalt parking lot of a supermarket?

that is foundational to the beauty of the Church, created a great dynamism. True beauty has a harmony with *ascesis*, the struggle to achieve union with God. As Kontoglou tells us:

> The works after the fall of Constantinople are often full of astonishing freedom, originality and religious passion, often more so than the works that were done at times of political and social flourishing of Byzantium.... The Hellenes who lived in that period underwent much hardship and suffering, and they withdrew into their own inner depths and there contemplated themselves directly. Their souls passed through the fire of martyrdom and were purified. For this reason, whatever they produced then, whether icons, or books describing the lives of saints, or dirges, or other songs, had the fragrance of Christian faith, which cannot be possessed by souls that have not become humble and wept.[xviii]

Bishop Anthony (Michaels) further elucidates this essential connection between true beauty and spiritual struggle in a letter written to the author:

> Aesthetics (the beauty of the Church) and ascetics (the spiritual disciplines of the Church) emerge from the one faith. The display of beauty on the one hand conveys the arduous spiritual work of reforming and artistically reshaping the soul on the invisible, inside of us, on the other. St Paul prayed that the Ephesian community might be "strengthened with might through the Holy Spirit in the inner man." By making beautiful vestments the visual Tradition of the Church frames the whole written Tradition, like an appropriate frame hugs a masterpiece and brings it out, reveals it as beautiful. The great ascetic Fathers who served parishes, although faithful to the monastic calling of being personally poor, spent money continually on stunning vestments and church adornment. Why? Because they

knew the sacramental dimension of the Church. Their own ascetic piety brightened the lives of the faithful. That brightness has to be seen, also, materially. It must be "on display." The Eucharist has a material vestment, bread and wine, and a glorious, eternal, beautiful Body and Blood of Christ. So, icons, vestments, etc. must be a visible medium of invisible grace—uncreated energy. In this way the Church as the Kingdom of God permeates the Church as the true Eden of Paradise. Fr. Pavel Florensky has written: "Asceticism produces not a good but a beautiful personality; the characteristic peculiarity of great saints is not the goodness of heart which is common among carnal and even very sinful men, but spiritual beauty, the dazzling beauty of radiant, light-giving personality, unattainable by carnal men weighed down by the flesh."[xix]

As Orthodox Christians, we are called to this mystical, holy beauty, both in our churches, where heaven is manifested through the sacraments and glorious adornment, as well as in our souls, which we must be striving to make truly beautiful rather than merely good.

When we take up the holy endeavor of adorning our churches we embrace a great and sacred source of repentance and salvation not just for ourselves, but also for the world around us. There is great power in the beauty of the Church and this "beauty will save the world."[xx] The beauty of the Church is a compelling means not only of repentance, but also of evangelism, particularly to those who find the dogmas and theology of the Church dry or difficult. In this modern world, with its ubiquitous ugliness and plainness, the startling and refreshing beauty of an Orthodox Christian church temple is an amazing witness to the Faith, a beautiful gate through which searching souls may enter. As St John of Damascus exhorts, "If someone asks you about your faith, do not start talking about dogmas, but show him the icons which you venerate."[xxi] True beauty is the essence of our holy Faith, a fulfillment of our longing for Paradise.

Endnotes

i. Constantine Cavarnos, *Byzantine Sacred Art* (Belmont, MA: Institute for Byzantine and Modern Greek Studies, 1985), 126.

ii. Paul Evdokimov, *The Art of the Icon* (Redondo Beach, CA: Oakwood Publications, 1990), 59.

iii. St Germanos, *On the Divine Liturgy* (Crestwood, NY: St Vladimir's Seminary Press, 1985), 63.

iv. Constantine Cavarnos, *Byzantine Thought and Art* (Belmont, MA: Institute for Byzantine and Modern Greek Studies, 2000), 63.

v. *The Lenten Triodion*, Mother Mary and Archimandrite Kallistos Ware, trans. (South Canaan, PA: St Tikhon's Seminary Press, 1994), 169.

vi. Cavarnos, *Byzantine Sacred Art*, 38.

vii. Bishop Kallistos Ware , *The Orthodox Way* (Crestwood, NY: St Vladimir's Seminary Press, 1996), 50.

viii. St Germanos, *On the Divine Liturgy*, Paul Meyendorff, trans. (Crestwood, NY: St Vladimir's Seminary Press, 1985), 95.

ix. St John of Damascus, *On the Divine Images*, David Anderson, trans. (Crestwood, NY: St Vladimir's Seminary Press, 1980), 23.

x. St Athanasius, *On the Incarnation* (Crestwood, NY: St Vladimir's Seminary Press, 1989), 26.

xi. St Athanasius, 39.

xii. St Athanasius, 43.

xiii. St John of Damascus, 31.

xiv. Evdokimov, 117.

xv. St John of Damascus, 54.

xvi. St John of Damascus, 41.

xvii. St Nikolai Velimirovic, *The Prologue of Ohrid*, Fr T. Timothy Tepsic, trans., Fr Janko Trbovic, the St. Herman of Alaska Serbian Orthodox Monastery, and the St Paisius Serbian Orthodox Monastery, eds. (Serbian Orthodox Diocese of Western America, 2002), 196–7.

xviii. Cavarnos, *Byzantine Sacred Art*, 81.

xix. Personal letter to the author, 2008.

xx. Fyodor Dostoevsky, *The Idiot*, Richard Pevear, trans. (New York: Vintage, 2003).

xxi. Cavarnos, *Byzantine Sacred Art*, 157.

Chapter Two

Of Tunics, Togas, and Tradition

At the present time it is man's fancy to dress hideously: he encases himself in five tubes, two for the arms, two for the legs, and one for the trunk (with a smaller connecting tube round the neck); and when he goes out, he puts on the top of his head a sixth tube which is so useless that it has to be protected by an umbrella. If we were not so accustomed to this absurd fashion of the past hundred years, we should see how ridiculous and undignified it is. We have only to imagine one of the Apostles thus bedizened in a frock-coat and a top hat, to see that in our hearts we do know that men look absurd when encased in dingy cylinders. It is clearly wrong for men to look like this, because they become ugly blots on the world which God makes with such infinite loveliness; so that earth and sky, trees and flowers, beasts, birds and insects are of ever varying beauty, and only man looks vile—man who should be the crown and glory of that visible loveliness which God provides with such care for the comfort, refreshment, and inspiration of our hearts.

The Rev. Percy Dearmer, *The Ornaments of the Ministers* (1908)

Prototypical Garments of Antiquity

The liturgical vestments employed by the Orthodox Christian Church in its divine services and rites are drawn from a tradition of immense beauty, rich theological significance, and profound historical continuity. The Church's ongoing usage perpetuates a garment tradition that originates at the very dawn of humanity with the postlapsarian clothing of Adam and Eve, continues with the prototypical garments of ancient Mesopotamia, Egypt, and Palestine, proceeds through classical Greek and Roman attire, and finally culminates and finds a standardized expression in the comprehensive Christian vision of the Byzantine Roman Empire. This is a tradition that has outlasted nations, empires and cultures—a truly remarkable pedigree when one considers that an Orthodox Christian priest today wears garments that have, in their essential type, been in use by mankind in one form or another for over 6000 years. Perhaps even more astonishing is the fact that many of the specific garments of Orthodox liturgical dress have enjoyed an unbroken chain of essentially unaltered design for the past 1500 years, making the prototypes of vestments worn by deacons, presbyters, and bishops today easily recognized in icons dating as far back as the sixth century in such historically significant churches as San Vitale in Ravenna and Sant'Apollinare in Classe.

Because the origins of Orthodox Christian liturgical vestments are found in some of the earliest garments of mankind, it is helpful to begin a study of Orthodox ecclesiastical vesture with an overview of the garments of the ancient world. To begin we will focus primarily on the clothing of ancient Mesopotamia and Egypt, since in these regions we have the greatest amount of information pertaining to early garment history. This is a radical departure from the time period considered by most writers on Church vestments, most of whom have contented themselves with observations on the historical antecedents of liturgical vesture beginning with the garments of ancient Greece and Rome. While the immediate precursors of Orthodox Christian vestments are to be found in the garments of these two classical civilizations, a study of the garments that in their turn influenced those of the classical age leads us to a greater and spiritually significant story that must be told. When one examines the earliest garments of civilized man—the archetypal garments that would develop into the daily dress of ancient Greece and Rome and, in turn, our Orthodox Christian liturgical vestments—one observes with startling clarity the common origins of this entire historical trajectory of clothing. The very garments that Adam and Eve used in the beginning to cover their nakedness are seen to be transfigured by time and through God's merciful economy into Orthodox Christian liturgical vesture: the garments of salvation.

In addition to the spiritual significance of a study of ancient garment history, it is also vital to understand ancient garments in their original forms so that we can observe how garment design adapts and changes from age to age and how such adaptation has affected Orthodox Christian liturgical dress. A thorough knowledge of the basic forms of ancient garments also obviates confusion when the usage of different historical epochs and varying geographical regions results in the designation of the same garment by a variety of names.

While some of the original garments of mankind were simple conventions for modesty's sake (such as the loincloth), garments that served a less practical but more stylistic function were introduced at a very early period. The essential garment of this type is the long tunic,[1] which is a length of cloth twice as long as the wearer, folded in half with an opening for the head cut along the fold. In addition to the circular aperture for the head there is also an extended opening which makes the garment easier to put on and which appears in one of two versions: either a vertical slit down the front neck, or an opening horizontally along the shoulders. In some instances the tunic has no sleeves, but rather allows the excess fabric simply to drape over the body. In other cases sleeve extensions are added to the tunic and the sides are shaped or curved to bring the fit closer to the body. An overview of Figs. 1 and 2 will readily convey the two basic design variations of this garment.

---

1. The English term "tunic" (derived from the Latin *tunica*) will be used interchangeably with the Greek *sticharion* signifying a long, robe-like garment.

44 ✦ Garments of Salvation

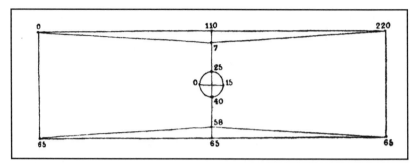

Figure 1. An Egyptian *kalasiris*, an early version of the tunic. The circle in the middle is an opening for the head. (Carl Kohler, *History of Costume*, Dover Publications, 55).

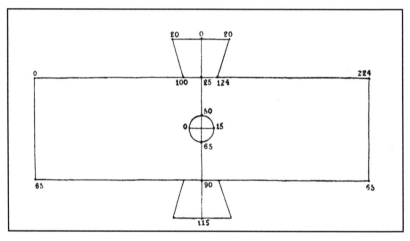

Figure 2. An Egyptian *kalasiris* shown with sleeve extensions (trapezoidal pieces at top and bottom of figure). (Carl Kohler, *History of Costume*, Dover Publications, 55).

In ancient times, the use of long garments was often, although not exclusively, reserved for the upper classes, since it required not only a certain amount of financial resources to own a voluminous, and therefore more costly, garment, it also meant that the wearer would not be participating in any strenuous physical labor which would be hindered by a flowing garment. Most slaves, soldiers, and those of the lower classes wore shorter versions of the tunic, in which it was easier to work and fight.

In Egypt the basic tunic was referred to as the *kalasiris* and was introduced shortly after the New Kingdom, c. 1000 BC. This simple tunic, with a variety of subtle variations, was widely used among ancient Mesopotamian peoples as well. Along the Upper Euphrates a form of this garment was worn by the Retennu-Tehennu peoples,[i] possibly by one specific clan or as the war-dress of this ancient people, but with an interesting addition: along seamlines and fronts it was covered with strips of colored material and the bottom hem was trimmed with tassels.[ii] The presence of this ornamentation illustrates one of the tunic's most compelling features: its adaptability to a wide variety of decorative schemes. As a blank slate the tunic is almost without equal among historical garments. In the ancient world ornamentation was used to denote status and wealth, with those higher up the social ladder wearing garments with more elaborate decoration.

Among the Hebrew people a variation on the tunic (see Fig. 3) appeared around the time of the Assyrian captivity and was most likely of Assyrian or Babylonian origin.[iii] This garment retained the general outline of the tunic, being a long rectangle with sleeve additions, but it modified the design with an opening extending along its entire front length in order to form a type of coat or caftan. It is interesting to note that this garment varies little in basic design from the *bekishes* still worn by Hasidic Jews (although the modern garment now has lapels and tailored sleeves). In both Assyria and Babylonia the usual dress was another variation of the tunic, similar to the Egyptian *kalasiris* which, while worn by all people from slave to king, was worn only to the knee by the lower classes, following the same general usage as other ancient cultures.[iv] This Assyrian and Babylonian tunic closely resembled the common garments of many other peoples in Western Asia and as far away from the Fertile Crescent as the Horn of Africa, where the Ethiopians also adopted a form of tunic for the upper classes.

While all the ancient peoples thus far considered wore garments made of woven fabrics, an interesting technological difference is observed with the garments of Media and Persia. The climate of these regions was colder and thus the primary clothing materials used by their inhabitants were animal hides which, due to their stiffness and resistance to drape, inspired a different direction in garment design. Median and Persian garments (see Fig. 4) usually consisted of hose or breeches with a type of blouse-like shirt that in some instances resembled a heavier, coat-like garment.

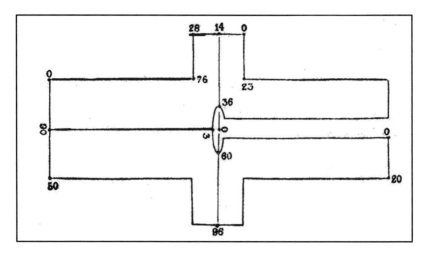

Figure 3. Hebrew caftan, shown with an opening from the neck (circle at center) to the front feet. (Carl Kohler, *History of Costume*, Dover Publications, 69).

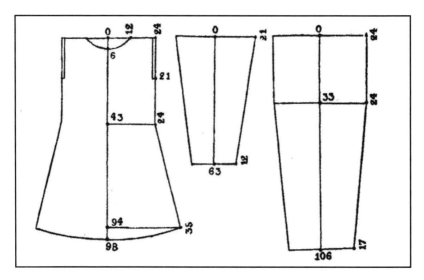

Figure 4. Median and Persian coat and breeches. The piece in the middle is the sleeve extension added to the coat. (Carl Kohler, *History of Costume*, Dover Publications, 75).

There is a basic division in ancient garment design depending on whether the primary material of a culture is leather or a fabric made of woven threads. Tanned hides do not behave in the same way as light and flowing woven fabrics and cannot be decorated with the same techniques (it is far more difficult to pierce leather with a needle than wool or linen). However, despite the necessity for adaptation given the limitations of a particular material, the basic design of hide garments and woven garments share similar qualities: the hide garment, when laid out for cutting, is still a rectangular shape with an opening cut in the middle for the head. The Persian coat was often much closer-fitting than the Egyptian *kalasiris* or the Hebrew caftan, but in its essential design was, once again, a modified rectangle with a hole in the center for the head.[2]

In any overview of ancient garment history, mention must also be made of the dress of the Minoan and Mycenaean civilizations (2100 BC to 1100 BC) since from these descended some of the garments of ancient Greece. Although their usual garments are distinctly different from those of Mesopotamia (men wore simple loincloths while women's dress was quite elaborate and involved skirts with ruffled flounces and tightly fitted bodices), there is also record of a "Mainland Dress"[v] worn by both sexes which was very similar to the tunics of Mesopotamia and was possibly reserved for either religious or ceremonial occasions.

With an overview of these various ancient garments we can see that, despite some variations in details or decoration, the basic design of the tunic appears almost universally among mankind. While there is not sufficient room here to explore ancient Asian and South American clothing, these venerable cultures also employed garments closely resembling the tunic. From the general category of the tunic was to originate the Orthodox Christian baptismal *sticharion*, deacon's *sticharion*, presbyter's *sticharion*, and even, though through a more circuitous route of

---

2. The dress of the ancient Persians will be familiar to Orthodox Christians from the depiction of the Magi in icons of the Nativity of Christ. Additionally, their attire can be observed in the mosaic of the Empress Theodora at San Vitale in Ravenna, depicted in the richly embroidered hem of her garment.

the tunic, evolving into the more elaborate form of the *colobium* (see below), the bishop's *sakkos*.

Garments of the Classical World

Moving forward in history, the same tunic-style garments are found in widespread use in ancient Greece and Rome and it is here that we must become familiar with the classical terminology used to describe them: the *chiton* and *tunica* respectively. Once again the basic form is a rectangle of material suspended from the neck and draped over the body, but now with interesting variations appearing, most notably those associated with the folding and arrangement of the voluminous fabric. The most common materials used for ancient Greek garments were wool and linen, and the quality of these fabrics ranged from coarse and heavy to light and flowing depending on the skill of the spinner and weaver, the status of the wearer, and the desired character of the finished garment. In ancient Greece we observe remarkable ingenuity in the varied methods of draping or folding the *chiton,* which could be worn open along the length of the shoulders with pins keeping the garment fastened (rather than having a hole cut for the neck opening). This allowed for a great width of cloth to be used and thereby resulted in magnificent drapes of fabric which are commonly depicted in Greek artwork of the early period. Some depictions illustrate draping around the shoulder area while others show a *chiton* that is much longer than the wearer and is drawn up into graceful folds around the waist area by the use of a girdle or belt. In this ornamental draping we see a foreshadowing of the elaborately folded garments that will later develop into specific garments of office in ancient Rome and Byzantium.

In addition to elaborate draping there were three general methods of decorating ancient Greek garments, all of which continue to be the forms of decoration used on Orthodox Christian vestments today. First is woven ornamentation in which a design is made while the fabric is being woven on the loom. This category can include an all-over woven design as well as highly decorated pieces of woven cloth that are made separately and then sewn onto a garment. (This latter option provided the flexibility of removing the ornamented sections or bands or placing them on new garments when the original garments wore out.) Second, while not very commonly used in modern times, is dye-painting, in which various designs such as the "wave pattern" or the "egg and tongue" were applied with dyestuffs, often in multiple layers and colors. The third category is embroidery, in which highly elaborate designs such as the "palmette" or floral and vegetative motifs were embroidered by hand using either wool or linen threads.[vi]

While it is in the ancient cultures of Mesopotamia and Egypt that we find the origins of the universal tunic, it is in ancient Greece and Rome that we first encounter an equally influential garment, the *himation* or *clamys,* a type of cloak.

Figure 5. Himation. (Mary G. Houston, *Ancient Greek, Roman, and Byzantine Costume*, Dover Publications, 68).

Various rectangularly shaped, cloak-like garments were in use simultaneously with the tunic throughout most of the ancient world, since cold or inclement weather necessitated a warm, outer wrap. But in classical Rome the ancient cloak reached the pinnacle of its design in the *toga*, that symbol of Roman citizenship and patriotism, "the chief and most distinctive feature of Roman costume in Republican and Imperial times," which developed out of the Greek *himation*.[vii] The standard *toga* was constructed of wool, almost always in its undyed, natural state which varied in color from ivory to parchment tones, depending on the breed of sheep from which the wool was derived (two exceptions to the undyed *toga* were the military *toga* which was dyed red and the mourning *toga* which was dyed a dark color). The *toga* was a flattened semi-circle of fabric, over eighteen feet long and seven feet deep, and was free of decoration except for decorative bands along its edges known as *clavi*. These *clavi* appeared sometimes along the long edge and sometimes along the curved edge of the *toga* (see Fig. 6).

Figure 6. A Roman *toga* shown draped on the body and laid out as a flattened semi-circle. (Mary G. Houston, *Ancient Greek, Roman, and Byzantine Costume*, Dover Publications, 91).

At the height of its usage in ancient Rome, there were eight separate types of *toga* ranging from those worn by ordinary citizens, to those worn in mourning, to the special *toga candida* reserved for use by candidates for public office. There was a specific *toga* to be worn by a victorious general (and later by emperors and consuls) and another worn by youths under sixteen. The *toga* was the garment *par excellence* among the Romans and they valued it greatly. Despite its simple shape, it was a complicated garment to wear because, in the time-honored fashion established by the ancient Greeks, it required a highly distinctive form of draping to be worn correctly. To give an idea of its complexity, garment historian Mary G. Houston gives these directions for its proper draping (see Fig 6):

> The method of draping is as follows: Begin by making toga into folds of about eight inches wide and arrange them so that the stripe [*clavus*] will show. Wind one end backwards from the wrist to shoulder of left arm so that the arm is entirely covered....Now pass over the left shoulder and draw it downwards across the back until it rests at right side of waist, and, having sufficiently loosened the folds to allow the curved edge to reach the ankles, draw the straight edge onwards across the front of waist, still keeping it in folds to prevent trailing. Continue round the back of waist until the right side is reached again. Now take the whole garment and throw upwards across the chest and over the left shoulder, taking care to display the band. Draw downwards across the back to the right side again. Now unwind the portion of toga from the left arm and allow it to hang down to the feet from the left shoulder. Last of all, take the still undraped portion of the toga and throw it across the front of the body and across the crook of the left elbow, the left arm being bent at a right angle to thus receive it.[viii]

In addition to the *tunica* and the *toga* there were other garments in use during Roman times that influenced Orthodox Christian liturgical dress and thus must be mentioned. The *colobium* was a version of the *tunica* that had shortened sleeves. It was worn by Roman men of free birth and eventually developed into the liturgical garment referred to in the West as the *dalmatic* and in the Orthodox Church as the deacon's *sticharion*. The *colobium* reached its most elaborate and ornamented version as the court dress of Byzantine emperors and empresses (as seen in early Byzantine mosaics) which garments in turn served as the source of the bishop's *sakkos* and, in a historically significant parallel development, influenced the court dress of almost every royal house in Western Europe.[ix] The *paenula*, a cloak of semi-circular shape, was worn by both men and women primarily for travel or in place of the *toga* in the case of those residing in the country, and it did not have the same high status as the *toga*. Another form of the cloak, the *pallium*, was a long, rectangular garment distantly related to the *toga* which, while rarely worn by ancient Romans, being considered too distinctly Greek (since it was identical with the Greek *himation*), came back into vogue sometime prior to the founding of Constantinople.

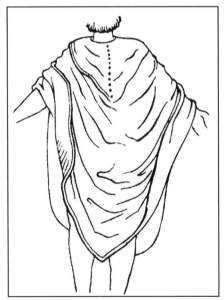

Figure 7. Paenula (Carl Kohler, *History of Costume*, Dover Publications, 115).

Garments of Late Antiquity

Thus at the beginning of the Christian era we see two distinct, major categories of garments: tunics and cloaks. All too often in the research of liturgical garments a critical error is made in envisioning ecclesiastical garments as far more complicated and convoluted in their evolution than they actually are. For instance it is vitally important to understand pre-Christian dress in order to ascertain the simple fact that tunics were often layered, a necessity in colder climates or for general comfort and modesty. A person wearing a *colobium*, a specialized type of tunic, must also wear a lighter tunic as an undergarment for modesty or warmth (or to protect the skin from the rough threads of a *colobium* embellished with metal thread embroidery), but despite the fact that they are two separate garments, in their essence they are the same design: both are tunics. When studying the history of Orthodox Christian liturgical dress, it is helpful to categorize garments according to their basic design and not necessarily by the various names that have been applied to them throughout different ages. In this way, a universality of design can be observed in Orthodox Christian vesture that illuminates its origins in ancient garments.

The Roman dress described thus far remained in use through the third century AD and the subsequent founding of Constantinople as the "New Rome," with one important exception. By the beginning of the second century AD the *toga* was confined to purely ceremonial use, having fallen out of favor with the average citizen who preferred the easier-to-wear *paenula*. During the "Transition Period" (approx. AD 285–324) which served as a bridge between the old Roman dress and the newer styles of Byzantium, the only form of the *toga* that remained in use was the ceremonial *toga picta* which was worn by Roman consuls (high-ranking officers of state) and which became lavishly ornamented, with the formerly narrow *clavi* (decorative bands) evolving into a single, eight-inch wide band of decoration perfectly displayed when the *toga picta* was folded into its customary eight-inch wide folds, thereby becoming what is known as the *toga contabulata*.[x]

The *tunica* continued in use, but the wider-sleeved version referred to as the *colobium* began to be more commonly adopted. It is at this point in the development of the tunic that many writers, in their analysis of garment history, begin referring to this wide-sleeved tunic as a "*dalmatic*," a term that can be misleading. The word "*dalmatic*" has been adopted as a description because a particular type of wide-sleeved tunic was the national costume of the inhabitants of Dalmatia (the eastern coast of the Adriatic Sea).[xi] In the West the wide-sleeved tunic bearing the name *dalmatic* became, in time, the distinctive vesture of Western Christian deacons, a circumstance which unfortunately complicates a discussion of Eastern Orthodox vestments since in Orthodox nomenclature the term *dalmatic* is never used. In reference to Orthodox vestments I prefer the more precise term "*colobium*," which denotes a wide-sleeved tunic which was always worn over a *tunica talaris* (the specific term for the narrow-sleeved, undergarment version of the *tunica*). During the Transition Period we find men wearing the *tunica talaris* with the *colobium* over it and then wrapping the *paenula* over all (see Fig. 8). For more formal occasions, the *pallium* might be worn over the *paenula* or in its place (the cloak in Fig. 8 is most likely a pallium as it is more rectangular in shape than a paenula).[xii] It is important to note that the *paenula* was used as a common, everyday garment whereas the *pallium* had an air of formality associated with its use (most likely from its common origins with the *toga*).

Figure 8. Depiction of an early Christian priest from the catacombs. He is wearing the *tunica talaris* (of which only the edge of the right-hand cuff is visible), *colobium* (note the dark bands which are *clavi*), and *pallium*. (Mary G. Houston, *Ancient Greek, Roman, and Byzantine Costume*, Dover Publications, 128).

By the early years of the Christian era men of the lowest classes, slaves, and soldiers would have worn short tunics with various types of cloak-like overgarments, such as the *paenula*. Men of higher social standing, including teachers and those in positions of authority (such as the Apostles and early Christian clerics), would have worn the longer tunic and *pallium*. In early Christian iconography, such as the grand mosaic of the Procession of the Martyrs in Sant'Apollinare Nuovo in Ravenna, the martyrs are depicted wearing this same combination of dress to identify not only their spiritual rank and the reverence due to them, but to underscore their position as "philosophers," i.e., "lovers of Wisdom" ("Wisdom" here being Christ himself). Alternately, they might have worn the *paenula* over the tunic, as we may surmise the Apostle Paul did, for he requests in 2 Timothy 4.13 "Bring the cloak that I left with Carpus at Troas when you come. . . ." In Greek, the word used for "cloak" in this passage is φαιλόνην (*phailoneen*) [accusative case], which nearly all authorities agree is the *paenula* since the two words are linguistically similar. In early iconography, the Apostles are frequently garbed in this classic *tunica, colobium* and *paenula/pallium* combination as a means of visually denoting their respected status within the Church.

In the early Byzantine mosaics of San Vitale and Sant'Apollinare Nuovo, many of the primary figures such as the Old Testament patriarchs, angels, and the martyrs are depicted wearing the *tunica* decorated with *clavi*, with the *pallium* over all, a fact that leads us to consider in greater depth that most common decoration of the tunic, the *clavi*. *Clavi* are narrow, embroidered or woven bands of decoration that were applied to the *tunica* and the *toga* to enhance their appearance and denote status. While there are multiple variations in the placement of such bands, they are most commonly depicted on the *tunicae* in early icons as two vertical stripes, one on either side of the center of the tunic, in a darker color that contrasts with the lighter color of the garment. Although they are shown in icons as solid bands of color, such as purple or deep red, they also sometimes incorporated ornate geometric, floral, or meander designs, a fact we may deduce from a few extant late-antique tunics (most notably those in the collections of the Victoria and Albert Museum in London and the Metropolitan Museum of Art in New York). In addition to decorating the garment, the *clavi* were a means of indicating the rank of the wearer, thereby utilizing decorations as symbols of status and vocation, a necessity when so many members of society dressed in similar garments.[xiii]

Garments of the Early Byzantine Age[3] and the Emergence of a Standardized Vestment Tradition

With the establishment of Constantinople as the "New Rome" in the early fourth century and the subsequent inauguration of the Byzantine era, the custom of specific garments or garment decorations having a purely ceremonial function, be it civil or religious, reached a pinnacle of standardization greater than any heretofore seen in the ancient world. In a thorough study of Orthodox Christian liturgical dress, it is imperative to reflect upon the Byzantine outlook and its effect upon the standardization of Orthodox Christian vesture in order to understand this usage in its proper historical context. This worldview is evocatively described in Robert Browning's *Justinian and Theodora*:

> When, in the early fourth century, Constantine was converted to Christianity—which soon became the dominant and then the official religion of the empire—a new dimension was added to the political idea of its citizens. The permanence of the Roman Empire was seen no longer as a mere matter of fact, but as an essential part of the divine plan for the salvation of mankind. The first step had been the unification of the civilized world under Augustus at the time of the birth of Christ. This was now seen to have been

---

3. It bears mentioning that at no time in history has there ever been a nation whose citizenry called themselves "Byzantines" or thought of themselves as such; rather, those people whom we call Byzantines would consistently have referred to themselves as Romans, emphasizing their continuity with the traditions and mindset of the classical world. For the sake of clarity, I have followed a convention common among an older generation of art history scholars of referring to the Christian Roman Empire (i.e., the period from the conversion of Constantine to the fall of Constantinople) as "Byzantine."

the necessary condition for the rapid spread of Christianity. Now the Roman state, from being a passive vehicle for the spread of truth—and sometimes, under bad emperors, actively hindering its spread—had become its active champion, foreshadowing upon earth the Kingdom of God which was to come in the fullness of time. As there was one God, so there could be only one empire and one emperor. These were the ideas which Justinian, like every man of his time, had inherited. It would never have occurred, even to a humble man, to question them.[xiv]

And from the same source, now referencing the many problems Justinian faced at the beginning of his reign:

A modern man, faced with a situation in which things seem to be going seriously wrong, would think in terms of reform, of fashioning something new. For a man of the sixth century, and especially for one as steeped in the traditions of the past as was Justinian, such an approach was impossible. 'Innovation' was a word with strongly pejorative overtones; in theological parlance it implied heresy. Neither the refinements of philosophical thought nor the clichés of popular expression had any room for the concept of progress or continuous change. Although Justinian . . . introduced much that was new into the Roman world, he could only do so by convincing himself and others that he was restoring the past. His grand idea was to correct the errors of the past century and to rebuild, in even greater majesty and glory, the empire, the Christian empire of Constantine.[xv]

It was precisely this creativity within the bounds of conformity to established patterns that led to what Byzantine scholar Gervase Mathews refers to as "one of the primary creative periods in human history, in thought and in literature as well as in architecture and art. . . . Fresh literary forms were created in hymns, in chronicles, and in lives of saints. There was nothing sterile in a literature which produced an orator as great as St John Chrysostom. . . ."[xvi] If the traditions of the ancient Roman Empire were a nascent bud, then in Byzantium they found their Christian flowering. For the Byzantine man the duty imposed by his society was not to throw away the grand traditions of old Rome, but rather to redeem and resurrect them in new and salvific forms.

As a point of contrast it is important to note that while Byzantine society was experiencing a renewed commitment to the perpetuation and revitalization of old Rome's traditions, in the Western Roman Empire such was not the case. With its precipitous decline in the years leading up to the fifth century and its final fall to the Ostrogoths in AD 476, the Western Roman world was effectively cut off from much of the redemptive work of synthesizing venerable cultural traditions that was such a noted feature of Byzantine life in both the civil and spiritual arenas.[4] It is only after the Western Roman world began to succumb to the incursions of the northern barbarian invaders that the beginnings of Western vestments (such as those worn in the Roman Catholic and Anglican communions) start to be described by Western Christian writers. This division between Western and Eastern modes of thinking and theology has hampered scholars who approach the study of ecclesiastical garments from a purely Western viewpoint, not taking into consideration the conscious absorption of ancient Roman traditions and garments into the vesture of Byzantium and the Eastern Church. Thus while there are numerous Western authors who argue for the late standardization of church vestments (their dating usually puts such standardization somewhere between the eighth and twelfth centuries), there is a compelling argument to be made from the study of Byzantine society and civil practice for the early standardization of Orthodox Christian vestments, perhaps as early as the third century and certainly no later than the fifth century.

---

4. It is interesting to observe that after the Fall of Rome, the ancient city's civil dress changed to correspond with that of the barbarian conquerors.

Evidence of an early-established vestment tradition may in fact be seen in an address to Paulinus, Bishop of Tyre, related by the historian Eusebius in the early fourth century. The oration begins, "Friends of God and priests clothed with the sacred vestment and the heavenly crown of glory, the divine unction and priestly garments of the Holy Spirit. . . ."[xvii] [5]

The Theodosian Code of AD 382 presents the most compelling evidence for early standardization, as it requires all civil servants to wear a badge of office.[xviii] In the sixth century the same approach to standardization of dress is apparent in Justinian's "hierarchy of clothing" which restricts the use of specific textiles and specific garments to certain social classes.[xix] In addition to its grounding in ancient Roman practice, such a strict, ceremonial delineation of clothing has its origins as far back as ancient Assyria where scarves of office were awarded to high-ranking officials.[xx] The ceremonial use of garments was simply an unquestioned fact of life from ancient times through the Byzantine era and constituted a strict regulation of what today we would call "uniforms."

In our modern age we are accustomed to view uniforms as something purely utilitarian and functional, such as a postal carrier's or soldier's uniform. Yet despite our assumption that uniforms must be practical, even our present-day military uniforms have remnants of "scarves of office" in their epaulets, the golden bands worn on the shoulders of officers' dress uniforms. These ornaments might seem to serve a purely decorative purpose, but in reality constitute an absolutely essential feature of the uniform: at a glance one can see the rank of the person one is facing. Such was the case in ancient times as well as modern.

The fact that a source as early as the Theodosian Code required all civil servants to wear a "badge" or sign of their office is one of the most compelling arguments for the early standardization of Orthodox liturgical vesture, because from the fourth

---

5. Eusebius completed his *History of the Church* most likely no later than AD 324 and perhaps earlier. Thus, the possible reference to specific, hieratic vestments in the address to Paulinus occurs within a decade of the founding of Constantinople and could be seen as evidence of the standardization of vestments *prior* to the Christianization of New Rome, although this cannot be stated unequivocally from a scholarly standpoint.

century onward servants of the Church were also servants of the Byzantine state.[xxi] At the Council of Laodicea in Phyrgia, at the end of the fourth century (AD 342-380), minor orders were forbidden to use the *orarion*, which demonstrates that the garment was already well established as an identifying mark of the clergy by that time.[xxii] In Canon 23, St John Chrysostom provides the first extant mention of the *sticharion* as a purely liturgical garment (although he refers to it as a *"chitoniskos"* which is linguistically related to *"chiton,"* the ancient Greek word for tunic).[xiii] Mosaics in the church of St George in Thessaloniki, dated to the time of Constantine, depict martyr-bishop Philip and a presbyter, Romanos, in *phelonia*.[xxiv] And mosaics at Ravenna in the churches of San Vitale and Sant'Apollinare in Classe, which were installed during the reign of Justinian, show a very structured use of liturgical garments, making it easy to distinguish which figures are bishops and which are presbyters or deacons. From these and other sources, it is clear to see that we can safely date the standardization of Orthodox Christian liturgical vesture to between the fourth to fifth centuries.

In addition to the widespread use of ceremonial dress, another argument for early standardization is found in the abundant evidence of generous Byzantine imperial patronage of the Church. As Gervase Mathews states, "Haghia Sophia was rebuilt by the Emperor not the Patriarch."[xxv] From AD 408 to 602 Byzantium enjoyed its greatest period of wealth and in this period imperial patronage played an integral part in Church life. Such patronage was motivated by reverence for the priesthood, eloquently stated by Justinian in his sixth novella:

> The greatest blessings of mankind are the gifts of God which have been granted to us by the mercy of Providence—the priesthood and the imperial authority. The priesthood ministers to things divine: the imperial authority is set over and shows diligence in things human; but both proceed from one and the same source, and both adorn the life of man. Nothing, therefore, will be a greater matter of concern to the emperor than the dignity and honour of the clergy; the more as without ceasing they offer prayers to God on

his behalf. For if the priesthood be in all respects without blame, and full of faith before God, and if the imperial authority rightly and duly adorn the commonwealth committed to its charge, there will ensue a happy concord which will bring forth all good things for mankind.[xxvi]

It is inconceivable that the same empire that would require all officers of state to wear specific signs of office would not require the same of its state-supported clergy. This understanding also puts to rest the occasionally proposed speculation that Christian clergy conducted their services in the clothing of the poor or lower classes—an emperor such as Justinian would simply not have allowed such a state of affairs, due both to his personally held beliefs regarding the dignity of the clergy as well as the fact that it would almost certainly have been illegal for a priest not to be somehow identified by his dress (as the Theodosian Code required of all persons of official rank). Additionally, the Byzantine civil service lasted until the middle of the fifteenth century, ensuring continuity in Byzantine art and culture for over 1000 years, which in turn safeguarded and solidified the early established traditions of Orthodox vesture.[27] Additions and ornaments might be added over the centuries, and certainly were, but it would have been profoundly anti-Byzantine to attempt to lessen, simplify or fundamentally alter the ceremonial dress of the clergy.

In very simple terms, the standardization and regulation of Orthodox Christian vestments begins with the *tunica (sticharion)*, which develops in two directions, first the undergarment (sometimes called the *"tunica talaris,"* which henceforward will be referred to as the *"sticharion"*) worn by the Orthodox Christian presbyter or bishop under his other vestments; and secondly as the wider-cut, fuller-sleeved *colobium*, which goes on to become the deacon's *sticharion* in the Church, the garb of the emperor in the civil sector, and then in turn develops into the bishop's *sakkos*. In its undergarment version the *sticharion* is often depicted in icons with the vertical *clavi* on either side of the center front. The earliest mosaic depictions present both deacons and higher clergy vested in *sticharia* with *clavi*, but hierarchs wear a *paenula* over the *sticharion*, thereby distinguishing the higher ranks from the deacons. The *paenula* is the garment from which the *phelonion* originates, both being names for a large, cape-like over-garment (this is the most visible garment when a presbyter is fully vested). In one of the most important early mosaics from a garment history standpoint, we see St Apollinare, in the Classe church bearing his name (Fig. 9), vested as a bishop, wearing first the *sticharion* with *clavi*, then the *phelonion* (which, it should be noted, is adorned with a beautiful and elaborate pattern), and then a curious garment draped around his shoulders with one end hanging down: the *omophorion* (which will be discussed further below).

Figure 9. Sant'Apollinare in Classe. Note how St Apollinare is vested as a bishop (Otto Von Simson, *Sacred Fortress*, Princeton University Press, Plate 22).

The *phelonion* originated as a very voluminous garment, originally worn almost to the feet in both the front and back of the body, essentially a large circle with an opening for the head in the center. Multiple examples of early phelonia are depicted in the mosaics of San Vitale and Sant'Apollinare in Classe. While the most famous mosaic in Sant'Apollinare is that of the titular saint as described above, the register of mosaics below this shows four episcopal successors, each of whom is depicted wearing the *phelonion* with omophorion. That the *phelonion* originally had a much longer front length than is currently used is further supported by the depictions of these four bishops; they all four have the *phelonion* hanging past the knee at their left sides as they cover their left hands holding the Gospel (factoring in the extra fabric to cover the left hand, the fully-draped length of the *phelonion* would have been almost floor-length). On their right sides, the excess drape of the *phelonion* is gathered into the crook of their elbow so that they may bless with their exposed right hand. Despite this original front length of the *phelonion*, practicality won out over time and the front of the *phelonion* began to be shortened so that the priest could more easily move about during divine services, the current length (typically to the waist) possibly being as late an adaptation as the seventeenth century, although it is unclear exactly when this transition occurred. It is just as likely that the *phelonion* could have been shortened very gradually over many centuries.

It is a feature of Orthodox liturgical dress that as a man advances through the major clerical orders, he does not lay aside his previous garments, but rather layers them one upon the other. Thus, the bishop is vested first in his *sticharion*, a sign of his diaconal vocation, then his *phelonion*, a sign of his presbyteral vocation, and finally his *omophorion*, the sign of his episcopal vocation.[6] It is interesting to note that this layering of garments is a visual reminder of the Orthodox understanding that with

---

6. Since the eleventh to twelfth centuries, it has become increasingly common for bishops to be vested in the *sakkos*—a specific form of the *colobium*—rather than the *phelonion*. While the *sakkos* has distinct imperial overtones (being the vestment of the emperor) and is a glorious garment, I have a complaint against its episcopal usage due to the fact that it displaces the *phelonion*, and thus is lost the symbology of the bishop taking on additional responsibility (i.e., oversight of the presbyterate) and suggests the laying aside of one office (the presbyterate) in order to assume another (the episcopate). The more ancient usage, in which the bishop assumes the *omophorion*, worn over the *phelonion*, emphasizes the proper ecclesial understanding in which the bishop is the head and overseer of the local synod of presbyters.

more service comes greater responsibility. It also underscores an important concept in Byzantine ornamentation, that of layering. This is frequently seen in Orthodox Church decoration, an aesthetic approach that can appear overdone to the modern eye, accustomed as it is to utilitarian simplicity, but wholly appropriate to the Byzantine view in which the Church on earth was seen as a mirror image of Heaven and, as such, should look glorious and multi-faceted.

Scarves of Office: Orarion, Epitrachelion, Omophorion

It is with the *omophorion* that we come to one of the most debated topics in the study of liturgical dress, that of the origin of the specific "garments of office" for the major orders of the clergy. For in addition to their *sticharion* or *phelonion*, each order (that is, deacon, presbyter, and bishop) has a corresponding "scarf of office": the *orarion, epitrachelion,* and *omophorion.* Most writers on this subject are at a loss to determine definitively the origins of these garments due to the lack of references in ancient texts and the often obscured, draped fabric folds depicted in iconography, ivory carvings, and mosaics. However, from a study of pre-Christian garments, Byzantine statecraft, and various ancient artworks, including early mosaics and consular diptychs, along with an understanding of the tailoring methods of producing these items, one may reach the conclusion that these three garments have their origin in two historical garments, namely the *toga* and the *pallium*, both of which had an either exclusively (in the case of the *toga*) or a primarily (in the case of the *pallium*) ceremonial or formal usage for at least two hundred years prior to the standardization of Orthodox Christian vestments.[7]

To begin with the deacon's *orarion*, this garment is a long, narrow band, usually five to seven inches in width, which is worn over the *sticharion,* suspended from the left shoulder and

---

7. While I have expended much effort in finding firm correlations, absolute confirmation continues to elude me in the shadows of history, and so I must be clear that these are purely my own theories, some supported by respected authors on the subject, such as Duchesne and Legg, and others not.

extending to the hem of the *sticharion* both in front and in back (the additional length wrapped around the torso and over the right hip, as is now in use in the Greek tradition, seems to be a later addition, and its initial use could have been reserved to archdeacons). In its general design the *orarion* is a very long rectangle, approximately nine feet in length (fifteen feet with the Greek hip loop). Some authors have attempted to trace its origins to the imperial "handkerchiefs" distributed by Aurelian to be waved in approval at the theatre or circus.[xxviii] According to this attribution the garment would carry, despite its imperial gifting, connotations of worldliness and entertainment, both of which ideas are strongly at odds with the deacon's primary role of service at the Divine Liturgy, such service being associated with the ministry of the angels in heaven. Several writers have tried to bolster the supposed connection of the *orarion* with Aurelian's handkerchief on the basis of speculative etymology. "*Os*" is Latin for "mouth" or "face," which some have taken to refer to the use of a scarf to wipe the face, thus suggesting that the *orarion* begins its liturgical service as a glorified napkin or sweat cloth.[8] Such explanations might well strike one as insufficient and slightly ridiculous. Previously we have noted the importance of studying the fundamental design of a garment when attempting to determine the origins of a particular piece of Orthodox liturgical vesture. A long, rectangular garment used for a formal purpose is more satisfactorily found in the ancient *pallium*, which we have previously seen was reserved for dignified settings and thus is far more appropriate in both its design and usage for the Divine Liturgy. As with most cloak-like garments, the *pallium* had two methods of wear: the first being to wrap the garment around the shoulders letting the ends hang down the front of the body; the second being to wrap the garment

---

8. The question of the source of the word "*orarion*" is a linguistic puzzle which is fascinating in its own right and may, or may not, shed light on the origins of the garment thus named. In addition to a derivation from "*os*," it has also been suggested that the name could derive from the Latin "*hora*" (referencing the deacon leading prayers at the services of the hours) or simply from the Latin verb "*orare*," meaning "to pray," and in this understanding could well have the meaning "the item one prays with," establishing it as a liturgical scarf of office and thereby differentiating it from a ceremonial or court scarf of office.

around the front and back of the body, covering one shoulder completely and fastening at the other shoulder with a pin or *fibula*. This latter style of wear is depicted on the courtiers in the Sant'Apollinare mosaics (see Fig. 10), yet more evidence of the use of the *pallium* as a mark of office and service, since courtiers were servants of the imperial court, an earthly corollary to the office of the deacon at the Divine Liturgy. If we take the *pallium* thus worn sideways, fastening at the left shoulder, and abbreviate it to a narrow strip (a natural evolution from ancient forms of folding and draping garments so that only the decorative border would be displayed), we have a garment identical to the deacon's *orarion*.[9] While there is no conclusive evidence proving this origin of the *orarion*, this theory best answers the foremost questions of suitability of use and consistency of design.

Figure 10. A mosaic from Sant'Apollinare in Classe depicting courtiers wearing the pallium. Note tablion worn by courtiers. (Otto Von Simon, *Sacred Fortress*, Princeton University Press, Plate 27).

---

9. If the form of the *orarion* does indeed come from the abbreviation of the full *pallium* to its decorative border edging, then another source for the word "*orarion*" is suggested: "*ora*" is a Latin word meaning "border" or "edge."

Moving on to the *epitrachelion*, the scarf of office of the presbyter, we may find its origins in the alternate wear of the *pallium*, that of suspending the garment around the shoulders and allowing the ends to hang down in front of the body. Once again, the *pallium* was associated with dignity and formality, as well as being the appropriate narrow, rectangular design, all of which points to the *epitrachelion* finding its origins in the *pallium*.[10] (In the West the name of the historic *pallium* eventually came to be associated with a badge of archepiscopal office, a fact which further underscores its revered position in garment history.) As the noted liturgical scholar Duchesne observes, "In the last analysis this scarf [the *pallium*] was, no doubt, a relic of the short mantle which had been brought into fashion in the Roman Empire by the Greeks. But the *discolora pallia* of the Theodosian Code were evidently scarves, and scarves of office, which were worn over the *paenula*...."[xxix]

In modern usage we are accustomed to seeing the *epitrachelion* held together with buttons up the front (or, more rarely, as a solid piece of fabric with a hole for the neck opening, sometimes referred to as the "Athonite" style due to its common use on the Holy Mountain), but this is a much later adaptation of the garment. The common form of the *epitrachelion* in early centuries was certainly that depicted in icons of the early Fathers, such as St John Chrysostom and St Basil the Great; in these depictions it is clear that the *epitrachelion* is a narrow, non-buttoned length of fabric hanging down from either side of the neck. In addition to these artistic representations there are also a number of extant, embroidered *epitrachelia*, many dating from as far back as the eleventh century, that are made in this non-buttoned style as highly embellished, narrow rectangles to be draped around the neck, all of which support the origins of the *epitrachelion* being traced to the *pallium* (see Fig. 11).

---

10. It is significant to note that, when laid out flat, an *orarion* and a buttonless *epitrachelion* without shaping at the neck are virtually identical, another argument for the common origin of both garments in the *pallium*.

Figure 11. Embroidered epitrachelion showing its origins in the pallium. (N. V. Drandakis, *Ecclesiastical Embroidery at the Monastery of Arkadi*, Holy Monastery of Arkadi, 67).

We now return to that garment which began our discussion of the various clerical scarves of office, the *omophorion*, the preeminent garment which identifies its wearer as a bishop. It is with the development of the *omophorion* that we find the most striking evidence of a conscious transference of symbolic garments from the civic to the spiritual realm. For in the *omophorion* of the Orthodox Church we find the last remnant of that great and quintessentially Roman garment, the *toga*. Other writers have opined that the origins of the *omophorion* are to be found in the *pallium*, but the widespread use of the *pallium* in late antiquity means that such a garment would not have been suitably commensurate with the status and respect accorded to bishops in the early Byzantine period. In order to better understand the elevated requirements of the bishop's particular badge of office, it is necessary to consider the authority accorded to the Christian episcopate as early as the Constantinian era:

> Under conditions, Constantine gave to the bishops the power of arbitration in certain suits; their findings were to be valid in the courts of the Empire, and it was enacted that the decrees of the Christian synods were to be upheld. Honorius later on enlarges the legislation of Constantine and gives to the arbitration of a bishop an authority equal to that of the Praefectus Praetorio himself, an officer second in importance only to the emperor. It would be thus quite natural

that a bishop being a high Roman official should adopt some of the ensigns of his civil duties.[xxx]

This official honor and authority bestowed by the emperor upon the Church's episcopate continued and expanded under Justinian:

> Although the emperor appointed his bishops, the Justinian Code conceded to them independence, immunity, and authority to an extent that must have made them sovereign lords wherever the imperial power was not immediately present. In the administration of the Byzantine Empire the bishop occupied a position second to no one except the emperor himself. In the city the bishop nominated the municipal officers, maintained fortifications, aqueducts, bridges, storehouses, and public baths; supervised weights and measures; and controlled the city's finances. In the provinces it was again the bishop who recommended candidates for the administrative posts and maintained a close watch on their activities, including those of the governor himself. In addition to these administrative powers, the bishop acted as judge. . . . The age did not distinguish between the two sources, spiritual and political, of the bishop's power.[xxxi]

For someone with authority as great as that wielded by a bishop, no mere *pallium*, however dignified, would suffice; he must wear the greatest symbol of office the ancient world had devised: the *toga*. We must remember that by the second century AD the *toga* was no longer used in its old senatorial form as a full cloak to cover the body, but as a purely ceremonial garment with distinctive folds, the *toga contabulata*, as shown in the consular diptych of Consul Anastasius in Fig. 12. In this diptych we see the consul wearing the *toga,* folded into a band approximately eight inches wide (this accorded with the eight-inch band of ornamentation along the edge of the *toga*), in the same

Y-shaped configuration as the present-day *omophorion*, with the exception that the back section of the garment is wrapped to the right front and draped over the left arm. (In modern usage, this section of the garment simply hangs down the back of the bishop and is not brought to the front of the body; this difference is most likely because bishops now usually wear the *omophorion* standing while all extant ivory consular diptychs show the consul seated.) This and other consular diptychs as well as iconographic depictions (see Fig. 13) provide a very strong visual argument for the *omophorion* originating from the *toga*, not the *pallium*. Further evidence is found in the Theodosian Code, where the *pallium* is bestowed upon lower-ranking officials, not those with the kind of overarching authority a bishop would wield.[xxxii] Yet again, we must look not only at the design of the garment, but also consider its appropriateness and suitability according to the mindset of the Byzantines. A garment which was seen as suitable to a consul in the secular realm would accord perfectly with the respect and honor due a bishop in the spiritual realm.[11]

---

11. It is likely that the *omophorion* began as a garment denoting the bishop's civil, rather than spiritual, authority. It is interesting to note that even in modern liturgical practice, the bishop wears the great *omophorion* until the reading of the Gospel at which point he removes the great *omophorion* and remains without *omophorion* until the end of the Great Entrance at which point he dons the small *omophorion* (an abbreviated *omophorion* of rather late development). This may well hark back to an early practice in which the bishop would have worn the *omophorion* until the Little Entrance (i.e. the start of the Divine Liturgy proper), at which point he would have removed it for the remainder of the Divine Liturgy, from that point forward being vested as a presbyter.

OF TUNICS, TOGAS AND TRADITION ✦ 71

Figure 12. Consular diptych. Note the *toga contabulata* worn in similar draping as the omophorion. (May G. Houston, *Ancient Greek, Roman and Byzantine Costume*, 125).

Figure 13. Icon of Christ the High Priest showing same draping as consular toga. Copyright © Holy Transfiguration Monastery, Brookline, MA, used by permission. All rights reserved.

Ancillary Vestment Pieces

Having surveyed the origins of the most significant pieces of Orthodox liturgical vesture, it now remains to consider a few auxiliary garments.

Zone (Belt)

The first of these is the *zone*, or belt, presently used by both presbyters and bishops. It is likely to remain impossible to establish this garment's precise time and place of origin since in any visual representation a *zone* would be hidden by overgarments and it is rarely mentioned in any early documents. This is an understandable omission, for such a small detail of clothing, while practical and necessary, is easily overlooked. However we can presume the *zone's* early usage due to the fact that many ancient forms of the tunic had folds held in place by some kind of girdle or belt, a necessary measure for the management of a voluminous garment. The *zone* almost certainly came into use as a practical garment but in time it took on symbolic significance. Its theological meaning was firmly rooted by the time of St Germanos (Patriarch of Constantinople from 715–730) who states, "The belt signifies that [the priest] wears the mortification of the body and chastity, having girded his loins with the power of truth."[xxxiii] The humble *zone* stands as a perfect example of how practical garments came to be imbued with theological symbolism in their evolution from daily wear to liturgical usage.

Epimanikia (Cuffs)

With the *epimanikia*, or cuffs, we find yet again a lack of precise information as to initial usage. We do know that they were first used by bishops who in later centuries then awarded the dignity of their use to presbyters and deacons. They were perhaps a fairly late addition as they are not mentioned in St Germanos' *On the Divine Liturgy* (eighth century) or any earlier documents; their first mention as a liturgical garment is not until 1054 in a letter written by Peter of Antioch.[xxxiv] However, this absence of mention may simply be due to the fact that unadorned cuffs could have been used in much the same way as the *zone*, that is to contain the voluminous sleeves of the tunic for practicality and, so may have not been considered a specialized garment associated only with vestments until they began to assume a highly embellished and decorative form which was more suitable to the character of an award piece. In the mosaics of San Vitale, Justinian is shown with bands around the sleeves of his *tunica talaris*, which could either be a decorative element of the actual tunic itself or removable cuffs worn to narrow the sleeves. Christ is depicted with similar bands, as is Melchizedek and the Evangelist Mark. In fact, it is interesting to note that in the mosaics of San Vitale, every single figure, whether male, female, or angelic, is depicted wearing some kind of banding at the wrist to gather in the full sleeves of their tunics (the only exception is the depiction of the four angels in the apse). At Sant'Apollinare in Classe the titular saint is shown with the same bands as those at San Vitale and the Emperor Constantine IV wears a more elaborate version of the cuffs that more closely resemble the *epimanikia* in use in modern times.

Epigonation

As with the *omophorion*, the origins of the *epigonation* have been a subject of much debate among scholars. Many authors trace its origins to a handkerchief or to the *maniple* of the West, but this appears unlikely. All evidence points to the consistent use of the *epigonation* as an award piece, given as a mark of service or favor. The piece was originally referred to as an *encherion*. From the earliest depictions of *epigonatia* in iconography, they are shown to be highly embellished, usually by heavy gold and metal embroidery and the use of jewels. This lozenge-shaped, stiff, lavishly ornamented piece is far removed from any square, limp handkerchief. Additionally, the purpose of a handkerchief or napkin does not readily suggest its adoption as a garment that is to be granted specifically as an award.

We find a very compelling alternate theory of the origins of the *epigonation*, however, if we consider the garments of the Byzantine court, specifically the cloak-like garment of courtiers, called the *paludamentum*, which was worn in the sideways fashion of the ancient *pallium*, resting upon the left shoulder and fastened at the right with a *fibula*. On this *paludamentum* was an often elaborate piece of decoration in the form of a lozenge situated over the right hip of the wearer, called the *tablion* (see Fig. 10), which was an integral feature of Byzantine male court dress from the fifth to tenth centuries. The most exquisite and elaborate decoration of the courtier's costume was often reserved for the *tablion* and in this the *tablion* exactly corresponds to the *epigonation's* use among the Church's vestments as that of a highly ornamented award piece.[12] Due to its limited size and its use as an award piece, some of the finest examples of Orthodox embroidered iconography are found on *epigonatia*, many of which are on display in museums and monasteries to this day. Central motifs can include Christ, the Theotokos, or any of the Great Feasts, and surrounding this primary motif are often intricate vinework and floral designs.

It seems certain that the *epigonation* was first bestowed upon bishops and "had become a regular item of liturgical dress. . . ."[xxxv] and then much later, most likely after the eleventh century, was awarded to presbyters for distinctive service.[xxxvi] Its modern usage underscores this ancient practice in that it is awarded to presbyters in various Orthodox jurisdictions for either the completion of formal theological training, the blessing of hearing confession, or in recognition of a lengthy and distinguished period of priestly service. In the *epigonation* may also be found the origins of the Russian *nabedrennik*, another presbyteral award piece, similar in size but in a horizontal, rather than trapezoidal, orientation and usually lacking the elaborate decoration that may adorn the *epigonation*.

---

12. J.W. Legg, in his *Church Ornaments and their Civil Antecedents,* is the only author I have found that argues for the origin of the *epigonation* in the *tablion*. While Legg's view is considered by one respected scholar "an intuitive leap without underpinnings from visual or textual sources" (Warren Woodfin, "On Late Byzantine Liturgical Vestments and the Iconography of Sacerdotal Power," doctoral dissertation, 1999, p. 30), as a tailor I find Legg's argument cogent and compelling given the perfect correspondence in size and usage between the *epigonation* and *tablion*, especially given the fundamental design differences between a garment that is supposed to drape (e.g., a handkerchief) and one that is supposed to be rigid (e.g., a tablion or epigonation). Draping and rigidity are completely opposed tailoring goals and require very different modes of construction.

Further Development of Bishops' Vestments

The last, significant piece of Orthodox Christian vesture that needs to be examined in a study of the origins of Church vestments is the bishop's *sakkos*. Up until the Middle Byzantine period (AD 867–1204) the bishop was vested in *sticharion, epitrachelion, zone, epimanikia, epigonation, phelonion,* and *omophorion*. Sometime around the eleventh to twelfth century, the episcopal *phelonion* underwent a new development and began to be made from *polystavros* material, a woven fabric with a geometric design of crosses ("*polystavros*" means "many crosses" in Greek). The use of this fabric for phelonia was the exclusive right of bishops, and, originally, only for the bishops in the sees of Caesarea, Ephesus, Thessaloniki, and Corinth.[xxxvii] By the fifteenth century, St Symeon of Thessaloniki refers to use of the *polystavros* as a privilege of all metropolitans[xxxviii] and from that point its use trickles down to all bishops and then, eventually, to presbyters as well. With this extension of the *polystavros phelonion* from certain episcopal sees to the entire episcopacy and thence to the entire presbyterate, we see how the award of vestments takes place and why, over time, vestments that originally were the prerogative of the episcopacy are now worn even by deacons (e.g., *epimanikia*).

Regarding the *sakkos*, sometime during the same period there comes a fascinating shift which results directly from the political fate of Byzantium. During the Middle Byzantine period the power of the emperors began to decline due to various socio-political developments, and the populace of Byzantium began to place more emphasis upon the power of heaven than upon the earthly power of the emperor. The idea of the court of Byzantium as a mirror image of the Heavenly Court became widespread and there was a freer interchange of symbology between earthly and heavenly.[xxxix]

It was during this time that the garment previously exclusive to the emperor, the *sakkos,* began to replace the *phelonion* in the episcopal liturgical attire, first of patriarchs, then gradually of all bishops. Just like the *polystavros phelonion*, there was a trickle-down effect: at first, only the patriarch was allowed the wearing of the *sakkos*, as is mentioned by Theodore Balsamon in the twelfth century, but by the fifteenth century, St Symeon of Thessaloniki recounts that all archbishops were allowed its use.[xl] All of the other historic garments such as the *sticharion* and *epitrachelion* continued to be worn by the bishop, but the *phelonion* was laid aside in favor of the imperial *sakkos* with its connotations of spiritual authority now eclipsing even the highest earthly authority.

In construction, the bishop's *sakkos* is a highly ornamented *colobium*. It is similar to the deacon's *sticharion*, but is worn shorter, most likely a necessary feature due to its use of heavy and ornate fabrics and also possibly so that any ornamentation on the *sticharion* and *epitrachelion* might be seen, an example of the layered fashion much beloved of the Byzantines. The sleeves of the bishop's *sakkos* are often shorter as well, the better to display the elaborately embellished *epimanikia* worn on the sleeves of the *sticharion* underneath.

Today, we most commonly see a bishop attired in *sakkos* with *omophorion*, now referred to as the "great" *omophorion* to distinguish it from an abbreviated form, the "small" *omophorion*. In the course of the Divine Liturgy, the bishop removes the great *omophorion* and replaces it with the much shorter *small omophorion* so that he is less encumbered for the Anaphora prayers and Communion. These two *omophoria* are nearly always matching in fabric and decoration since they are essentially two forms of the same garment.

The episcopal miter, the heavily ornamented crown featuring metal-thread embroidery and iconographic depictions, was a quite late addition to Orthodox Christian practice. Originally, the use of headgear during a liturgical service was reserved as a special right of the patriarch of Alexandria and the use of the miter was only taken up by other bishops when the patriarch of Alexandria was translated to Constantinople in the seventeenth century.[xli]

Conclusion

With this overview of ancient garment history, culminating in the standardization of Orthodox liturgical vesture in the early Byzantine Roman Empire, we clearly observe a methodical and ordered development, particularly in the transformation of Roman imperial, ceremonial garments into Orthodox ecclesiastical garments. Contrary to popular and some scholarly opinion, Orthodox Christian vestments did not emerge from a random evolution, but rather are the result of a focused development stemming from a conscious endeavor to redeem the garments of the pomp of the world and transform them into the glorious, heavenly garments of salvation. Our beautiful vestment tradition is no mere accident of history but rather an important facet of the story of salvation and, as such, cannot be relegated to the realm of aesthetic preference, but must take its proper historical and spiritual place as a visible testament to our theology, an expression of the love and mercy of God, and the proper adornment of the Church of Christ.

Endnotes

i. Carl Kohler, *A History of Costume* (Mineola, NY: Dover Publications, 1963), 66.
ii. Kohler, 67.
iii. Kohler, 69.
iv. Kohler, 70.
v. Mary G. Houston, *Ancient Greek, Roman, and Byzantine Costume* (Mineola, NY: Dover Publications, 2003), 16.
vi. Houston, 75.
vii. Houston, 87.
viii. Houston, 93.
ix. Houston, 135.
x. Houston, , 92.
xi. Houston, 120.
xii. Houston, 126.
xiii. Kohler, 116.
xiv. Robert Browning , *Justinian and Theodora* (New York, NY: Praeger Publishers, 1971), 89.
xv. Browning, 89.
xvi. Gervase Mathew, *Byzantine Aesthetics* (London: John Murray, 1963), 62.
xvii. Eusebius, *The History of the Church* (London: Penguin Books, 1865), 306.

xviii. J.W. Legg, *Church Ornaments and Their Civil Antecedents* (Cambridge: Cambridge University Press, 1917), 25.
xix. Robert Sabatino Lopez, "Silk Industry in the Byzantine Empire," *Speculum*, Vol. 20, No. 1 (January 1945): 1–42.
xx. Kohler, 71.
xxi. Louis Duchesne, *Christian Worship: Its Origins and Evolutions* (London: SPCK, 1904), 384.
xxii. Duchesne, 391.
xxiii. Archimandrite Chrysostomos, *Orthodox Liturgical Dress* (Brookline, MA: Holy Cross Orthodox Press), 37.
xxiv. Chrysostomos, 45.
xxv. Mathew, 53.
xxvi. Browning, 98.
xxvii. Mathew, 54.
xxviii. Chrysostomos, 40.
xxix. Duchesne, 386.
xxx. Legg, 1.
xxxi. Otto G. Von Simpson, *Sacred Fortress, Byzantine Art and Statecraft in Ravenna* (Princeton, NJ: Princeton University Press), 40.
xxxii. Duchesne, 386.
xxxiii. St Germanos, *On the Divine Liturgy*, Paul Meyendorff, trans. (Crestwood, NY: St Vladimir's Seminary Press, 1985), 69.
xxxiv. Christopher Walter, *Art and Ritual of the Byzantine Church* (London: Variorum Publications Ltd, 1982), 20.
xxxv. Walter, 21.
xxxvi. Warren Woodfin, "Late Byzantine Embroidered Vestments and the Iconography of Sacerdotal Power," doctoral dissertation (Urbana, IL: University of Illinois at Urbana-Champaign, April 2002), 31.
xxxvii. Walter, 14.
xxxviii. Walter, 14.
xxxix. Henry Maguire, ed. *Byzantine Court Culture from 829 to 1204* (Cambridge, MA: Harvard University Press, 1997), 247.
xl. Walter, 17.
xli. Walter, 29–30.

Chapter Three

The Garments of Salvation

My soul shall rejoice in the Lord, for he hath clothed me with the garment of salvation, and with the robe of gladness hath he encompassed me. As a bridegroom he hath set a crown upon me, and as a bride hath he adorned me with ornament, always, now and ever, and unto ages of ages. Amen.

Vesting prayer for the donning of the sticharion (Is 61.10)[i]

Present-Day Usage of Orthodox Christian Vestments

Now that we have examined the origins of Orthodox Christian liturgical garments, we turn our attention to the garments as they are used today. While Orthodox Christian vestments have changed little through the centuries, making it easy to observe the basic form of their precursors in even the most contemporary vestments, please note that this chapter will focus specifically on Orthodox ecclesiastical vesture as used in North America in the early twenty-first century. Here we will describe in close detail the venerable tradition of Byzantine vesture as it is expressed in a particular time and place.

While the information provided in this chapter is as complete as possible so that it may inform current usage and provide an accurate record for posterity, the information contained here is *not* intended to be a do-it-yourself guide to making vestments. The study of vestment construction is no different from the other arts of the Church, such as iconography or chant, and therefore must be based upon the traditional apprentice and master model in which one desiring to learn the craft of vestments must study with a master tailor for a period of several years. During this training period, the apprentice learns how to select brocades and finishings based upon traditional color usage, is taught the correct methods of construction, and studies how the finished garments should fit and drape. An apprentice's work is checked thoroughly by the master and in this way the apprentice learns to create vestments that fit correctly and do not deviate from traditional forms, colors, and ornamentation, thereby maintaining the long-standing stability that is so important with Orthodox Christian liturgical vesture. While this apprentice and master model may seem outdated, it is vital that this traditional method of educating ecclesiastical tailors be maintained, because it is only by handling, sewing, and working with brocades and finishings under the tutelage of an experienced master craftsman that a novice tailor learns to tell high quality from low, the valuable from the valueless, true gold from dross.

A significant difference between ancient and contemporary vestments is notable primarily in the fabrics used for their construction. Following on the heels of the discovery and commercialization of synthetic dyestuffs in the late nineteenth century (for more on this topic, please see Chapter Five), the rapid adoption of synthetic fibers such as rayon and polyester in the mid-twentieth century almost entirely eclipsed the use of the traditional fibers of silk, wool, and linen in the matter of a few short decades.[1] This accounts for the widespread use of modern, synthetic fabrics such as polyester brocades, rayon brocades, polyester satins, and even such recent innovations as polyester athletic wicking fabrics used for cassocks. As with all materials used for the adornment of the Church, conscious attention must be paid to ensure that when synthetic fibers are used they are of a good quality and made with traditional designs and colors.

---

1. This is particularly true in the use of silk brocades. Historically, silk was the fiber of first choice for over one thousand years, whereas in my twenty years working as an ecclesiastical tailor I have made fewer than 15 sets of silk vestments. Happily, silk brocades from India based upon historic designs are now available to the North American market and I look forward to seeing more of these truly remarkable fabrics taking their rightful place in beautifying the Church once again.

Computer-design technology has made this much more attainable, especially in the arena of machine-embroidered fabrics, so that we are now able to employ historic designs produced with modern technologies and materials.

Baptismal Robe

The baptismal robe is the universal garment of the Orthodox Christian Church and its basic design forms the foundation of many vestments, serving as a visible testament to one's baptismal regeneration, whether the wearer is a newly illumined layman, altar server, deacon, presbyter, or bishop. This garment is a long tunic, worn to the feet or ankles with wide sleeves approximately twenty inches in circumference. The neck placket is comprised of a circle for the head with a long slit coming down eight to ten inches along the center front, thus facilitating the garment's passage over the head. This neck placket is finished with galloon (decorative trim) under which the raw edge of the fabric is pressed and sewn in place to create a clean border (not with a facing as in modern garment construction). When made to fit an adult, it is cut from one whole piece of cloth with small extensions sewn onto the sleeves to add length, but when sized for infants or children, the sleeve extensions are unnecessary. A four-inch to six-inch cross is sewn to the back of the garment between the shoulder blades, which position is symbolically close to the heart. For those who are baptized in adulthood the baptismal robe may be kept to be used as a burial shroud upon death.

The baptismal robe of the Orthodox Christian originates from what is arguably the most basic of ancient, civilized garments: the tunic. As delineated above, while there have been various lengths and styles of tunics throughout human history, the tunic that the Orthodox Christian baptismal robe is based upon is the *sticharion* of Byzantium ("*tunica talaris*" in Latin). The long profile is a pre-Christian symbol of high rank or status which, in the Church's usage, came to bespeak the Christian's adoption as a son of God, thus being given the highest possible human rank by adoption into the family of God.

This garment is always white to symbolize purity and new life and is made from either cotton or a polyester-cotton blend, silk broadcloth, linen, or synthetic polyester satin. The neck placket is finished with either half-inch, one-inch, or one-and-a-half-inch wide galloon and the cross on the back can be either gold, silver, white, or red, depending on preference and local custom.

The baptismal robe of an Orthodox Christian is bestowed at his baptism, immediately after he emerges from the font. The

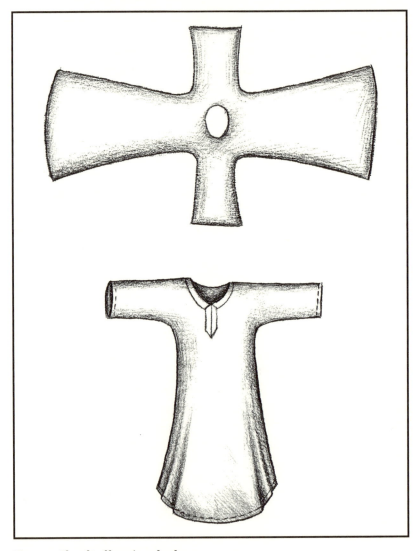

Figure 1. Sketch of baptismal robe.

robe is blessed by the priest and given to the infant's godparents to clothe him or, in the case of adult baptism, given to the sponsor to assist the newly illumined.[2] In many traditions the baptismal robe is worn to the Divine Liturgy for a period of time following the baptism: forty days, three consecutive Sundays, or some other length of time specified by local custom.

Vestments of the Minor Orders

In the Orthodox Christian Church, there are both minor and major clerical orders. The minor orders are blessed or tonsured to a specific realm of service in a particular parish (e.g., reading, chanting, serving at the altar) and these offices comprise acolyte, reader, chanter, and subdeacon. The major orders are ordained and are comprised of the offices of deacon, presbyter, and bishop.

A reader or chanter does not wear vestments properly speaking. Rather both the reader and the chanter wear, while exercising their offices within the church, some form of either the inner or outer cassock (see the subsequent section on cassocks for more information on these garments).

An altar server, also known as an acolyte or taper-bearer, wears the garment referred to as the *sticharion*. This garment is quite similar in overall design to a baptismal robe, being a long, tunic-type garment, but in the case of a brocade *sticharion* it is not made from one whole piece of cloth (due to the bulkiness of the fabric) but is rather made from a front and back cut from brocade and sewn together at the shoulders and the sides. This brocade *sticharion* is the same garment whether worn by altar servers, subdeacons, or deacons, but the altar server's and

---

2. For infants, modern usage allows for more ornate, embellished baptismal robes in the style of Western christening gowns, although these are typically reserved for female infants and are usually embellished with lace, embroidery, and other finery. In modern usage, male infants are often clothed after their baptism in miniature suit coats and pants. While the female christening gown closely approximates a traditional baptismal robe, the practice of putting a male infant in what is essentially nineteenth-century adult male attire is not reflective of the Orthodox Christian ethos and should be eschewed. Tradition requires a baptismal *robe*.

subdeacon's *sticharion* is typically made with less ornamentation than the deacon's and with sewn sides rather than button sides. An altar server's *sticharion* features a galloon neck placket, double bands of galloon at the sleeves and hem, and a simple cross sewn to the back between the shoulder blades. While the color and design of the brocade can vary widely, it is considered seemly that such brocade is never more ornate or lavish than that worn by a deacon or presbyter in order that the vestments of the minor order not eclipse those of the major.

A subdeacon vests in a brocade *sticharion* just like the altar server's, but with the addition of a subdeacon's *orarion*, a long, rectangular garment which is a simpler version of the deacon's *orarion*. Because the width of the *orarion* is a historic indication of rank (the wider the *orarion*, the higher the rank), the subdeacon's *orarion* is narrow, typically four inches wide. It varies in length depending on the wearer, but can be anywhere from thirteen to sixteen feet long. Its ornamentation is a simplified variation on the deacon's *orarion* and typically features three crosses (one placed at the center and one at each end), galloon around the perimeter, and no fringe. The *orarion* is usually made from brocade to match the *sticharion*, but can also be made of different-colored brocades or solid-colored velvets which can then be worn in conjunction with a bright brocade *sticharion* to conform to color rubrics (e.g., in Great Lent a subdeacon could wear a gold brocade *sticharion* with a dark burgundy *orarion*).

The subdeacon's *orarion* is worn over the brocade *sticharion* in the following manner: the center of the *orarion* is wrapped around the waist and both ends are taken to the back where they are crossed over the shoulder blades and brought to the front of the wearer; these ends are then crossed and tucked through the portion of the *orarion* that is wrapped around the waist in order to secure them. Wearing the *orarion* in this manner partially conceals the cross on the back of the *sticharion*, but this is distinctly preferable to placing the cross much lower down the back because such lower positioning places the cross directly behind the lower organs instead of near the heart and thus does not retain the symbolism of the cross being worn adjacent to the spiritual center of the man. In some cases, if a subdeacon is preparing for imminent, diaconal ordination, he will wear the more ornate deacon's *sticharion* and *orarion* (without cuffs) in order that he need not purchase separate sets of vestments, but he will still wear the *orarion* in the subdiaconal fashion.[3]

Figure 2. Photograph of altar server's robe.

---

3. In modern Greek practice a bishop will sometimes bless child altar servers to vest with the *orarion* in the manner of a subdeacon, but the use of the *orarion* for altar boys is a recent innovation (due to the decline, in some places, of the subdiaconal order) and not part of the traditional practice of the Orthodox Church, which typically does not appoint immature children to the serious and permanent responsibility of any order within the Church.

Figure 3. Photograph of altar server's robe with subdeacon's orarion.

Vestments of the Major Orders

As mentioned above, the major orders of the Church are deacon, presbyter, and bishop.[4] Their vestments are more ornate and comprised of more garments than the minor orders and are typically made from more splendid fabrics and finishings. We will examine the vestments of each order in turn.

---

4. For the sake of precision, I prefer to use the term "presbyter" to refer to the second major order of the Church. There is room for confusion with the use of the common English word "priest" (even though "priest" is linguistically derived from "presbyter"). In Greek there are two distinct words that may be translated as "priest": "πρεσβύτερος" ("*presbyteros*," literally "elder") which in ecclesiastical usage denotes specifically a member of the second major order of the Church, and "ἱερεύς" ("*ierefs*," meaning "minister" or "cleric") which may be used to denote a member of any of the three major orders, especially either a bishop or a presbyter. To be clear, I use "presbyter" when speaking specifically about the second order, reserving "priest" for instances where a statement may be understood to apply to both presbyters and bishops.

Vestments of the Deacon

The deacon vests in a *sticharion*, typically of brocade material, which is almost exactly the same in design as the brocade *sticharion* of the altar server or subdeacon, but is finished in a more ornate manner. Whereas the altar server's *sticharion* is finished with simply sewn sides and galloon trim at only the hem and sleeves (and is sometimes unlined), the deacon's *sticharion* is finished not only with these same decorative bands at hem and sleeve, but also has galloon sewn around the entire perimeter of the garment and the garment is then fully lined. The sides are held together by either buttons and loops or buttons sewn through both sides of the garment. This method of finishing emphasizes the ancient symbolic shape of the garment which forms a cross when it is unbuttoned and laid out flat.

In general design, the deacon's *sticharion* is quite similar to the baptismal robe from which it is derived, but it has been tailored to reduce the bulk of the brocade from which it is made and thus has become more like the ancient *colobium* which was also a heavier garment than a common tunic. The deacon's *sticharion* features wider sleeves, twenty-eight to thirty-four inches in circumference, and it is common for the final button holding the sleeves together to be placed not at the very end of the sleeve (near the wrist), but several inches back in order that the cuffs may be better displayed.

The upper bands of galloon sewn to the sleeves and hem serve both a decorative and practical purpose: because brocade is usually no wider than sixty inches it is not wide enough to cut the entire front or back of the *sticharion* with the necessary sleeve length, so extra pieces of brocade must be sewn to the *sticharion* to extend the sleeves. The galloon hides the seam of these extensions, giving the appearance of the garment being made from one entire piece of cloth.

In Greek style the deacon's *sticharion* has the traditional neck placket and the galloon bands as described above along with the perimeter galloon, but in the Russian style a further galloon embellishment is often added by sewing a square, or "bib," of galloon on the front and back of the upper torso area. When the galloon bib is used the cross on the back of the *sticharion* is centered within this square. Further ornamentation can be added by variations which incorporate solid-colored velvet into the brocade *sticharion*. Velvet can be sewn into the entire area of the galloon bib in the case of the Russian style, or it can take the place of the brocade in the sleeve extensions. When velvet is used for the sleeve extensions, there is usually a coordinating band of velvet sewn between the bands of galloon at the hem of the garment.

While the deacon's *sticharion* of today is nearly always made from brocade, be it polyester or real-metal brocade, this is conjectured by scholars to be a rather late development. Prior to the use of brocade it would have been typical for solid-colored silk or wool to be used (or possibly linen, although this is less likely due to its impractical tendency to wrinkle). It is difficult to pinpoint the exact moment of transition from solid-colored textiles to brocades and more scholarship is necessary to determine the point of this change and even the veracity of such a transition. (Because silk brocades were so heavily in use throughout the entire Byzantine Empire one wonders how, while all other vestments were made from patterned silk, the deacon's *sticharion* would have been somehow exempted from this practice.)

A variety of fabrics are currently used for the deacon's *sticharion:* these include synthetic brocades (polyester or rayon), real-metal brocades (polyester base with metallic fibers woven throughout), silk brocades, machine-embroidered polyesters, machine-embroidered velvet, and both synthetic and cotton velvet (the latter is greatly preferred due to its more historic appearance). Less-ornate versions can be made of fabrics with woven designs (typically polyester-cotton blends) or machine-embroidered embellishments. These styles made from lighter fabrics are often left unlined for greater comfort.

The *orarion* is the scarf of office for the deacon, typically a very long and narrow garment (nine to fifteen feet in length and five to seven inches in width) worn over the *sticharion*. In Greek practice (and in the case of Russian archdeacons or protodeacons), it is worn in a particular looped fashion (this looped form of the garment may be termed a "double *orarion*"): starting at the left back heel, the *orarion* is brought up to the left shoulder, comes down across the chest draping diagonally to the right hip whence it is wrapped around and brought across the upper back to the left shoulder once again, and then drapes over the left shoulder to the front of the body and hangs down to the left front foot. From this position the front section is then taken up and remains either draped over the left forearm or held in the right hand for the intoning of petitions. The Russian practice is for the *orarion* to be worn from the left back heel up to the shoulder and then draped down to the left front foot from whence it is taken up over the left arm or held in the right hand. Because there is no hip loop in the ordinary Russian usage (excepting deacons who have been elevated to preeminent rank) the Russian *orarion* is typically six feet shorter than the Greek *orarion*, making it approximately nine to ten feet in length (this shorter form of the garment may be termed a "single *orarion*").

Whether the *orarion* is worn in the looped, Greek fashion or in the straight, Russian fashion, its draping is changed by the deacon prior to his receiving Holy Communion and assisting with the distribution of the Holy Gifts to the laity (ordinarily this change is made at the recitation of the "Our Father" in the Divine Liturgy). The center of the *orarion* is drawn to the front of the waist and the ends are brought to the back, crossed over the shoulder blades, brought over the shoulders and tucked, crossed, through the center front at the waist, so that the *orarion* assumes the same configuration as that used by a subdeacon. This secures the ends of the *orarion* so that the deacon's hands are free for the reception of the Holy Gifts and to better assist with the ministration of the chalice.

The *orarion* is interfaced to provide stability and durability, lined, and finished with galloon around its entire perimeter and double rows of galloon and fringe at each end. There are seven crosses which are sewn in the following manner: one at the center of the *orarion* (worn at the bottom of the hip loop in the Greek practice and worn at the top of the left shoulder in the Russian practice), and then three crosses sewn to the front and three crosses sewn to the back. These seven crosses represent the seven gifts of the Holy Spirit.

The archdeacon's or protodeacon's *orarion* is awarded to a deacon when he is elevated to preeminence within the diaconate. It is wider than the standard *orarion*, typically six to eight inches wide, and approximately fifteen feet long since the hip loop is employed in both Greek and Russian practice. Because the archdeacon's or protodeacon's *orarion* is an award given after many years of diaconal service or on account of a deacon's leading liturgical role, it is a much more ornate garment, often lavishly embroidered with a design scheme comprised of grapevines to symbolize the deacon's service during Holy Communion, the monogram "Holy, Holy, Holy" (Is 6.3), and iconographic representations of cherubim and seraphim which call to mind the correspondence of the deacon's role at the earthly Altar to the position at the heavenly Altar of the higher angels, who continually cry "Holy, Holy, Holy." Due to the elaborate embellishment of the archdeacon's or protodeacon's *orarion*, there will often be fewer crosses, usually reduced to three in order to symbolize the Holy Trinity. These elaborately embellished award *oraria* are made either of a deep blue or burgundy ground fabric of velvet or silk and are then worn with all of the deacon's *sticharia*, regardless of the color or design of the *sticharion*. They may also be made from brocade to match existing deacon's vestments.

The last pieces of the deacon's vestments are *epimanikia* (cuffs), and these will be discussed in more detail in the "Vestments of the Presbyter" section below. Cuffs were not a part of the ancient diaconal vestments but are a fairly late addition, granted by episcopal award.

When the deacon's vestments are made as a set comprised of *sticharion, orarion,* and *epimanikia,* each of the pieces is made from matching brocade, lining, and galloon. Often the crosses will be a matching set, with the crosses on the *orarion* and cuffs being smaller versions of the main cross on the back of the *sticharion.* However, it is also common practice for a deacon to vest with various-colored *oraria,* either brocade or velvet, worn in conjunction with either a bright or dark brocade *sticharion,* to be in conformance with the rubrics or local color traditions. Not only an economical practicality, this can be a very beautiful expression of the Orthodox Christian approach to color usage: a deacon can wear a white and gold *sticharion* with a deep blue velvet *orarion* or a red *sticharion* with a gold *orarion*—the variations are limitless and reflect the historical approach to color found within the Orthodox Christian Church (for more information on color, please see Chapter Five).

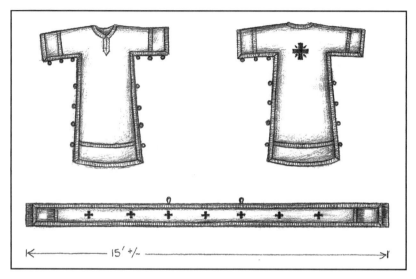

Figure 4a. Sketch of deacon's vestments, Greek style.

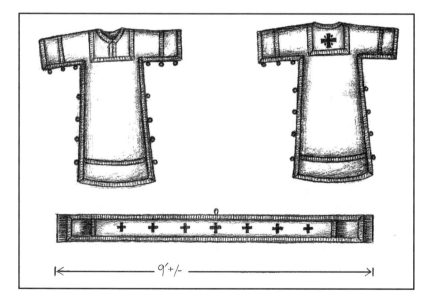

Figure 4b. Sketch of deacon's vestments, Russian style.

When serving the Divine Liturgy and assisting at the Prothesis, the deacon is fully vested with *sticharion, orarion,* and *epimanikia*. For Great Vespers he vests in the *sticharion* and *orarion,* but does not wear cuffs. Deacons typically do not serve at daily Vespers, but when they are called upon to serve they wear—in the Greek practice—the *exorason* with *orarion* (this is also the practice for other minor services or blessings). For baptisms, weddings, and funerals, the deacon vests in *sticharion* and *orarion.* (It should be noted that in the modern Russian practice the deacon is usually fully vested for all services.) For Pascha and Bright Week the major orders are fully vested for every service, which means the deacon wears *sticharion, orarion,* and *epimanikia.*

Vestments of the Presbyter

The presbyter's vestments include the *sticharion, epitrachelion, zone, epimanikia,* and *phelonion.*[5] Special award pieces may also be worn, which are discussed below. The presbyter begins vesting by putting on his *sticharion* which is identical in design to the baptismal robe but is finished with more galloon ornamentation that often coordinates with the galloon used on the rest of the vestment set. The *sticharion* represents his baptism garment and thus is typically white or off-white (though in Greek practice the fabric of the *sticharion* sometimes matches the color and fabric of the lining of the vestments) and can be made from cotton, cotton-polyester blends, synthetic satin, silk broadcloth, or occasionally linen. Just like the baptismal robe it is made from one piece of cloth which, when laid out flat, forms the shape of a cross and has extensions sewn to the sleeves to make the garment the required width since most fabric used for *sticharia* is not wide enough to reach from wrist to wrist. The priest's *sticharion* has the typical galloon neck placket and is finished with a six-inch cross on the back sewn between the shoulder blades and various arrangements of galloon banding at the hem. These hem banding variations can range from double rows of either one-inch or one-and-a-half inch wide

---

5. *Zone* is pronounced *"ZOH-nee"*—two syllables with the accent on the first.

galloon spaced four to six inches apart to a single, three-inch wide band of galloon sewn at the very edge of the hem, to more elaborate embroidery designs worked along the lower eight to twelve inches of the garment (when this type of embroidery is utilized, it sometimes takes the place of any galloon embellishment). There is also a special variation in which an approximately six-inch band of the brocade of the vestments is sewn to the hem of the *sticharion*, bordered on either side by a band of galloon. The sleeves of the priest's *sticharion* are open from the elbow to the wrist and have a piece of cording sewn to the back of the sleeve which allows the priest to overlap the sleeve edges around his wrist, taking up the excess fabric, wrapping it around the wrist, and securing it with the cord. The most traditional *sticharia* have only side seams so that they retain the design feature of being made from one piece of cloth, but it is not uncommon to see *sticharia* with additional vertical seams in order to provide the necessary width if the given fabric is not wide enough for the garment or to reduce the overall girth of the garment if a more tailored fit is desired. Regardless of the number of vertical seams, there are always slits along the side seam, approximately ten inches long, so that the priest may place the *zone* around his waist over the *sticharion* in the front and tie the ends of the *zone* under the *sticharion* in the back.

The *epimanikia* are curved rectangles, being narrower at the wrist and wider at the forearm. They serve to embellish the sleeve ends of the *sticharion* at the same time as they help contain the voluminous sleeves. These cuffs retain their ancient garment design by wrapping around the wrist and fastening with a system of seven metal rings through which a long piece of cord winds, beginning at the wrist and proceeding alternately through each ring to the forearm, after which the remainder of the cord is wrapped around the forearm to secure the cuff in place. While *epimanikia* are typically made from brocade and galloon to match the set of vestments, there is also a beautiful tradition of cuffs being highly embellished with embroidery which is most likely a feature of their smaller size and their origin as a gift or award piece. One of the most historically significant embroidery motifs for this application is a representation of the Annunciation in which the Mother of God is portrayed on the right cuff and the Archangel Gabriel on the left. When the priest moves his hands together the action symbolizes the Annunciation and becomes a type of living icon.

The *epitrachelion* is the scarf of office for the presbyterate. While this garment began as a long band, approximately three to six inches wide, that simply wrapped around the neck and hung down the front of the body almost to the floor, in current usage it features a curved, fitted neck and the two bands reaching to the floor are held together with seven buttons sewn down the center front. It is usually made from the same brocade and galloon as the vestment set and features seven crosses, once again referencing the seven gifts of the Holy Spirit. Six of the crosses, usually three to four inches in size, are sewn in confronted pairs spaced evenly along the front and a seventh, smaller cross is sewn at the back of the neck. This back neck cross is the one which the priest kisses when he vests. There are typically two banks of galloon and fringe sewn along the bottom of the *epitrachelion* with the bottom bank even with the edge of the garment and the upper bank positioned eight to fourteen inches above this, depending on the priest's height and the motif repeat of the brocade. The fringe, with its multiple, tiny threads, symbolizes the many souls under the priest's care.

There are variations of the *epitrachelion*, most notably the one-piece style in which a single breadth of fabric takes the place of the two bands fastened with buttons. This so-called "one-piece" *epitrachelion* features a galloon neck placket (just like that on the *sticharion*) for ease of vesting and is typically finished with three crosses, four to six inches in size, along the front in place of the six smaller crosses (the small cross at the center back neck is retained). The origins of this variation are unclear, but its usage likely began in monasteries since the overall design shows a marked similarity with the *analavos*, the symbolic garment which is bestowed upon monastics when they are tonsured to the great schema. Its one-piece design could also have come about due to its width providing a much better format for brocades with large-scale motifs; whereas the standard style necessitates cutting down the brocade into a five- to six-inch section which is then further obscured by the addition of vertical bands of galloon leaving barely four inches of brocade visible, the one-piece style allows for an almost ten-inch swath of brocade to be seen.

Similar to the *epimanikia*, *epitrachelia* may also be ornately embroidered and such decorated *epitrachelia* feature some of the most spectacular examples of traditional Orthodox Christian liturgical embroidery preserved in our monasteries and museums. Virtually covered with embroidery, these historic *epitrachelia* feature embroidered iconography of saints and scenes from the life of Christ, vinework and floral motifs, birds of paradise, elaborate cross designs, pearl work, and similar motifs. Truly breathtaking in their complexity, richness, and sheer beauty, these pieces are to honored, treasured and—one hopes—emulated by future generations of ecclesiastical artisans.

Figure 5. Embroidered *epitrachelion* from Holy Monastery of Iveron (Eleni Vlachopoulou-Karabina, *Holy Monastery of Iveron Gold Embroideries*. Mt Athos: Holy Monastery of Iveron, 67).

The *zone* is essentially a belt which serves the practical purpose of containing the broad girth of the *sticharion* and restricting the movement of the *epitrachelion*. Sewn from brocade to match the set of vestments, it is heavily interfaced to provide stability and durability and is finished around its entire perimeter with galloon to match the set of vestments and a small cross sewn at the center front. Ribbons are sewn between the brocade and lining on either end for fastening. The *zone* is worn over the *epitrachelion*.

Of the basic vestments of the presbyter, the final and most impressive garment is the *phelonion*. This large garment is made from a twelve-foot length of brocade and is similar in design to the cape from which it originates (the *paenula* of antiquity), hanging from four to eight inches above the floor in the back and cut away in front. It features the classic galloon neck placket and a band of galloon sewn around the perimeter. A large, ornate cross is sewn to the back between the shoulder blades (occasionally an embroidered icon may be used in the place of a cross, but it should always be an icon of Christ or an icon of the Mother of God with the Christ child). The *phelonion* is most commonly fitted by means of deep darts at the shoulder (typically one five- to six-inch dart on each shoulder) and can be made either fully lined or unlined (in the case of machine-embroidered fabrics, woven *polystavros* fabrics, or lightweight silks). In order to create its conical shape, the *phelonion* is made from a center panel, typically the entire width of the brocade, and then additional side flanges are attached to the center panel to create the necessary width. When made from brocade, the seams of these side flanges must be motif-matched in order that the seams are virtually invisible on the finished garment. When made from lightweight, embroidered fabrics or woven *polystavros* fabrics, the side flanges are eliminated since these materials are specially milled to be exceptionally wide, typically ten feet in width. Once the requisite width is achieved, the *phelonion* is sewn along the center front seam. While most contemporary *phelonia* feature a front that is much shorter than the back (usually waist length or higher), the fronts of historic *phelonia* were often worn to the knees or lower. For *phelonia* in which the front is significantly shorter than the back, two lengths of sturdy ribbon are sewn to the inside of the garment at the bottom of the galloon neck placket so that the wearer may secure the *phelonion* by tying the ribbons behind his back. This keeps the presbyter from being choked as the shorter front is pulled backwards by the greater weight of the longer back of the garment. Occasionally, a system of buttons and loops is employed along the front edge of the *phelonion* so that the wearer can fasten the front up for freer movement during the Proskomedia and critical portions of the Divine Liturgy.

Like other vestment pieces, there are multiple variations of the *phelonion*, but they can be divided into two basic categories: the so-called "low-back" variation described above which is fitted around the neck by means of shoulder darts, and the "high-back" or "Athonite" variation which is made without any darting, resulting in a large section that stands up behind the neck area, often to the middle of the back of the head. To provide stability and shape to this excess fabric, a large piece of interfacing must be sewn into the garment in the entire upper portion and this interfacing is held in place along its bottom edge by an additional "bib," or square, of galloon sewn in the upper torso area along the front and back. The high-back *phelonion* is commonly used in both the Russian practice and in the monasteries of Mt Athos. It is a wonderful canvas for the display of elaborate, heavy, real-metal brocades with large-scale motif repeats and has the advantage of fitting multiple, variously-sized wearers since the neck and shoulders are unfitted (this may well account for the popularity of this style in monasteries where the same *phelonion* may be used by multiple hieromonks in rotation). In some variations the interfaced portion may be made with inset velvet, which is referred to in Russian as an "*opelchye*." This velvet can be finished with an eight-inch cross or more elaborate embroidery, occasionally covering the entire ground of the velvet.

Many people have wondered and speculated which form of the *phelonion* is the original: the low-back or the high-back variety? An examination of the historical record (limited as it is) yields the paradoxical answer: both and neither. Judging from what we can observe of the back section of *phelonia* in historic icons (always a limited view, since the priest wearing the garment faces the observer) and judging as well from very old (though not quite ancient) *phelonia* that are preserved in museum collections, it seems clear that the early form of this garment was conical in shape with an aperture for the head at the top of the cone. Fabric was cut away for the neck opening on the front side of the garment, leaving a certain amount of material to fall down and pool behind the neck of the wearer. Apparently, in time more shaping of this area of the garment came to be desired and tailors devised two different methods of dealing with this excess fabric. One method was to remove the excess by the use of shoulder darts; thus the low-back style emerged. An alternative was to stiffen the excess fabric with interfacing so that it would stand upright, thus yielding the high-back profile. Clearly both styles are fully traditional and in conformity with accepted Orthodox Christian liturgical usage.

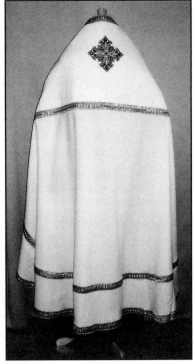

Figures 6.a and 6.b. Historic, conical *phelonion* with interfacing, front and back views.

Figures 6.c and 6.d. Historic, conical phelonion without interfacing, front and back views.

On both the low-back and high-back variations, there are a variety of galloon embellishment options. On the low-back *phelonion* this is typically limited to a single band of galloon sewn to the entire perimeter of the garment along the edge. Sometimes a second band of galloon is added six to eight inches above this for further ornamentation and this second band is almost always employed in the high-back version. Occasionally, coordinating velvet will be sewn between these two bands and can be a very successful design feature. Additionally, the high-back style will also feature the galloon bib that secures the stiffening interfacing. In place of additional, decorative galloon banding, some machine- or hand-embroidered *phelonia* may feature an embroidered border of four to ten inches in width which follows the entire perimeter of the *phelonion*. This "border style" is quite common in Greece and is beginning to make its way into North American usage.

A variety of fabrics are used currently for the presbyter's vestments including synthetic brocades (polyester or rayon), real-metal brocades (polyester base with metallic fibers woven throughout), silk brocades, machine-embroidered polyesters, machine-embroidered velvet, and both synthetic and cotton velvet. Less-ornate versions can be made with simpler, woven fabrics, typically polyester-cotton blends, and these styles are often unlined for greater comfort.

In addition to the vestment set comprised of *sticharion, epimanikia, epitrachelion, zone,* and *phelonion,* there are two distinct award pieces that may be worn with an Orthodox Christian presbyter's vestments: the *epigonation* (in Russian, *palitsa*) and the *nabedrennik.* The *epigonation* is a lozenge-shaped piece, heavily interfaced to provide a rigid shape, approximately twelve to fourteen inches wide and twelve to fifteen inches long, and often made from the same brocade and galloon as the rest of the vestment set. It is finished with three tassels, one at the bottom and one at each side corner, and a long loop of ribbon or cord is sewn to the top. The priest slips the loop of ribbon or cord over his left shoulder allowing the *epigonation* to hang at his right knee with the ribbon placement then secured by the *zone.* The cross sewn to the center of the *epigonation* is medium in size, midway between the larger cross sewn to the *phelonion* and the smaller crosses used on the lesser vestment pieces.

Because the *epigonation* originated as an award piece and continues to function in this capacity, there are also very heavily embroidered versions that feature vinework and floral designs, various icons of Christ, saints, or feasts, and decoration with pearls, semi-precious stones, and synthetic gems. This type of more ornate *epigonation* is intended to be worn with multiple sets of vestments, not necessarily matching only one set, and so tends to be rendered in a versatile palette, either burgundy velvet with gold metal thread embroidery or multi-colored embroidery work on an ivory ground fabric.

The use of the *epigonation* varies among Orthodox Christian jurisdictions: it can be used as a sign that a presbyter has completed a course of higher theological education, has been blessed to hear confessions, or has served a specific number of years. In this manner the *epigonation* fully retains its historical significance of being a piece specially awarded to the presbyter by his bishop.

The *nabedrennik* is an award piece restricted to Russian usage only and its origin is unclear, although it is likely that it began to be employed during the period of Tsarist Russia in which clergy were official state employees and therefore awarded various crosses, vestment pieces, and other distinctions to correspond with the multiple pay grades of civil servants. The *nabedrennik* is rectangular and approximately eleven inches wide by sixteen inches long and features galloon around its entire perimeter and double banks of galloon and fringe along the bottom edge, similar to the finishing of an *epitrachelion*. It features a three- to four-inch cross sewn in the center of the upper section and has a ribbon or cord sewn to the two top corners and is worn in a manner similar to the *epigonation,* suspended from the left shoulder and resting above the right knee. Like the *epigonation* it is often made to match a vestment set, but it can also be made in a more versatile palette or style so that it can be worn with various sets of vestments. In the Russian tradition a presbyter may be awarded both the *nabedrennik* and the *epigonation (palitsa)* in which case the former is worn on the left side and the latter on the right.

For the Divine Liturgy, a presbyter is fully vested with *sticharion, epimanikia, epitrachelion, zone, phelonion,* and any appropriate award pieces (*epigonation,* and/or *nabedrennik,* and pectoral cross). For Great Vespers, he begins the service wearing the *exorason* (see Cassocks below) and *epitrachelion,* but dons his *phelonion* prior to the Entrance. For Daily Vespers, the Hours, Compline as well as other minor services, the presbyter wears the *exorason* and *epitrachelion.*[6] For baptisms, the oldest tradition is for the presbyter to be fully vested as for Divine Liturgy; a more recent custom has arisen of the presbyter wearing only his *exorason, epitrachelion,* and *phelonion* (for convenience some omit even the *phelonion*). At weddings, the oldest

---

6. If a presbyter either enters or exits through the Holy Doors, then custom requires that he be vested with his *phelonion*. Because of this requirement, the presbyter wears his *phelonion* at any service that has an entrance, a Gospel reading from the *solea,* or a great dismissal.

tradition is for the presbyter to be fully vested as for Divine Liturgy; a more recent custom has arisen of the presbyter wearing only his *exorason*, *epitrachelion*, and *phelonion*. For funerals, the presbyter wears his *exorason*, *epitrachelion*, and *phelonion* (though in some local practices the *phelonion* is omitted for funerals). For baptisms, weddings, and funerals archimandrites may, by local custom, substitute their monastic veil for the *phelonion*. During Pascha and Bright Week, the presbyter is always attired as for the Divine Liturgy since the major orders are fully vested for every service during this season.

Figure 7.a Vestments of the presbyter: low-back phelonion

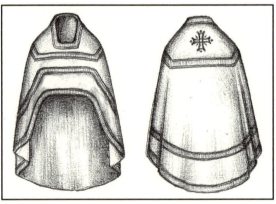

Figure 7.b Vestments of the presbyter: high-back phelonion.

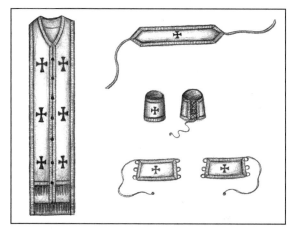

Figure 7.c Vestments of the presbyter: epitrachelion, zone, epimanikia laced and unlaced.

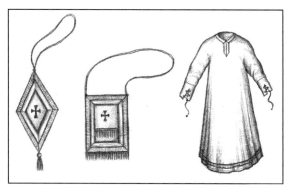

Figure 7.d Vestments of the presbyter: epigonation, nabedrennik, sticharion.

Vestments of the Bishop

The bishop wears the priest's *sticharion, epitrachelion, zone, epimanikia* and *epigonation* as described above, and over these pieces dons the *sakkos*, a garment adopted fairly late in the Church's history as has been described in Chapter Two. While these garments are almost identical in design and ornamentation as when made for a presbyter, there are some slight differences, most notably in the priestly *sticharion* worn by bishops serving in the Russian church: because Russian practice is for the bishop to be vested in the middle of the nave this garment features sides that fasten with buttons and loops for easier vesting.

The *sakkos* worn by Orthodox Christian bishops is identical in design to the imperial *sakkos* of Byzantium, which was based upon the colobium, a shortened, more heavily ornamented type of tunic. In its overall design it is simply a shortened version of the brocade sticharion, being finished in an almost identical method with galloon around the entire perimeter and additional galloon bands at the sleeves and hem. A large cross or icon of Christ is sewn to the back of the sakkos, but placed slightly lower than the shoulder blades so that when the omophorion is worn over the sakkos it does not obscure the cross or the icon. Because the sakkos is the garment of the highest office in the Orthodox Christian Church, the episcopacy, it is correspondingly the most ornate and embellished of all the vestments. It features the typical galloon neck placket, galloon around its entire perimeter, and additional rows of galloon at the hem and sleeves. The upper bank of galloon above the hem can feature fringe sewn under the bottom edge, and the sleeve extension area and bottom hem area can be made with velvet insets similar to those sometimes used for diaconal sticharia.

Due to its episcopal use the *sakkos* is often quite lavishly ornamented. It is typically made of the best-quality brocades or embroidered fabrics. The decoration on the back may be a hand-embroidered, metal-thread-work cross or a silk-floss embroidered icon. The galloon is usually a wide or extra-wide size, either one-and-a-half or three inches wide. The sides are fastened with buttons and loops and a common practice is to sew small bells in place of buttons at the wrist and hem edges. The *sakkos* presents the ecclesiastical tailor with a wonderful canvas and many elaborate fabrics can be employed featuring interesting color combinations (such as ivory, gold, blue, burgundy and multiple combinations thereof) with bold and striking motifs including flowers, vines, and birds, or with other magnificent decorative schemes rendered upon ornate, heavily embroidered velvet. Although the general design is nearly always the same across the Orthodox Christian world, the ornamentation and embellishment can be quite varied. Russian *sakkoi* may have a galloon bib sewn in the upper torso area (usually circular rather than square). Due to their value and historical significance, many distinctive *sakkoi* are featured in museum collections throughout the world.

The great *omophorion* is an eight-inch wide by approximately fourteen-foot long band of fabric, interfaced, lined, and finished with a particular scheme of crosses, badges, and appliqué stars or icons. It is worn in a very distinctive fashion, identical to that of the *toga contabulata* worn by Roman consuls of the second to fourth centuries. It has a unique "half vs half" design in which its two halves are constructed separately and then sewn together so that, when laid flat, the right half is seen brocade side up and the left half is seen lining side up and, when turned over, vice versa. When worn, it resembles a "Y" shape with crosses over the chest area and a large star or icon sewn to the center back neck area. It is finished in a manner similar to the deacon's *orarion* or the presbyter's *epitrachelion* with galloon around the entire perimeter and extra galloon and fringe bands sewn to each end. The great *omophorion* typically features four crosses and one star (or icon) as well as rectangular badges sewn towards the ends of the garment.

The great omophorion is worn as follows: beginning at the left front knee, the omophorion goes up to the left shoulder, wraps around the back of the neck to the right shoulder, drapes down to the middle of the chest, is then folded back upon itself forming a "Y" at the chest level, brought back up to the left shoulder and then draped down the back of the wearer to the back left knee. Buttons and loops are sewn at various positions along the omophorion to keep it firmly in place when worn. Some of the buttons fasten to corresponding loops on the omophorion itself while others fasten to loops on the sakkos. Such fastening is necessary in a garment so large and bulky in order to keep it from slipping off the shoulders.

The small *omophorion* is an abbreviated version of the great *omophorion* used during portions of the Divine Liturgy when the great *omophorion* would be too cumbersome, and used as well (in conjunction with the *epitrachelion*) for sacraments, blessings, and lesser services. The small *omophorion* generally features two large crosses, one star (or icon) at the center back neck, and badges. It is as wide as the great *omophorion* but only eight feet in length. Instead of being worn in the Y-draped fashion, it is simply draped around the bishop's neck and hangs down the front of the body to almost knee-length with a button and loop positioned at the center chest to hold the two sides together and prevent the *omophorion* from slipping. In some cases it is cut away and shaped around the neck to allow it to lay flat upon the shoulders. Because of its abbreviated length, it typically features only one cross on each side (instead of two as for the great *omophorion*) and may or may not have badges.

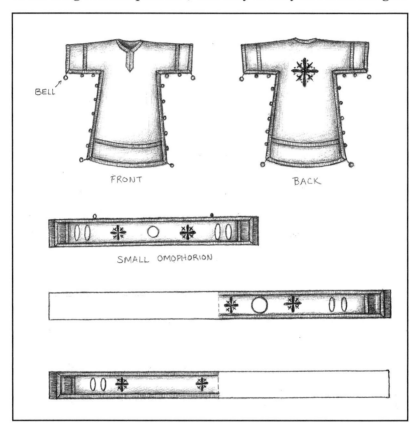

Figure 8. Vestments of the episcopacy.

Just as the *toga contabulata* was the civil garment of highest rank in late antiquity, the *omophorion* holds highest rank within the usage of liturgical vesture in the Orthodox Christian Church. It bespeaks honor and authority as well as responsibility for the souls under the care of its wearer (in Byzantine times bishops were not only responsible for the spiritual welfare of the souls "under their *omophorion*" but oftentimes their physical well-being also, since during times of foreign attack or siege bishops were required either to muster military defenses or move their people to a safe location). It was the garment *par excellence* of the late-antique Roman and early Byzantine world and continues to hold this position even today in its usage within the Church.

In addition to the major pieces of episcopal vesture, there may also be a cover for the *paterissa* ("pastoral staff"), a small rectangular piece of brocade finished to match the vestments which has a casing at the top with a cord threaded through that is tied around the episcopal staff under its crosspiece. This piece is most likely a rather late addition to the accoutrements of the bishop (originating from a protective cloth wrapped around the *paterissa*) and is not universally used. Similarly there are also accoutrements referred to simply as "candle ribbons" which are small circles or octagons of brocade to which are affixed two decorative tails, all of which is fashioned out of a brocade or velvet to coordinate with the vestments of the bishop. These are attached to the candles of the *dikerotrikera* (the two-candle and three-candle candelabra which the bishop uses to bestow blessings). These candle ribbons have small pieces of regular ribbon sewn to their reverse which allows them to be affixed to the candles. These are also a very late addition to the episcopal vestment collection (as an elaboration of simple ribbons used to hold the candles together) and are not utilized in the practice of many local churches.

The last garment worn by the bishop we shall consider is the *mandyas*. The episcopal *mandyas* derives from the monastic *mandyas* ("mantle"), which is a historic garment representing prayerful protection of the monk from spiritual attack and is likened to angels' wings.[7] The episcopal *mandyas* is a truly magnificent garment with multiple pleats sewn into an interfaced collar and cascading down the back of the very long garment, typically spreading out behind the wearer in a three-foot to five-foot train. The fronts can be either pleated or

---

7. St. Germanos, appointed Patriarch of Constantinople in 715, remarks that the "loosely unfolding mantle recalls the winged angels." St Germanos of Constantinople, *On the Divine Liturgy* (Crestwood, NY: St Vladimir's Seminary Press), 69.

plain, but always feature buttons at the collar and another set of three buttons at the hem to fasten the garment about the bishop (these are the only closures on the *mandyas*; it is otherwise open all along the front). The lower buttons of the *mandyas* may be replaced with small bells like those on the bishop's *sakkos*. On either side of the upper fronts are affixed *tablia*, embroidered tablets, typically with angelic representations of cherubim or seraphim, or crosses. An additional pair of *tablia* are sewn to the bottom front corners at the hem and these feature either angelic representations or, in a specifically Russian tradition, the monogram of the bishop who wears the garment. Running from the center front across the sides and around to the back in parallel, horizontal lines are multiple rows of galloon or ribbon which are referred to as *potamoi* ("rivers").

The bishop wears the *mandyas* in processions and when he presides at a service officiated by a presbyter. The overarching symbology of the *mandyas* is the image of a cocoon or protective sheath, being fastened at the neck and hem and without sleeves, keeping the wearer self-contained and defended from spiritual assaults. The galloon *potamoi* represent the gospel teaching flowing out from the apostolic office into the world. There are variations in color usage: Greek practice typically employs burgundy for all bishops regardless of rank; Russian practice uses burgundy or purple for bishops or archbishops, light blue for metropolitans, and green for the patriarch. In Greek use the *potamoi* are fashioned from gold galloon, while in Russian practice they are made of red and white ribbons.

When a bishop celebrates the Hierarchical Divine Liturgy he wears the *sticharion, epitrachelion, zone, epimanikia, epigonation, sakkos* and the great *omophorion* (replaced in the latter half of the Liturgy by the small *omophorion*), the pectoral cross, *engolpion* (icon pendant), miter, and he carries the *paterissa*. If a bishop celebrates the Divine Liturgy simply (in accordance with the rubrics for a presbyter[8]) he wears all the presbyteral vestments (*phelonion* instead of the *sakkos, sticharion, epitrachelion, epimanikia, zone, epigonation*) with the *omophorion*, but with no miter. If he is presiding over a service officiated by a presbyter

---

8   Russian practice may differ in details.

he wears the *mandyas* and dons the *epitrachelion* and small *omophorion* to partake of Holy Communion or for moments of particular solemnity when he assumes the role of officiant (e.g., for the blessing of the five loaves at an *Artoklasia*). For Great Vespers, Daily Vespers and minor services the bishop wears the *mandyas* only. For baptisms, weddings, and funerals he wears the *mandyas*, *epitrachelion* and small *omophorion*. During Pascha and Bright Week if the bishop is celebrating or officiating he vests for every service fully as for the Hierarchcal Liturgy; if he is presiding then he dons the *mandyas* only.

Figure 9. Bishop's mandyas

Cassocks

There are two types of cassocks used in the Orthodox Christian Church: the inner cassock and the outer cassock. While "cassock" is the word most commonly used in English for the robe worn by the major orders and monastics for daily use and certain services and by minor orders for their specific tasks within the church building, other languages have specific terms for the inner cassock and the outer cassock respectively. Thus the inner cassock is commonly *"anteri"* or *"zostikon"* in Greek and *"podryasnik"* in

Russian, whereas the outer cassock is *"exorason"* in Greek, and *"ryasa"* in Russian.⁹

The simplest way to understand how the inner and outer cassock are utilized is to think of the inner cassock as analogous to a dress shirt and tie and the outer cassock as analogous to a suit coat—in a setting in which a man might wear just a dress shirt and tie the inner cassock alone is worn, but in settings which demand a suit coat over a dress shirt an outer cassock is worn over an inner cassock. Cassocks are typically worn over black pants and a white shirt.¹⁰ Both minor and major orders wear the cassock as well as male and female monastics (when the Greek-style *zostikon* is worn by monastics, the drawstring belt is omitted to allow the use of a leather belt). Etiquette requires the minor orders to restrict their usage of the cassock to the parish church in which they serve (i.e., they do not wear the garment in public or when visiting another parish, but only when they are performing their specified work within their assigned church; this is a practical consideration so that they are not confused with members of the major orders). Priests and deacons wear the *zostikon* or *podryasnik* as their primary garment, both in the church building as they are serving or performing their duties there as well as for general street wear. For the sake of decorum it is generally deemed proper for priests and deacons to wear the *exorason* (outer cassock) or, in its

---

9. In Greek, the inner cassock may also be referred to as a *"rason,"* an *"esorason,"* an *"imation"* or a *"chiton."* In the recent past *"anteri"* was the most popular colloquial term (pronounced *"an-te-REE"*), though this word is of Turkish derivation and is consequently beginning to fall out of favor in present Greek usage. *"Zostikon"* (pronounced *"zo-sti-KO,"* an abbreviated form of *"zostikon rason,"* i.e., "girdled *rason*") is emerging as the preferred term due to the common use of this word on the Holy Mountain. *"Esorason"* is perhaps the most technically precise name as it specifies the "inner *rason*" (i.e., "inner robe"). The outer cassock may also be referred to simply as a *"rason"* but also as an *"epanorason,"* a *"mandorason,"* or a *"pallion,"* with *"exorason"* being both commonly used and technically precise as it specifies "outer *rason*." (On historical use of Greek terminology for cassocks in the early twentieth century, see N.F. Robinson, *Monasticism in the Orthodox Churches* (London: Cope and Fenwick, 1916), 37.

10. In a capitulation to North American clerical fashion of the twentieth century, priests or deacons might wear a black shirt with a clerical tab collar under the cassock, but this usage is beginning to wane.

place, the *kontorason* (vest) over the inner cassock. The inner cassock is usually worn under the liturgical vestments of the major orders. While inner cassocks are derived from the tunics of antiquity, they have undergone significant design changes to make them fit closer to the body, a necessity for a garment worn daily in various settings (imagine getting in and out of a car in a voluminous *tunica talaris*).

The Greek *zostikon* is a garment worn almost floor-length, comprised of a rectangular front and back to which side sleeve panels are then attached. The overlapping front pieces, which are fully reversible, are angled from the center of the collar to just above the hip and fastened by a button tab over which a drawstring belt is tied to bring in the extra fullness in the garment. The tailored sleeves, complete with upper and under sleeve, have a chevron cuff with three functioning buttons. There is a lozenge-shaped gusset sewn to the underarm of the sleeve which provides greater freedom of movement, an important feature in a roomy garment such as this. The back of the garment has a casing through which the belt is drawn, gathering up the back slightly and providing shape and containing the extra ease built into the design of the garment. The collar has several variations: mandarin (a collar which meets at center front and has rounded edges), cross-over (a collar which overlaps at center front and has squared-off edges), or various combinations of these two. Cross-over styles can vary widely in the distance they are overlapped, but range from one-quarter of an inch to an inch and a half. The collar is fully tailored with both interfacing and an inner collar (the inner collar is typically finished with a French binding). There are pockets sewn at chest level on each front and welt pockets positioned at hip level of the side sleeve panel. The hem is usually deep, with about two and a half inches of hem allowance total (a generous hem is a must in a garment worn floor-length as it allows for the garment to be lengthened or shortened with relative ease).

The Russian version of the inner cassock, the *podryasnik*, is usually worn about two to three inches higher than the Greek *zostikon* (it is interesting to note that most Russian-style liturgical garments and cassocks are worn higher than

Greek-style ones; some have speculated that this might be an accommodation to the need to wade through the snow of Russian winters). The *podryasnik* features a distinctive back construction with the body of the garment being tailored with inverted pleats and a very wide sleeve gusset, creating a narrow, V-shape from the shoulders to the waist. The overall fit of the torso section is designed to be worn much more fitted than the *zostikon* (the *zostikon* has a six-inch to ten-inch ease whereas the *podryasnik* has a two-inch to five-inch ease), while the skirt of the garment is A-line in design and therefore much fuller at the hem than the *zostikon*. The front pieces are less angled, coming to a position midway between hip and center front waist, but still fastening with a button tab. The collar is stiffer, often finished with a double layer of interfacing. The sleeves sometimes have buttons, but more often are finished without a button placket. The hip pockets have a large faced flap that is topstitched in place. There is no belt attached to the Russian *podryasnik* since its closer fit requires none (though monastics will still wear a leather belt over the garment).

The *zostikon* most likely has its origins in the tunics of ancient Greece and Rome and has developed its more sophisticated tailoring over time, possibly with some folk-costume influence. The Russian *podryasnik* seems to have adopted its stylistic differences from Russian folk costumes since it shares many design features with these garments, in particular the close-fitting, V-shaped torso section with distinctive sleeve gussets. Originally the *zostikon* was almost certainly a light color due to its being made from undyed cloth. This can be observed in historic icons depicting monks in which a light-colored tunic can be observed under the more voluminous, darker-colored *mandyas*. Most likely, darker-colored *zostika* began to be worn due to practicality (they show dirt less) and the greater availability of darker-dyed fabrics. The most typical color for an inner cassock is black, but other colors may be worn which include navy, blue (in various hues), burgundy, white or off-white (typically reserved for the Paschal season), taupe or khaki, gray, and forest green.

A variety of fabrics can be used for making cassocks. The most common are polyester blends (either polyester/cotton or polyester/wool) and wool, but new fabrics utilizing technological advances in fiber development are beginning to be used such as stretch-wool blends, wicking polyesters, and even hemp. Real silk crepe is also coming back into vogue and its excellent properties make for beautiful cassocks (it is the most breathable of the natural fibers and very comfortable to wear). While cotton is often perceived to be the most comfortable of fibers, it is not ideal for cassocks for several reasons: it is prone to wrinkling and it does not retain black dye without a lead mordant (lead mordants are currently banned in textile production because of health concerns).

For the Greek *zostikon*, the edges of the fronts, the chest pockets, the cuffs, and the collar are often finished with decorative stitching and one-eighth inch cording or braid attached to the edges of the fronts (extending from collar to waist), the edges of the collar, and the edges of the cuffs. The decorative stitching at the collar is often a type of tailor's signature with each tailor using a distinctive pattern. The most common type of Russian *podryasnik* has no decorative stitching; however, more elaborate versions of the garment can incorporate lavish decorative stitching with grapevines being the most-favored motif.

In addition to the Greek *zostikon* and Russian *podryasnik*, there are other cassock styles in different parts of the world. These garments feature slight differences in cut, placement of seams, method of collar fastening, and variations upon the decorative stitching and include, but are not limited to, styles identified as Romanian, Serbian, and Syrian.

In local churches that still employ the minor order of reader, the reader may be blessed by the bishop to wear the inner cassock. While a clergyman of the major orders may wear this garment in various colors, a reader always wears a black cassock. In the case of the subdeacon, for any service in which the presbyter dons his phelonion the subdeacon is attired in brocade sticharion and orarion; for lesser services in which the presbyter does not wear the phelonion, he is clad in inner cassock alone.[11]

The outer cassock, known as the *"exorason"* in Greek or *"ryasa"* in Russian, is the more voluminous form of the cassock and is worn over the inner cassock in semi-formal, formal, and liturgical settings. Of elegant design, the *exorason* features the same front and back construction as the *zostikon*, but instead of angled fronts a triangular-shaped section is sewn to each front and the particular cut of this piece allows the fronts of the garment to overlap along the center without any closure, save for the hook-and-eye closure at the mandarin collar (whereas the *zostikon* has multiple collar variations, the *exorason* invariably features a mandarin collar). These front edge panels are fully lined so that, when they fall open as the wearer walks, the back side of the piece is as beautiful and finished as the front side. The garment employs the same general sleeve panel arrangement as the *zostikon*, but instead of a tailored sleeve-and-gusset combination it has a very large kimono sleeve sewn to a side panel which has eight-inch vents at the hem to allow greater freedom of movement while walking. The width of the sleeves is an indication of rank: chanter's width sleeves are approximately thirty-six inches in circumference, the deacon's and presbyter's are forty-eight inches, and the bishop's width is sixty inches. The sleeves have a six-inch deep lining that is made from the same fabric used for the lining of the front edge panels. The sleeves are worn long, typically two to three inches longer than inner cassock sleeves and thus covering the hands entirely when the wearer stands with his hands at his side.

---

11. There has been some confusion about the practice of subdeacons wearing the inner cassock beyond the church confines in recent years. Because the office of the subdeacon is limited to the sphere of the Altar of a specific church, his use of clerical garments should be limited to that location. Subdeacons do not wear cassocks, kontorasa (clerical vests), or other clerical garments anywhere besides the church in which they serve. Much confusion and embarrassment has ensued when a layperson approaches a subdeacon clad in clerical attire to request a blessing and must be rebuffed. It is necessary that the service of the office is considered foremost and that clerical garments are not abused by wearing them for personal aggrandizement.

The Russian-style *ryasa* is a more fitted garment than the Greek-style *exorason* and it does not feature the front edge panels, but rather fastens with a button tab at the waist in the same manner as the *podryasnik*. The sleeves of the *ryasa* are wider than the *podryasnik* but much narrower than those of the *exorason*, being typically twenty to twenty-four inches in circumference.

While the *exorason* features elements of very ancient garments like the kimono, evincing oriental and Persian influence, it does not appear to come into Orthodox Christian usage until much later than the *zostikon*, perhaps as late as the fifteenth or sixteenth century. The relatively late beginning of its ecclesiastical usage can be surmised based upon how late its use came to monasteries. Prior to the adoption of the *exorason*, the plain, black *mandyas* was the outer garment worn over the *zostikon* for attendance at divine services and at communal meals in monasteries. Even into the early decades of the twentieth century the *mandyas* was still the preferred garment in many monasteries, only gradually giving way to the use of the *exorason*. It is significant that the *mandyas* and the *exorason* (also called the *"mandorason"*—note the etymological similarity to *"mandyas"*) have many features in common in their general design and the *exorason* may have developed as a simpler, more tailored version of the *mandyas* adopted for daily wear by monastics, or possibly a more practical version of the *mandyas* adapted for use by the secular clergy.[12] (Its similarity to other, voluminous, oriental-influenced, outer robes in use during the Ottoman period may well have encouraged its widespread adoption by secular clerics.) The Russian *ryasa*, on the other hand, has much more design affinity with the *podryasnik* and appears to have followed a similar developmental trajectory to the *podryasnik*, most likely borrowing its distinctive design features from Slavic folk costume.

In the Greek tradition the *exorason* is worn for services by chanters and sextons (liturgical assistants) with the narrowest-

---

12. The adjective "secular" is used to denote those clergy (married or widowed) who live "in the world," i.e., clergymen who are not monks.

width sleeves and with no inner cassock underneath.[13] In both Greek and Russian tradition the outer cassock is worn by bishops, presbyters, and deacons over the inner cassock both liturgically and as the top layer of street wear (in current Greek practice the major orders often wear the same width of sleeve, but historically, there would have been separate widths for each of these ranks with the deacon wearing narrower sleeves and the bishop wearing the widest sleeves; in current and historical Russian tradition, there is no variation in sleeve width based upon rank). In traditional Orthodox lands a bishop, presbyter, or deacon does not appear in public in any official setting without both the inner cassock and the outer cassock, which is akin to the custom of semi-formal attire consisting of tailored shirt and suit jacket. For this reason, the collar of the outer cassock is slightly larger than that of the inner cassock to accommodate this layering.

Due to the front edge panels and the wider sleeves, the *exorason* requires a fabric with good draping qualities, so the fabrics typically used are polyester, polyester/wool blends, wool (both lighter and heavier weights), and real silk crepe. Occasionally, a polyester-cotton blend will be employed, but its lack of drape renders this a very poor choice for the *exorason*. The *ryasa*, with its more structured design, can be made from fabrics such as those listed above as well as fabrics with a crisper finish.[14]

The most distinctive feature of the *exorason* is its quality of regality, from the extremely wide sleeves to its elegant drape to its graceful, overlapping fronts. In this it is unique among the articles of Orthodox Christian clerical dress in that its overall design serves as its ornamentation and it does not rely upon any additional augmentation of fabric or stitching, aside from the

---

13. Orthodox faithful in North America are sometimes puzzled by this liturgical use of the *exorason* by members of the laity, particularly when it is worn by women chanters. In this regard it is helpful to note that the narrow-sleeved version of the *exorason* is essentially the traditional Greek Orthodox Christian version of a choir robe. In Greece the chanter's *exorason* is often made distinctive by the placement of galloon or colored, decorative banding upon the collar.

14. There are even a few photos from the late nineteenth century showing Russian hierarchs wearing *ryasas* made from elegant black brocades.

elaborate stitching at the collar which serves more a utilitarian than decorative purpose as multiple rows of stiches are required to hold the collar interfacing in place.

As we have observed, historical Orthodox Christian practice is for both the inner cassock and outer cassock to be worn by the major orders for street wear, but this practice can become rather burdensome in warm climates since these two garments are comprised of a sum total of twelve yards of fabric and weigh four to eight pounds when combined. The attendant discomfort of wearing two such heavy garments in a Mediterranean climate, combined with the considerations of modern modes of transportation (as noted before, getting in and out of automobiles takes some skill when wearing multiple, floor-length garments) has brought about a further development in the *exorason*. Over time the heavy weight of the *exorason* was mitigated by first shortening the garment to knee length or to the waist (the use of this garment still continues and is often worn as a type of coat in cooler seasons) and then eventually losing its distinctive, yet cumbersome sleeves. This abbreviated version of the *exorason*, known as the *kontorason* ("short *rason*") has become quite popular in recent times. Wearing the *kontorason* the priest or deacon is considered appropriately dressed for daily wear without the heavy bulk of wearing two voluminous garments.

The *kontorason* in its most common form is virtually identical to a sleeveless vest. It has a front button placket with the buttons either visible or hidden by an extended facing. It can be lined or unlined and features pockets, usually two towards the bottom front of the garment and, occasionally, one or two smaller pockets sewn at chest level. While collared styles may be seen, the most common version is collarless, which makes it easier to fit over the *zostikon*. Heavy-weight versions also exist, made of wool coating fabric, and these will have some design differences due to the different construction techniques required by the bulk of the substantial fabric. The coat version of the *kontorason* is usually made with sleeves wide enough to easily accommodate the sleeves of the *zostikon* (although not so wide as a standard *exorason*) and with some form of collar. Because it is worn as a substitute for the *exorason*, the same rules apply to the usage of the *kontorason* as apply to the *exorason*, notably that it should be worn only by members of the major clerical orders or by tonsured monastics.[15]

Since the *kontorason* is a shorter, less bulky garment, there is a greater range of fabrics that can be employed in its construction than can be used for the *exorason,* although typically it is made from the same type of fabrics as those used for cassocks. Often the *kontorason* will be made with an inner cassock as a matching set. Because it is an abbreviated *exorason,* however, the *kontorason* will nearly always be black, the invariable color of the *exorason.* The *kontorason* vest does not include any decorative stitching though the coat version may have decorative stitching at the collar. The simpler, unlined vest typically has patch pockets whereas the more formal, lined version has welt-finished pockets on each side. The heavy, melton-wool vest has bias-bound edges and patch pockets finished with bias-binding.

Figure 10. Sketch of Greek *zostikon* and Russian *podryasnik*.

---

15. Since many people in North America are unaware of the origins of the *kontorason,* its use is sometimes usurped by members of the minor clerical orders who think of it simply as vest. This practice arises out of ignorance and should be curtailed.

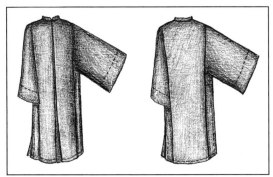

Figure 11.a Sketch of Greek *exorason*.

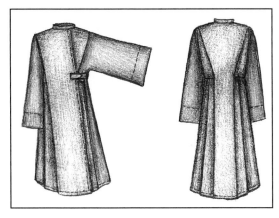

Figure 11.b Sketch of Russian *ryasa*.

Figure 12. Sketch of Greek kontorason over a zostikon.

Headgear

In traditional Orthodox Christian practice there are two basic types of headgear worn: the casual *skufos*, and the formal *kalymmafchion*. Although significant design and color variations of these hats can be seen in various places throughout the Orthodox Christian world, most hats worn by the major orders or monastics fit into these two general categories.

The *skufos* in its most typical Greek form it is made from a single rectangle of fabric that is folded in thirds to create an approximately four-inch band of fabric surmounted by a circle of pleats (these pleats serve to take up the excess fabric) topped with a fabric-covered button. The band of the *skufos* can be decorated in any number of styles, from plain rows of topstitching to scallops, lozenges, or other decorative stitching design schemes. The middle fold of the rectangle is lightly interfaced to provide some stability and shape, while still creating a hat that can be folded up and stowed in a pocket. The *skufos* is typically made from polyester-cotton blends, polyester, wool, or cotton velveteen. Hand-knit versions (often given the diminutive appellation "*skoufaki*") are also worn as a very casual headcovering; these have the same general shape, but the top portion is shaped with knitting decreases rather than pleats. The Greek *skufos* also exists in a more structured version with stiff sides. This version is almost identical in overall design to the soft *skufos*, but it is made somewhat taller and is heavily interfaced with buckram, which gives it a more formal aspect. It is typically made of felt (either synthetic or wool) or velvet and is entirely lined. It is often decorated with bands of geometric or braid-type stitching designs or elaborate embroidery designs such as grapevines, floral borders, or the egg-and-dart design. The *skufos* (both soft and hard-sided) is an informal hat and is worn by the major orders when a headcovering is required in a nonliturgical setting.

The second type of traditional Orthodox Christian headcovering is the *kalymmafchion*. This hat exists in three basic variations. The Greek monastic *kalymmafchion* is a tall, stiff cylinder with a flat top, which is surmounted by a monastic veil for liturgical use or any wear within the church or in formal settings (though hierodeacons remove the veil when vested for services). Sometimes a hard-sided *skoufos* may be substituted for the monastic *kalymmafchion*. The Russian version of this hat, called the "*kamilavka*" (worn by monks and nuns as well as by secular members of the major orders of the clergy), is slightly flared from bottom to top. Bishops, monks and nuns wear a veil over the hat with the entire ensemble being termed the "*klobuk*." The Greek *kalymmafchion* as worn by secular priests and deacons (as well as often by monastic clergy when serving outside their monastery) is a stiff cylinder with a slightly domed top and a brim that extends beyond the central drum of the hat by about one inch all around. Bishops, archimandrites and hieromonks may wear their monastic veil over the brimmed *kalymmafchion* (this combination of hat and veil is called the "*epanokalymmafchion*").

The *kalymmafchion* is the formal headcovering of the Orthodox Christian Church and is used by the major orders in a liturgical fashion. Because the *kalymmafchion* is used liturgically, customs regarding its use are more complicated than those pertaining to the less formal *skoufos*. Greek practice permits that during any service the *kalymmafchion* may be worn outside the iconostasis, but never within the Altar precincts. There is one exception to this general rule, and that is for any cleric who wears a veil with his hat, such as bishops, archimandrites or hieromonks; in the case of these ranks the headcovering may be worn in the Altar except for during the most solemn portions of the Divine Liturgy. It should also be noted that a priest, deacon, or monk removes his *kalymmafchion* (or *epanokalymmafchion*) during the reading of the Gospel, when he himself reads priestly prayers, and when venerating the gospel book or holy relics (some also remove it for the veneration of icons).

The Russian usage of headgear differs considerably from the Greek practice due to the custom of specific styles and colors of headgear being utilized as part of a system of awards. A soft *skufia* is used similarly to the Greek practice as a general, informal headcovering but may also be worn liturgically; the shape of the Russian *skufia* (a peaked hat constructed of four fabric panels) is distinctly different from the Greek *skufos* pattern. The Russian *skufia* and the *kamilavka* can be either black, purple, or crimson, with the latter colors being awarded as a mark of distinction to secular presbyters and deacons. In Russian practice both the *skufia* and the *kamilavka* may be worn within the Altar.

It should be further noted that the *skufos* and the *kalymafchion* also exist in various other styles, both black and in differing colors. These variations are worn in accordance with the local traditions of the various regional Orthodox churches.

Figure 13. Skufos and kalymafchion.

Monastic Garments

Orthodox Christian monastic garb varies somewhat from monastery to monastery depending on a wide range of factors, which can include the setting of the monastery (rural settings demand more rugged attire; urban settings less rugged), whether or not the monastery has access to skilled tailors or seamstresses in their midst, and adaptation to a given region. The basic monastic habit worn perpetually by both monks and nuns is some variation of the inner cassock. Some nuns wear cassocks that are more dress-like in style, others will wear a long, full skirt with a type of shortened *exorason* over this (called a *"kontoraki"*). While black is always used for garments worn by tonsured monastics in church and usually for daily wear as well, blue or other lighter-colored garments are sometimes worn by novices or by monastics as work attire. Cassocks worn on a daily basis and used for various tasks around the monastery need to be made from tough fabrics, such as denim or polyester-cotton poplin since the strenuous work of gardening, fishing or construction requires durability. Monastics wear a leather belt over their cassock (in place of the usual drawstring belt) in imitation of St John the Baptist.

The full Orthodox Christian monastic habit is comprised of the following garments: inner cassock, belt, *mandyas* (often replaced by an outer cassock for convenience), *kalymmafchion* with a veil (nuns in the Greek tradition wear the veil without a hat underneath), the *paramandyas*, the *analavos* and the *polystavrion*. The two types of cassock and the headcoverings have been described already. The *paramandyas* is a fabric square decorated with an image of the Holy Cross that is worn over the inner cassock and under the outer garment with cords that tie around the body. The *analavos* (sometimes called the "great *schema*") is a mantle that drapes around the neck and over the shoulders, hanging partway down the back and to about the knees in the front. It is elaborately decorated with embroidered emblems of the Holy Cross, the instruments of Christ's passion and sacred texts. This piece is held in place by the *polystavrion*, a cord with many small crosses plaited into it that is wrapped about the arms and the body as a sort of yoke. The *analavos* and *polystavrion* are worn over the inner cassock by monks and nuns who have been tonsured to the great *schema*, the final and most solemn level of monastic profession. In the Russian tradition, monks and nuns of the great *schema* set aside the usual monastic hat and veil replacing them with the *koukoulion*, a peaked cowl worn upon the head which descends into lappets, adorned with images of the seraphim, that drape over the shoulders.

There is much variation among local churches and different monasteries as to which garments are bestowed at the various levels of monastic profession as well as concerning which garments are worn strictly for divine services and formal occasions as opposed to which are worn as part of the habit for work and informal occasions. Each monastery will have its own typikon which governs such matters according to an established pattern. A thorough discussion of traditional Orthodox Christian monastic garb may be found in N.F. Robinson's *Monasticism in the Orthodox Churches*.

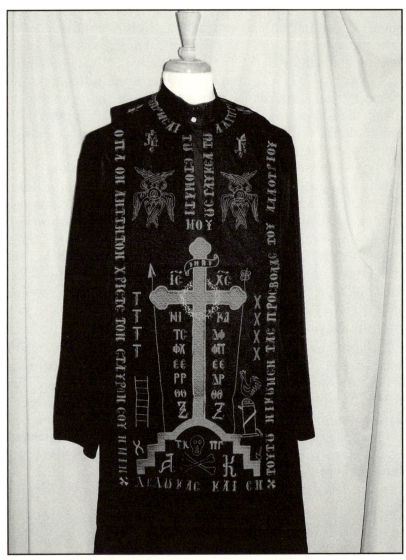

Figure 14. Photo of the *analavos*.

Vestment use of the minor and major orders

	Subdeacons	Russian Deacons	Greek Deacons	Arch/Protodeacons	Presbyters	Bishops
Sticharion	X	X	X	X	X	X
Single Orarion	X	X				
Double Orarion			X	X		
Epimanikia		X	X	X	X	X
Epitrachelion					X	X
Zone					X	X
Nabedrennik					*	
Epigonation					*	X
Phelonion					X	s
Sakkos						X
Omophorion						X

*Worn only if awarded

s Worn only in the special case of a bishop serving a presbyteral Liturgy

Endnotes

i. Rt. Rev. Bishop Basil (Essey), trans., *The Liturgikon* (Englewood, NJ: Antakya Press, 1989), 231.

Chapter Four

The Paraments of Paradise

Architecture, liturgy, hymnody, as well as vestments and liturgical furnishings, processions, icons, relics, and reliquaries were created to echo and amplify one another as palpable founts of holiness so that worshippers might fully enter into a holy realm.

Kathleen McVey[i]

Paraments Defined

No survey of the liturgical vesture of the Orthodox Christian Church would be complete without a discussion of those vestments used to furnish and adorn the interior of the church building. From very early in the history of the Church, it was expected that beautification would not be limited solely to the adornment of the clergy, but that the church building itself would also be endowed with beautiful textiles that would convey the glory and majesty of the Holy Trinity worshipped therein. In practice, the church building is seen as a distinct spiritual entity, complete with its own suitable garments, specifically known as "paraments."[1] The use of such paraments manifests a rich symbolic tradition as, together with the vestments of the clergy, they serve to express visually two major theological tenets of the Church: that the salvation of mankind through the

---

1. In historical usage, the terms "vestments" and "paraments" have often been used interchangeably, but for the sake of clarity within this book I use the term "vestments" for liturgical garments that are worn by people and "paraments" for all other church adornments made of fabric.

crucified and risen Lord is actually experienced in the Eucharistic Liturgy and that the earthly church building makes manifest the reality of the Kingdom of Heaven.

The paraments of an Orthodox Christian church include the holy table cloths, liturgical veils (such as the chalice and *diskos* covers, *aer,* and *epitaphios*), liturgical cloths with specific, practical uses (such as the *antimension* and *eiliton*), decorative veils (such as the *podea* and other drapings for icons and icon stands), free-standing banners with embroidery and iconography, decorative hangings displayed on walls and pillars featuring embroidery and/or iconography, and, finally, cloths of various types and sizes which adorn auxiliary church furniture such as the *proskomedia* table, the *tetrapodion* table and the like. All of these cloths and veils are used to edify, educate, and beautify, and some of the finest existing examples of Orthodox Christian textiles (in particular embroidered work) are shown to great advantage in the remarkable paraments produced in earlier historical periods. In the outfitting of the Orthodox church building we encounter once again the Byzantine celebration of the sense of sight. The highly ornamented textiles of the Church's parament tradition have been designed to awe the beholder with their technical perfection and the richness of their threads and, at the same time, spiritually encourage the viewer by their subject matter, which often features scenes from the life of Christ and depictions of the Great Feasts.

Early Christian Worship and Its Influence on Church Textiles

Before we can consider these wonderful textiles in detail, some attention must be given to the early history of Christian worship. For many people, mention of the early Church brings to mind the image of a small band of Christians, constantly persecuted and in hiding, without a permanent place of worship. In this imagined scenario, early Christian worship is exceptionally simple and only marginally liturgical. However, this popular image has come under serious scrutiny in recent times, especially as a result of the important archaeological discoveries at Dura Europos in the early decades of the twentieth century. This border city, captured by the Romans in AD 165 and held until AD 256 when it was abandoned following a Sassanid Persian siege, was built in what is present-day Syria. It is unique among archaeological finds in that it was covered by sand storms shortly after its capture by the Persians and the entombing sands marvelously preserved the ruins of Dura Europos, leaving not only buildings but even such details as wall paintings largely intact. Among the buildings excavated in the early twentieth century are a *mithraeum* (a temple to the god Mithras, whose cult was popular among Roman soldiers), a Jewish synagogue, and a Christian church. The co-existence of these three separate buildings devoted to worship have illuminated our understanding of the general approach to religious tolerance in pagan Rome. Just over a century after the life of Christ, rather than evidence of a constantly persecuted, always-on-the move band of destitute Christians, we find a small, yet well-appointed Christian worship space (built within the framework of an existing house), complete with an adjacent room suitable for meetings and meals, not unlike many missions in North America today. The walls of the house church are adorned with iconography, much of which is in a fine state of preservation due to the building being filled with rubble just prior to its capture.

From the discovery of this building with its iconographic decorations as well as from fragments of scrolls with Christian Eucharistic prayers which were also found in the ruins, a more complete picture of early Christian worship has emerged. Despite periodic waves of persecution by the pagan Roman authorities at various locales throughout the empire, we find evidence in Dura Europos of an established Christian community, secure enough in its Roman surroundings to permanently adorn its worship space.[ii] Even at this very early date, between the second and third centuries, we discover Christian church architecture that is dedicated to liturgical worship and features much of the same sort of adornment—albeit on a far smaller and more modest scale—that went on to grace such architectural masterpieces as Agia Sophia in Constantinople, the famous Byzantine churches of Thessaloniki and the *katholika* of Mount Athos.

During this same period of late antiquity, textiles were ubiquitously used as hangings and curtains in well-appointed homes since they could function not only as a means of decoration, but also as screens and doors. Ancient buildings, typically made of stone, could be cold and spare and textiles warmed, beautified, and demarcated space even within relatively modest dwellings. If one considers the late antique world's use of textiles in conjunction with the evidence of Dura Europos, it is easy to surmise how early Christians would have instinctively turned to woven and embroidered textiles to adorn and beautify their churches, whether the setting was a modest house church in a border town like Dura Europos or, eventually, the grand space of a great cathedral. This awareness of the common use of textiles in daily life along with a fuller understanding of early Christian worship must inform our exploration of historical paraments. While it is difficult to make any absolute assertions based upon extant pieces, we can begin to visualize a more historically correct picture of the important role textiles played in Christian worship from the very beginning.

The Standardization of Orthodox Christian Paraments

As time went on and persecutions ceased with the legalization of Christianity in AD 313, Christians found themselves living within an empire in which church building and beautification gained momentum and then flourished, reaching a zenith under Justinian with the construction of Agia Sophia in Constantinople in AD 532–537 (after earthquake damage in 553 and 557, its rebuilding was completed in 562). The Church now had full and unfettered opportunities to express its theology of the physical church building as the Kingdom of Heaven on earth and did so with enthusiasm, not only in the great cathedral of Agia Sophia, but in churches throughout the Byzantine Empire. The attention given to the architecture and adornment of Byzantine churches was not haphazard, but rather reflective of a considered and systematic program pursued by a society that endeavored to proclaim its faith in the might and glory of God by utilizing the media of woven and embroidered textiles, which it was accustomed to encounter in daily, civic life. Such focus on material adornment was not merely a type of outward religious demonstration, but was deeply rooted in a symbolic system in which the physical elements of the church embodied complex layers of mystic metaphor. The esteemed liturgical scholar Robert Taft illustrates the functioning of this system of symbols with a particularly rich example:

> The precise genius of metaphorical language is to hold in dynamic tension several levels of meaning simultaneously. In this sense, one and the same Eucharistic table *must be* at once Holy of Holies, Golgotha, tomb of the resurrection, cenacle [chamber of the Last Supper], and heavenly sanctuary of the Letter to the Hebrews.[iii] [2]

This thoroughly Christian worldview imbued each piece of furniture used within the church with a symbolic meaning, and by extension, the adornments of such furniture as well. The cloths placed upon the altar were no mere fancy drapery, but became in very essence the shroud of the lifeless Christ, the napkin covering His face, and, finally, the glorious robes of the resurrected King.

Giving full weight to the importance of the physical space and furnishing of the Byzantine church, it becomes apparent that the cloths and draperies used for adornment would have assumed standardized forms rather early in the Church's history, a development parallel to the early standardization of liturgical vesture described in Chapter Two. Despite the lack of extant liturgical cloths prior to the eleventh century, we know of

---

2. It is important to note that as recently as the mid-twentieth century, many scholars of Byzantine art evinced the attitude that the assignment of symbolic meaning to the various elements of the physical space of a church may be dismissed as "somewhat far-fetched and abstruse symbolical interpretation. . . ." (Cyril Mango, *The Art of Byzantium*, 4). More recent scholarship has embraced a fuller appreciation of the Byzantine era's symbolic approach to church architecture and adornment (note especially the collaboration between Princeton University and the Museum of Byzantine Art in Thessaloniki in their *Architecture as Icon* exhibit in 2009–2010). Scholars have even begun to explore how such symbology influences the portrayal of architecture within given icons. One of the most evocative examples of this appreciation for the multilayered nuances of symbolic "language," is a reading of the icon of the Forty Holy Martyrs of Sebaste in which the four rows of ten martyrs are understood to be the "walls" of the church, thereby underscoring that the people within the church are the "living stones" of Christ's earthly dwelling.

such standardization from writings on liturgical practice, most notably those of St Germanos, Patriarch of Constantinople from AD 715 to 730.

In his work, *On the Divine Liturgy*, St Germanos gives a very thorough list of the various vestments and paraments used in the liturgy and their associated symbolism, and from this list we observe two things pertinent to a study of Orthodox Christian paraments: first, the historic names and specific functions of certain liturgical items, and second, the multi-faceted approach to symbology common to the liturgical piety of his day.[3] It is important to remark upon this multi-faceted approach to symbology because in the study of paraments one finds multiple symbolic meanings attached to the various liturgical cloths and veils and it is imperative that we comprehend that such seemingly conflicting meanings can co-exist harmoniously within the liturgical imagination of the Church, and indeed, that they are a marked feature of Orthodox Christian theology. Taft further elucidates this idea:

> The problem of later medieval liturgical allegory consists not in the multiplicity of systematically layered symbols, such as we find here [in St Germanos' writings] and in patristic exegesis. The later one-symbol-per-object correspondence results not from the tidying up of an earlier incoherent primitiveness, but from the decomposition of the earlier patristic mystery-theology into a historicizing system of dramatic narrative allegory. All levels— Old Testament preparation, Last Supper,

---

3. Some scholars feel that St Germanos' work is too imaginative or allegorical to offer a clear picture of Orthodox Christian theology; however, Robert Taft ably refutes this viewpoint in his informative article "The Liturgy of the Great Church." For those wishing to study St Germanos in more depth, this article is essential reading for its balanced and historically accurate approach to St Germanos' writings. St Germanos' work is but one link in a chain of lavish and imaginative symbolic interpretation that held a prime position in Orthodox theological and liturgical exposition for well over 1000 years. We find, over a great span of history, an inclination on the part of Orthodox Christian commentators to seek maximum symbolic value in every aspect of Christian faith and praxis. When it comes to symbology, within the Orthodox Christian *phronema*, more is always better than less.

accomplishment on Calvary, eternal heavenly offering, present liturgical event—must be held in dynamic unity by any interpretation of the eucharist. To separate these levels, then parcel out the elements bit by bit according to some chronologically consecutive narrative sequence, is to turn ritual into drama, symbol into allegory, mystery into history.[iv]

Delving into the history of Orthodox Christian paraments will frequently uncover seemingly disparate symbological associations with the various pieces, but we can proceed with confidence knowing that such overlapping symbological associations can coexist mystically and harmoniously within the Church.

A Walking Tour of the Church

We will now embark upon an imaginary walking tour of an Orthodox church building to visualize the paraments therein and become familiar with their names and purposes before discussing them individually in more depth.

Immediately upon entering the doors of the church, we encounter in the narthex icons displayed on *proskynitaria*, or icon stands.[4] The adornment of these icons takes the form of decorative veils (referred to simply as icon stand covers or *proskynitarion* covers) which are typically long, rectangular pieces of brocade or velvet placed under the icon and draping down the front of the stand (and often down the back as well).

Moving forward from the icons in the narthex, we come into the nave of the church and as we look around, we see additional *proskynitaria* with variously decorated covers, but we also view large banners, free-standing on tall poles, in various positions around the church, most often somewhere near or on the *ambon* (in present-day usage, the elevated floor area just in front

---

4. There is sometimes confusion about the correct name for an icon stand. Often such stands will be termed *"analogia"* but properly speaking, an *analogion* is a stand used for reading from a book. The correct term for a stand holding an icon (or a Gospel book displayed for veneration) is *"proskynitarion,"* i.e., "veneration stand."

of the *iconostasion*). There can be a great deal of variety in banners, but one of the most typical styles is made from burgundy velvet with an icon (either painted on canvas or embroidered) in the center of the banner and three long, narrow fabric pendants draping down from the bottom half of the banner. Other banners may dispense with the tail-like pendants and be a straightforward square or rectangle made from velvet or brocade, but the universal feature of banners is a central icon surrounded by some kind of textile adornment. While these banners remain stationary during most liturgical services, their poles can be removed from their stands and the banner may then be carried in processions upon appropriate occasions throughout the Church year.

As we approach the *iconostasion* (icon screen), we now have our first glimpse within the altar (the sanctuary area behind the *iconostasion*) of the holy table, and it is here that we must devote the majority of our focus. To begin with, there are two layers of adornment placed upon the holy table at its consecration, hidden from view thereafter. First, four small linen cloths are placed upon the corners of the holy table, each having either the name or the image of one of the four evangelists stamped upon it (in current usage paper icons are often substituted). Second, a finely woven linen cloth called the *"katasarkion"* is placed over the holy table and cinched tightly over the top edges of the table with cords. Because the holy table is symbolically understood to be the tomb of Christ, the *katasarkion* represents the burial shroud of Christ, and, in a further layer of meaning, is sometimes also referred to as the baptismal garment of the altar table. After being positioned during the consecration, the *katasarkion* is never removed from the consecrated table. Once the *katasarkion* is in place, the next cloth laid on top of the holy table is the *endytei*, more simply referred to as the "altar cloth." This cloth (or set of cloths as is sometimes the case) has the widest scope for variety of embellishment of all Orthodox Christian paraments and should be the finest piece of textile artistry, among both the vestments and paraments, in the entire church building, thereby visually underscoring the Orthodox Christian theological emphasis on holy table as the throne of Christ as He is present in the Eucharist. Usually made of the finest brocade or velvet, the altar cloth is ornately finished with galloon (metallic trim), fringe, and often tassels at the corners. Frequently a top cloth, hanging down six to twelve inches from the top of the table, is placed over a bottom cloth which reaches all the way to the floor.

Once vested with the corner evangelists, *katasarkion*, and altar cloth (or cloths), the fully dressed holy table has the Gospel book enthroned front and center. When the table is not in use for a liturgical service, the Gospel book is covered by its own veil ("Gospel cover"), a square or rectangle of fabric made to match or complement the altar cloth. With the celebration of the Divine Liturgy, additional paraments will come into use: the *eiliton*, *antimension*, and the chalice veil set (which comprise two small *kalymmata* veils and one *aer*), all of which will be described in more detail in the section below.

As we turn to leave the church to end our tour, we are finally arrested by the sight of the stunning *epitaphios* in its traditional position on the west wall of the nave. The *epitaphios* is a large liturgical veil which has its origins in the *aer* (described below) and which is used ceremonially on Great and Holy Friday. It is the most prominent of all the pieces of embroidered iconography in the Orthodox Christian Church, featuring an image of the lifeless body of Christ, either alone surrounded by angelic symbols, or with a full complement of mourning figures—a composition known as the *"threnos"* ("lamentation").

With this introduction to the position and names of each of the paraments complete, it now remains for us to consider them separately in detail, examining their history as well as their current usage. We will begin with the paraments used liturgically and then work our way outwards to those serving a decorative function.

Paraments Piece by Piece

Antimension

Historically speaking, one of the earliest textile pieces used in Orthodox Christian worship is the *antimension*, a rectangular piece of cloth which from ancient times served as a portable holy table cloth that could be folded up, transported easily, and laid out on any table, thereby making it suitable for the celebration of the Mysteries of Christ. While some authors have speculated that this piece was formerly embellished with embroidery, this theory is problematic because a cloth covered with raised surface embroidery would not function well liturgically, potentially causing a chalice to tip or trapping small particles of the consecrated bread in its intricate threads.[v] The decorations on the *antimension*, which were most likely painted, seem to have begun with a simple "IC XC NIKA" monogram around a cross and an inscription by the hand of the consecrating bishop. In accord with its use as a portable holy table, relics would be sewn into the *antimension*. Eventually, other liturgical motifs were added to the decoration, such as the lance and the sponge of the Passion. In current usage the *antimension* is usually adorned with the design scheme of the *epitaphios threnos* ("lamentations at the tomb") which includes the lifeless body of Christ, the Theotokos, the Apostle John, St Nicodemus, St Joseph of Arimathea, angels, and the symbols of the four Evangelists.

Figure 1. Modern *Antimension* (photo used with permission of St. George Greek Orthodox Church, Greenville, SC).

The current *antimension* differs little from its historical antecedents. It is a painted or silk-screened piece of cloth that features the *epitaphios threnos*. The design is printed in either black or multiple colors on a light-colored silk or linen background fabric and the cloth is consecrated and signed by the diocesan bishop of the local church.⁵ Modern *antimensia* may have relics enclosed within their seams, but this is not a universal practice.

Katasarkion

As soon as early Christian communities were able to establish and consecrate permanent holy tables on which to serve the Divine Liturgy (like the holy table that undoubtedly stood in the house church at Dura Europos), these altar tables began to be vested with specific cloths. The earliest permanent covering for the holy table is the *katasarkion*, a white linen cloth draped over the table and secured with tightly bound cords. This cloth began as a symbol of the linen in which Christ's body was wrapped for burial but, as with so many things in Orthodox Christian tradition, it has taken on additional layers of symbolic meaning throughout the centuries and so is sometimes also referred to as the baptismal garment of the altar.

Endytei (Altar Cloth)

The more elaborate cloth placed over the *katasarkion* has historically borne many names, most prominently, "*endytei*," but in English is typically referred to simply as an "altar cloth." This elaborate cloth, made from either woven or embroidered textiles was already in established use by the late sixth century and, given our exploration of early Christian worship and the late-antique world's use of textiles, quite likely to have been in use centuries earlier.

Of all of the paraments in an Orthodox Christian church, the altar cloth stands at the very center, both liturgically and physically, being symbolically the resurrectional garment of the risen Christ and adorning the most prominent furnishing in the church, the holy table upon which the Eucharist is celebrated. Due to this elevated and honored position, the altar cloth should

---

5. Customarily, when a diocesan bishop performs the consecration of a new holy table, he will at the same time consecrate and sign multiple *antimensia* to keep in reserve and distribute to his parishes as old ones become worn and need to be replaced.

be the most elaborate parament within the church building, featuring elaborate embroidery work (either hand-embroidery or machine-embroidery) and the highest quality materials such as real metal brocades, velvets, and silks. The tradition of outfitting the holy table in such a regal and awe-inspiring fashion can be firmly traced as far back as the reconstruction of the dome of Agia Sophia in AD 562. At the rededication of the great cathedral, an officer of the imperial household, Paul the Silentiary, delivered a famous encomium in praise of the building's architecture and decoration, in which he describes in lavish detail the altar cloth adorning the holy table of what was, at the time, the most admired and influential church building in the whole world. Given the sheer splendor of the cloth he chronicles, it is worth recounting his description in full:

> Whither am I carried? Whither tends my unbridled speech? Let my bold voice be restrained with silent lip lest I lay bare what the eyes are not permitted to see. But ye priests, as the sacred laws command you, spread out with your hands the veil dipped in the purple dye of the Sidonian shell and cover the top of the table. Unfold the cover along its four sides and show to the countless crowd the gold and the bright designs of skilful handiwork. One side is adorned with Christ's venerable form. This has been fashioned not by artists' skilful hands plying the knife, nor by the needle driven through cloth, but by the web, the produce of the foreign worm, changing its colored threads of many shades. Upon the divine legs is a garment reflecting a golden glow under the rays of rosy fingered Dawn, and a chiton, dyed purple by the Tyrian seashell, covers the right shoulder beneath its well-woven fabric; for at that point the upper garment has slipped down while, pulled up across the side, it envelops the left shoulder. The forearm and hand are thus laid bare. He seems to be stretching out the fingers of the right hand, as if preaching His immortal words, while in His left He holds

the book of divine message—the book that tells what He, the Lord, accomplished with provident mind when His foot trod the earth. The whole robe shines with gold: for on it gold leaf has been wrapped round thread after the manner of a pipe or a reed, and so it projects above the lovely cloth, firmly bound with silken thread by sharp needles. On either side stand two of God's messengers: Paul, replete with divine wisdom, and the mighty doorkeeper of the gates of heaven [St Peter] who binds with both heavenly and earthly bonds. One holds the book pregnant with holy ordinance, the other the form of the cross on a golden staff. And both the cunning web has clothed in robes woven of silver; while rising above their immortal heads a golden temple enfolds them with three noble arches fixed on four columns of gold. And on the hem of the veil shot with gold, art has figured the countless deeds of the Emperors, guardians of the city: here you may see hospitals for the sick, there sacred fanes [churches]. And elsewhere are displayed the miracles of heavenly Christ, a work suffused with beauty. And upon other veils you may see the monarchs joined together, here by the hand of Mary, the Mother of God, there by that of Christ, and all is adorned with the sheen of golden thread. Thus is everything clothed in beauty; everything fills the eye with wonder.[vi]

The "purple dye of the Sidonian shell" refers to the color of the background cloth of the altar covering, a color akin to that which we call "burgundy," profoundly esteemed for its rich hue and great value (see Chapter Five for more information on Tyrian purple). From the limited record of extant, old iconography, it can be surmised that this deep, red-burgundy color was from early times considered most appropriate for altar cloths. The fresco icons of the ordination of St Nicholas in Agios Nicholaos Orphanos in Thessaloniki, the fresco icon of the Communion of the Apostles in Agia Ekaterina in Thessaloniki, as well as the mosaic icons of Abel and Melchisidek in San Vitale in Ravenna all depict altar tables with cloth of this color, a traditional use still to be observed throughout the Church worldwide as altar cloths are most frequently made from burgundy or deep red fabrics.

Paul the Silentiary's account describes the cloth as being made from woven silk, "by the web, the produce of the foreign worm" and augmented by metal-thread embroidery work: "The whole robe shines with gold: for on it gold leaf has been wrapped round thread after the manner of a pipe or a reed, and so it projects above the lovely cloth, firmly bound with silken thread by sharp needles." This astounding outlay of some of the most costly materials known in human history along with the great number of figures and scenes described attests to this cloth's superior workmanship and its surely astonishing beauty.

From the Silentiary's comments and other historical evidence, it seems certain that both woven and embroidered iconography and decoration were used for altar cloths and other paraments.[vii] This is not surprising given the overall scheme of adornment within an Orthodox Church: with the mystical understanding that the physical church serves as a meeting place between heaven and earth, it would be deemed right and proper that multiple surfaces—from walls to domes to tables themselves—should be covered in various iconographic media, placing before the viewer a material image of the spiritual reality of the presence of holy saints and angels and calling to mind that he was no longer "in the world" but in the Kingdom of Heaven.

While modern altar cloths can rarely be made from the kind of materials and with the impressive workmanship of the Agia Sophia altar cloth, they are still made from ornate materials and finishings in a similar design and with similar motifs. In current usage, varieties of altar cloths have developed, but all these variations can still trace their origins back to the cloth described above and its contemporaries.

There are currently two basic styles of altar cloth used in North America: the fully dressed altar cloth, which is comprised of a bottom and a top cloth, and an abbreviated form in which only the top cloth is utilized. The fully dressed altar cloth begins with a cross-shaped cloth that has a center square or rectangle (depending on the dimensions of the holy table) to which four panels are attached forming the "arms" of the cross. This bottom cloth is centered over the *katasarkion* after which the panels hang down each side of the holy table and are held in place with buttons and loops, much like the description given above: "Unfold the cover along its four sides and show to the countless crowd the gold and the bright designs of skilful handiwork." The front of this cloth is typically highly embellished and features a central motif, usually a cross surrounded by an arch of grapevines or floral work, with additional similar decoration around the entire perimeter of this panel. The three other sides of the cloth are generally left unadorned since they are not visible from the nave. Once this bottom cloth has been placed upon the table, a matching top cloth is placed over it and this cloth covers the entire top of the holy table and hangs down on each side six to twelve inches. This top cloth is decorated similarly to the bottom cloth around its entire perimeter and typically finished with galloon and fringe around the perimeter and a heavy bullion tassel at each corner. When so arranged, the bottom and top cloth are viewed as a "set," but, occasionally, a multi-purpose ivory-colored or gold-colored bottom cloth can be used with variously colored coordinating top cloths that may be changed depending on the liturgical season.

In the case of the abbreviated form, only the top cloth is placed upon the altar table and the bottom cloth is omitted. This style of covering is most often used when there is some kind of adornment on the holy table itself, such as iconography, carved marble, or mosaic work which would be hidden by a bottom cloth. While both styles are used in North America, generally speaking the abbreviated top cloth is used most often in Greek practice and the fully dressed style is used most often in Russian practice (although this is beginning to change as the fully dressed style is gaining favor in North American Greek practice due to a greater interchange between America and Greece—in Greece the fully dressed altar is the prevalent style).

One additional, but infrequently used, style of holy table cloth is that in which a single top cloth hangs all the way to the floor (instead of the set of separate bottom and top cloths) and is finished with galloon around its perimeter. This style creates an attractive "pooling" of fabric at the corners of the holy table, but is not often used due to its expense (even a standard 42-inch by 42-inch altar would require a ten-and-a-half foot square altar cloth made from eleven yards of fabric).

Figure 2. Fully dressed altar cloth.

Regardless of the style employed, it is imperative and in keeping with Orthodox Christian tradition that parish communities use the finest materials and finishings for their altar cloths so that "Thus is everything clothed in beauty; everything fills the eye with wonder."[viii]

Figure 3. Top cloth altar cloth, St. Demetrios Greek Orthodox Church, Libertyville, IL.

Eiliton

With the flowering of Christian architecture, the holy table was no longer dependent upon the small, portable *antimension*, but became a permanent, consecrated piece of furniture within the church, adorned with its own *katasarkion* and *endytei*. Because this *endytei*, or altar cloth, was made from elaborate materials and was thus difficult to remove from the holy table, for practicality's sake a linen top cloth was placed upon it to catch any stray particles of Holy Communion. This linen cloth, called the "*eiliton*," was made from white linen and finished without elaborate decoration so that it could be easily gathered up from the table and cleaned as needed. In practical terms it served, on a consecrated holy table, a purpose analogous to that of the *antimension* on an unconsecrated table, i.e., a cloth that reverently contains and preserves any spilled elements of Holy Communion.

In the present day there is much confusion regarding the *eiliton* and its relationship to the *antimension*. Historically speaking, when the Divine Liturgy was celebrated on a consecrated holy table the presence of an *eiliton* was deemed sufficient, whereas when the Divine Liturgy was celebrated on an unconsecrated table an *antimension* was required. In modern usage, however, it has become customary to use the *antimension* at every Divine Liturgy, even on a consecrated holy table (though this practice might seem strange from a historical perspective as it is the layering of a portable, consecrated table cloth upon a permanent, consecrated table). The modern *antimension* has come to be understood as making the altar table complete and no Orthodox Christian Liturgy can be served without it. The term *eiliton* has thus come to refer to a cloth that wraps the *antimension* when folded and lies under it when unfolded, still serving the same purpose of catching stray portions of Communion, but often made from a double layer of burgundy satin and, occasionally, permanently sewn to the *antimension*. In an alternative (and sometimes parallel) usage, the term *eiliton* has also come to be applied to a white linen cloth made to cover the entire top of the altar table (usually finished with a small border of either hand-made or machine-made white lace) which serves to protect the *endytei* and which may be removed and cleaned as necessary.

Gospel Cover

The Gospel cover is a liturgical parament of modern usage that covers the Gospel book (and sometimes also the blessing cross) when the holy table is not in use. It is either a 24-inch by 24-inch square, or a 24-inch by 36-inch rectangle. It is finished with galloon around the perimeter and a cross is either sewn or embroidered in the center of the piece (no fringe is used). The Gospel cover is made to match or complement the holy table cover.

Figure 4. Gospel Cover.

Liturgical Veils

Once the holy table is vested, the next liturgical cloths which come into use are the *aeres*, in present day referred to collectively as a "chalice veil set" or "*kalymmata* set." Originally, these were named "the great *aer*" and the "little *aeres*," with the little *aeres* being further delineated as the *diskokalymmata* (cover for the *diskos*) and the *potirokalymmata* (cover for the chalice).

To properly discuss these pieces, we need to examine them separately—first the little *aeres* and then the great *aer*. Due to their smaller size the little *aeres*, now referred to as "*kalymmata*," "veils," or "chalice veils," were in past times often lavished with embroidery. The Communion of the Apostles was a favorite early design scheme. Later it was replaced in prominence with a depiction of the infant Christ laid in the *diskos*, known as the *"amnos"* or "Lamb of God."[ix] The veils served not only a liturgical function but also a practical one by protecting the sacred bread and wine from any kind of pest or contaminant.

While the little *aeres* had a circumscribed purpose—covering the holy vessels—and thus could not develop in size given the limitations of this usage, the great *aer* (today referred to simply as the "*aer*") became larger in size and more lavishly ornamented and developed into two distinct variations with separate uses, the *aer* and the *epitaphios* (which will be described below). The first use of the *aer* was identical to its current usage: practically, as a protective cloth to cover the Holy Gifts as they rest upon the *prothesis* table and, later in the Liturgy, upon the holy table and, liturgically, draped over the shoulders of the deacon during the Procession of the Holy Gifts during the Divine Liturgy. Historically, this cloth often had a design of the Body of Christ attended by angels. There are a number of extant *aers* that feature lavish hand-embroidery work, their size making them an ideal canvas and their liturgical use making them an appropriate venue for intricate ornamentation.

Hand-embroidered *aers* or veils, such as the historical examples described above, are now the exception rather than the rule. Modern chalice veil sets are often made from the same types of brocades and machine-embroidered fabrics as the vestments of the priest. While historical chalice veil sets were seen as "stand-alone" pieces due to their intricacy and great worth, modern chalice veil sets follow one of two paths: they are either made to match the priest's vestments (this is far more common in Russian practice) or they are made to match or coordinate with the altar cloths. Given their historical development, the latter seems to be the more traditional approach. A chalice veil "set" consists of one *aer* with a matching *diskos* veil and a matching chalice veil with all pieces being finished with either galloon and fringe, or simply fringe (as is the case with the majority of the velvet, machine-embroidered type). In Greek practice, the *aer* has ribbons sewn to the top corners that allow it to be tied around the shoulders for the Great Entrance whereas Russian practice omits the ribbons in favor of draping the *aer* over the shoulder of the deacon or (in the absence of a deacon) the arm of the presbyter.

In design, the *aer* is a rectangle, varying in size from 18–20 inches deep and 24–30 inches wide. The veils are made in various shapes, from simple small squares that drape over the chalice and the *asteriskon* ("star cover") of the *diskos* to the more common cross-shaped veil, which, when laid flat, is an equilateral cross with the central "square" being approximately five inches by five inches. The arms of the cross can also be square, but are often curved or come to a gradual point. The central square is heavily interfaced to prevent the veil from sliding off the chalice or *asteriskon*.

Figure 5. Chalice veil set.

Figure 6. Communion of the Apostles aer (International Congress of Byzantinists, *Medieval Pictorial Embroidery: Byzantium, Balkans, Russia*. Catalogue of the XVIIIth International Congress Exhibition (Moscow: International Congress of Byzantinists, 1991.).

Communion Cloth

The term *"kalymma"* (plural *"kalymmata"*) has also become attached to another cloth, simple in design but of great practical importance, the "communion cloth." When Holy Communion came to be distributed to the laity by means of a spoon (in the ninth century) it became necessary to employ a cloth which could be extended from the edge of the chalice and held under the chin of the communicant to contain any accidental spillage of the consecrated mixture of the mingled sacred bread and wine. (Similar cloths would likely have been in use even earlier as a type of napkin when the laity as well as the clergy received the sacred wine by sipping directly from the chalice.) This practical, liturgical cloth is typically 18–20 inches square, made of red, wine-colored fabric (a highly absorbent cotton is best for this application), usually with a gold-colored cross embroidered on one corner. When not in use for the distribution of the Holy Gifts it lies folded under the liturgical spoon or rests upon the top of the chalice. It also serves the important function of being used to wipe the chalice clean after the consumption of the Holy Gifts by the deacon or presbyter at the conclusion of the Divine Liturgy.

Sponge

While not a parament, strictly speaking, since it is not made of fabric, the liturgical sponge is also an important, practical item in liturgical usage. A section of a natural sea sponge which has been flattened into an irregular shape approximately two inches by three inches through the careful application of heat and pressure (using a heated iron), the liturgical sponge remains folded within or resting upon the *antimension* at all times and is used for sweeping particles of the consecrated bread from the *diskos* into the chalice as well as for sweeping up and collecting stray particles from the surface of the *antimension*. An additional sea sponge, not flattened but in its natural, spherical shape, is also employed at the prosthesis table, being placed in the chalice, after its cleansing, to absorb any residual moisture.

Epitaphios

An additional, highly important, parament which developed from the *aer* is called the *"epitaphios"* and is used principally on Great and Holy Friday. The evolution of one textile piece, the great *aer*, into two distinct pieces, the *aer* and the *epitaphios*, came about thus: In addition to being used during every Divine Liturgy, the *aer* was also used on Great and Holy Friday to wrap the Gospel book which was carried on the priest's shoulder to represent the body of Christ, with the *aer* symbolizing a burial shroud. Beginning sometime around the late thirteenth or early fourteenth century (in the Paleologan period, AD 1261–1453), the *aer* used on Great and Holy Friday began to be made into its own separate cloth with a fuller design scheme, the Body of Christ being augmented by lamenting figures such as the Mother of God, the myrrh-bearing women and St Joseph of Arimethea.[6]

These two pieces, *aer* and *epitaphios*, while having a common origin have developed quite differently in both size and decorative scheme. Whereas the *aer* remains a small rectangle and has become less ornate over the centuries, the *epitaphios* became a much larger piece with average sizes ranging from 20 to 36 inches high by 30 to 48 inches wide and, sometimes even larger: one of the most glorious of all extant *epitaphioi*, the "Thessaloniki *epitaphios*," is truly life-size at almost six-and-a-half-feet wide by over two feet high.[7] These types of extraordinarily elaborate *epitaphioi* "represent the quintessential creations of the Late Byzantine art of embroidery"[x] and form the cornerstone of the canon of embroidered iconography within the Church. Although one may argue that embroidered *epigonatia* and *epimanikia* are just as elaborate, the larger scale of the *epitaphios* makes these textiles much more impressive examples of embroidered iconography. Due to their limited use (and thus excellent preservation) and their heavy gold-work, many historical *epitaphioi* remain in the collections of museums in Greece, the Balkans, and throughout Europe, and their workmanship, quality, and sublime beauty make them one of the highpoints in the history not only of the needle arts of the Orthodox Church, but of embroidered textiles in general.

While design schemes vary widely among *epitaphioi* from about the fourteenth century onwards, the *epitaphios* originally depicted the body of Christ upon a dark background, most often a deep, burgundy silk. Beginning in the thirteenth and fourteenth centuries, a fuller cast of characters began to be depicted, resulting in the now well-known "Lamentations at the Tomb"

---

6. There has sometimes been confusion about the terminology connected with these two distinct cloths. Here is my preferred usage: the *"epitaphios sindon"* ("burial/tomb shroud") denotes the *aer* because originally it depicted only the Body of Christ whereas the *"epitaphios threnos"* ("lamentations at the tomb") refers to the Great and Holy Friday *epitaphios* since it depicts mourning figures attending to the body of Christ.

7. The plural of *"epitaphios"* is *"epitaphioi."*

image which can include up to twelve figures as well as various angelic representations surrounding the lifeless body of Christ.[xi] Additionally, the apolytikion of Great and Holy Saturday (or a portion thereof)—"The pious Joseph brought down thy pure body from the tree, wrapped it in pure linen, embalmed it with ointment, arrayed it and laid it in a new tomb"—came to be embroidered as a border around the lamenting figures along with various floral motifs and vinework.[xii]

While their most prominent usage is in the processions of Great and Holy Friday and their solemn enthronement upon the holy table for the forty-day Paschal season, *epitaphioi* have also come to occupy an honored symbolic position in the church building and are now commonly displayed throughout the church year on the west wall of the nave, often hung in wooden cases or on drapery rods so that they may be readily observed.[8] Such strategic positioning is almost certainly due to a Byzantine fascination with the ceremonial rites of Jerusalem and, more specifically, with the Church of the Resurrection. The main altar of the Church of the Resurrection is oriented to the east, but if one turns from the altar and faces west then one is facing the chapel of the Holy Sepulchre, the very tomb of Christ. With an understanding of the earthly church building representing the Heavenly Jerusalem, the west wall is the most suitable location for the lifeless body of Christ, as portrayed on the *epitaphios*. At the time of the rise of the elaboration of the *epitaphios* in the Paleologan period, there was close contact between Byzantium and the Holy Land and this, along with an awareness of the church as the Heavenly Jerusalem, meant such symbolic placement of the *epitaphios* would not have been lost upon the viewer each time he departed the church building.[xiii]

While historical *epitaphioi* feature some of the finest textile craftsmanship in the history of the Orthodox Christian Church, it is unfortunate that the same can be said of only a fraction of the *epitaphioi* produced for use in the Church today. Many

---

8. The laity are often unaware of the fact that the *epitaphios* is placed upon the holy table (under the *antimension*) at the conclusion of the Orthros of Holy Saturday (the "Lamentations Service") and remains there through the leave-taking of Holy Pascha.

feature crudely worked machine embroidery, utilizing low-quality materials and threads. The designs and figures are almost cartoonish and, due to the technical difficulty of executing faces and the severe lack of trained embroiderers, painted paper is often inserted into the embroidery, which stands the test of time poorly, becoming worn and tattered in a few short years. These modern *epitaphioi* tend to have cheap velvet as their background fabric and are finished with embroidered outlines rather than filled gold-work designs as of old. They are usually finished with poor-quality, metallic-paper-wrapped fringe (as opposed to the old style fringe whose threads were wrapped in real gold) and some even feature metallic rick-rack or military braid in the place of better-quality finishings.

It is primarily due to the advent of poor-quality, synthetic "metal" threads and the desire for inexpensive products that this situation has arisen, but it is also due in part to a lack of understanding and awareness of the Church's long history of beautifully crafted, exceptional-quality textile pieces which are typically on display only in museums or in monasteries outside of North America. It takes only one generation to lose awareness of a fine craft and such is the sad case of the production of *epitaphioi* in North America today. It is not too strong a statement to remark that of all Orthodox Christian art forms, the *epitaphios* is the one that has sunk the lowest. But, despite this grave situation, there is some hope that this craft is slowly being revived by skilled embroiderers who are beginning to educate a new generation, and such work is to be highly commended.

Of the few high-quality *epitaphioi* being produced, they typically follow the old designs and are still made from historical metal-thread and split-stitch techniques. Better-quality *epitaphioi* feature heavier embroidery, more elaborate and finely executed figures (particularly the faces), and more ornate borders such as intricate grapevines, floral vinework, or angelic representations. These styles are rarely finished with any kind of fringe since the beauty and intricacy of the design need no further adornment and fringe tends to degrade quickly.

One derivative form of the *epitaphios* that is beginning to grow in use is the *epitaphios* dedicated for use on the feast of the Dormition of the Theotokos. This type of *epitaphios* is usually embroidered on a blue background and features an icon of the falling asleep of the Mother of God. These *epitaphioi* are displayed and venerated during the liturgical celebrations of the Dormition on August 15.

Decorative Veils

The next category of paraments for consideration is that of the various cloths that may be grouped under the heading "decorative veils" (as opposed to "liturgical veils"). These typically comprise cloths that are draped on icon stands (*proskynitaria*) and feature the widest variety of size, materials, and design of almost any category of Orthodox Christian parament.

Due to the great variation in size and overall design of *proskynitaria*, the cloths that cover them come in a range of sizes and designs—some cover the stand to the floor, others only come down partway in the front; some consist of a two-piece arrangement in which a smaller cloth is layered over a larger, longer cloth. In the latter instance the smaller cloth is often of high-quality linen and features finely hand-worked filet crochet lace, sometimes with symbols such as chalices, grapevines, or monograms like the Chi Rho forming a border along the front. It can also feature multi-colored cotton or silk embroidery on white linen, or be made from a more elaborate piece of real-metal brocade. In one variation, this top cloth is square rather than rectangular, and thus is placed under the icon on the diagonal so that a triangular-shaped section is glimpsed under each edge of the icon. Such cloths are typically made by hand by pious women and manifest a great amount of needlework skill and investment of time.[9]

---

9. I have been charmed by these wonderful linen cloths in my visits to Greece and I have gone out of my way to take photos and chat with women about their design and manufacture. They are a wonderful gift of love and devotion on the part of the women who make them and I am hopeful that this tradition will become normative in North America, providing women another means with which to dedicate their handcraft skills to the adornment of their churches. The most common forms of adornment are filet crochet (worked with fine-gauge crochet thread), but silk embroidery or hand-knit lace would also be suitable for this purpose.

Decorative veils made from brocade are typically finished with galloon, fringe, and often crosses, whereas those made from white linen or various-colored silks can be more elaborate and feature hand-embroidery work. Machine-embroidered velvet is occasionally used for decorative veils, with this type of decorative veil being sometimes matched to the holy table cloth and sometimes adorned with a different design altogether.

Figure 7.a *Proskynitaria* cover from Greece.

Figure 7.b *Proskynitaria* cover from Greece.

Podea

While this species of decorative cloth has rarely been seen in parishes in North America, it is gradually coming back into use, especially in Orthodox Christian monasteries, so mention of it should be made. It is important to note that its usage has never died out on Mt Athos and the parament collections of the Holy Mountain contain excellent examples of these beautiful embroideries. The *podea* is a type of decorative veil that hangs just below an icon, either affixed to the iconostasis or attached to an icon stand. Its primary function is to further adorn the icon and, as such, it serves as a permanent feature of the church interior. The podea's specific historical usage is further described by Pauline Johnstone:

> A podea belonged to a particular icon, was consecrated in its honour and sometimes presented as a thank offering to the saint it represented. . . . A podea could be any kind of decorated cloth. . . . The subject chosen was always connected with the icon for which the cloth was intended, but it was not a copy of the icon. Thus a sermon . . . described an icon showing a half-length portrait of the Virgin Hodigitria, of which the podea was represented as covering her feet, that is the lower half of her dress. In this way the faithful could benefit by touching the hem of her garment. In the same way the podea of the famous icon of Christ of the Khalki was described as recalling the story of the woman diseased with an issue of blood, who was cured by touching the hem of the Saviour's garment.[xiv]

While historical *podea* often featured complex embroidery, most modern *podea* are typically a rectangle of fabric which can be as simple as brocade finished in galloon or can be made in a more ornate fashion with a liturgical design machine-embroidered on velvet or silk. In its most ornate form, it is hand embroidered with iconography, and this iconography forms a complement to the icon it adorns. Due to its historical place in the collection of Orthodox Christian paraments as well as its excellent ability to provide yet more scope for the use of textiles in the Church, it is to be hoped that the *podea* will be given more prominence in North American parish usage in future generations.

Figure 8. Podea in St Katherine's, Thessaloniki, Greece.

Banners

The final, general category of Orthodox Christian church textiles is comprised of banners and embroidered hangings for pillars and walls. Historically, these large-scale textiles often featured various iconographic scenes and were designed to be yet another medium in which to portray the saints and the feasts of the Church, complementing the other elements in the church building and harmonizing with them, from vestments to woodcarvings. Hangings and banners were often worked on silk backgrounds with the typical stitches and methods of Eastern Orthodox embroidery as described below. Their finishings could have included various galloons, fringes, and tassels as some extant embroidered pieces can be seen to have been completed; however, it is conjecture to speak in any detail about how the grandest hanging textiles would have been embellished and there was most likely a wide variety for the finishing ornamentation adorning the great decorative pieces now lost.

Banners were a common fixture in earlier centuries, an essential feature of the many seasonal liturgical processions of Constantinople and other Orthodox Christian cities and a ubiquitous feature of well-appointed ancient church buildings. While the use of banners is beginning to be resurrected in modern times, textile hangings for walls and pillars have generally died out in current usage. This is primarily due to the historical development of the iconostasis. This evolution is succinctly described by Byzantine scholar Slobodan Curcic:

> From the very beginnings of church architecture, the area with the altar table was set aside as the Holy of Holies. Initially separated by a low chancel screen, by the fifth century this grew into a columnar screen, referred to as a *templon*. It is still debated how and when the intercolumniations of such a screen began to be closed. Generally, it is thought that initially curtains may have hung between columns, and that they could, at given moments, be opened, exposing the sanctuary area to full view of the assembly of the faithful. By the Middle Byzantine period, possibly as early as the ninth century, the templon began to be closed by icons—depicting Christ, the Mother of God, and other saints—thus rendering the interior of the sanctuary completely invisible to the congregation. This trend continued in the later centuries with the enclosing sanctuary screen, now referred to as the iconostasis, rising first by the addition of one, and later by two or more, tiers covered by individual icons.[xv]

An additional reason that the use of large-scale hangings died out was their prodigious size and, thus, great cost. Even during the height of imperial and noble patronage in Byzantium, these pieces would have been extremely costly to produce and they would be considered prohibitively expensive for most parish communities today. However, the use of smaller, portable banners is on the rise in North America with such banners being made in all levels of quality, from mass-produced types featuring paper iconography and lower-quality fringe, to lavish, hand-embroidered styles with either painted or embroidered iconography. Banners are typically displayed on poles mounted in stands and can be carried during processions. As with *podea*, it is gratifying that these textiles are making a small yet steady comeback and it is to be hoped that many more parish communities will embrace and fund the production of these forms of processional icons in years to come.

Figure 9. Photo of banner (photo used with permission of Alpha Omega Church Supplies, New York).

Miscellaneous Cloths

In addition to the covering of holy tables with textiles, auxiliary tables or furnishings such as the *prothesis* table, the *tetrapodion* (a "four-legged" table placed upon the *solea* for various services), niches, etc. are also covered with variously decorated cloths. If these are freestanding pieces of furniture, the cloth usually hangs down four to ten inches on all sides and is finished with galloon and fringe similar to the top cloth of the holy table, but in an overall simpler style so as not to compete with the holy table cover. In the case of a niche, in which the surface to be covered is part of the structure of the building, then the cloth typically follows the contours of the building at the back and sides, hangs down three to eight inches in front, and is finished with galloon around the perimeter, but fringe only along the front.

Iconostasion Curtains

A beautiful gate curtain (also known as a "holy door" curtain) is commonly used in Orthodox Christian churches and dates back to the architectural development of the *iconostasion* (or "iconostasis") as described above. Such a curtain hangs behind the double doors of the beautiful gate (the central and main opening of the *iconostasion,* directly in front of the holy table) and is typically made of burgundy velvet or silk and finished with a footed-style cross sewn in the upper, central portion of the curtain. It can also feature other ornamentation such as grapevines, the Greek key, flowers, or other nonfigural designs worked as borders along the sides and bottom of the curtain and, in more elaborate examples, a hand-embroidered or machine-embroidered icon of Christ or a very elaborate cross in the upper, central portion. Diaconal door curtains are used when an *iconostasion* does not have structural doors for the north and south openings. These are made using the same materials and finishings as the attendant beautiful gate curtain and thus form a matched set.

Most of these types of curtains are made from high-quality, cotton or cotton/silk velvet, or a high-quality, dense silk (although the use of silk for curtains is far less common than velvet) and the curtain is then lined with a suitable lining fabric. These curtains are installed on the altar side of the *iconostasion* by means of standard drapery hardware such as a drapery rod and ring system. Care should be taken in the choice of drapery hardware as the final selection will produce a distinctive sound when being opened and closed. Wooden drapery hardware is preferable as it produces a more mellifluous tone than metallic systems.

Figure 10. Beautiful gate curtain.

Paraments as Furnishings

With an understanding of the full range of Orthodox Christian textiles as well as an appreciation of the symbology of Christian architecture, it is vital to note that, historically, the textile adornments of the holy table and the church building had a design scheme different from the vestments of the clergy, a scheme more in alignment with the other permanent adornments of the church such as woodcarvings, painted and mosaic iconography, and metalwork. Then, as now, such textiles were expensive and lavish and their cost alone would have put them in the same category as the more permanent adornments of the church building.

In modern times there is sometimes a misconception that the holy table cloth and other church paraments must be identical in fabric and trimmings to the vestments worn by the clergy, thereby constituting a matched set. It is worth noting that this is a very late development in Orthodox Christian practice, most likely originating in the late Tsarist Russian period, an epoch in which there was a great fascination with Western European culture and art, including Western liturgical practices such as matching sets of vestments and paraments. At the height of this period of Western influence, North America saw many immigrant Orthodox Christian communities being founded with little opportunity for commerce with the Orthodox homelands, thereby compelling such parish communities to rely on Western church goods suppliers to outfit their churches, even though the available Western liturgical brocades and finishings had an aesthetic foundation markedly different from historical Orthodox Christian practice, particularly in the more rigid approach to color usage (for more information on color usage, please see Chapter Five). Despite the healthy and open interchange that now exists between "new" and "old" Orthodox Christian nations—an interchange that allows even the newest immigrant Orthodox Christians ready access to traditional liturgical materials—Western influence is still apparent in the paraments of many Orthodox churches in North America. A return to the older, more traditional practice of treating the paraments as part of the furnishings of the church and not as extensions of the clergy's vestments would be not only a practical measure (since commissioning multiple sets of paraments to match the clergy's vestments can be quite costly) but, more importantly, would inspire a rediscovery of the glorious tradition of highly embellished, iconographic textiles that has existed from the Church's early history, a textile tradition that encompasses almost every cultural expression of Eastern Orthodoxy from Byzantium to the Balkans, Russia, and beyond. With such a return to tradition, the new flowering of textiles would truly "fill the eye with wonder."

Materials and Methods of Historic Liturgical Embroidery

Having completed an overview of the paraments of the Church, it now remains for us to engage in a brief examination of the techniques and materials used in the highest expression of such textile adornments, those comprised of gold-work embroidery. From such an examination one comes away with great awe and respect for the artisans and workshops which produced such wonders.[10] Given the high value assigned to textiles in the Byzantine era (they were often given as diplomatic gifts and, in some instances, even used for political influence), it is a somewhat naïve assumption that an average noblewoman or even a princess would necessarily have possessed the kind of technical knowledge and skill to produce embroideries of such scope and quality. While, doubtless, there were many women proficient in the needle arts, these textiles are very much "workshop" pieces, designed and executed in a manner beyond amateur effort and requiring a crew of skilled workers to produce them in a reasonable amount of time.[11]

It is important to note that gold-work embroidery has been in use almost continuously from the earliest days of the Church. While certain forms of textile production collapsed completely after the fall of Constantinople, embroidery scholar Eleni Vlachopoulou describes the continuance of gold-work embroidery following the conquest of the imperial city:

> The numerous clergy of the Balkans, the Patriarchate and the great monastic centres (the Holy Mountain of Athos, Meteora, Sinai) needed gold embroideries, so there was no break in the continuity of this art; on the contrary, it gained in prestige and developed in a creative manner.

---

10. It is important to note that though many, myself included, have conjured up the charming image of a noblewoman plying her needle in the comfort of her own home, until at least the sixteenth century the type of textiles discussed in this chapter were typically produced in professional workshops that took great pride in the technical mastery of their craft (Johnstone, *Byzantine Tradition in Liturgical Embroidery*, 57).

11. Even today, it takes two or three months for a crew of skilled hand-embroiderers to produce a single *epitaphios* of average size.

> The art of gold embroidery changed little in the post-Byzantine era.[xvi]

The primary technique of Orthodox Christian liturgical embroidery is gold and silver embroidery work (also known as metal-thread embroidery). This type of embroidery employs a type of "thread" that is actually a silk floss core around which long, paper-thin sheets of gold are wrapped to create a golden thread. In traditional, Byzantine embroidery the silk core was either a color chosen to complement the gold, such as yellow, or a shading color which would be slightly visible through the wrapped gold and would thus add an additional dimension to the gold "thread." This ability to shade via the silk core was used to great effect in pieces designed almost entirely of gold-work as it broke up the tonal monotony of such pieces and lent a delicacy to the coloration.

As this type of gold "thread" was too bulky to be continually passed through cloth in the manner of regular silk floss, a type of embroidery known as "couching" was utilized. In this method, an awl made a small puncture in the background fabric and the gold thread was brought to the front of the fabric from the back and then laid entirely over the surface of the background fabric, being held in place by means of tiny silk floss stitches which went from the back to the front of the cloth and served to anchor the gold thread. These anchoring stitches themselves could be worked in elaborate patterns, often herringbone, chevron, or diagonal, in order to create yet more textural interest and complexity, and even a cursory perusal of textiles that employ such designs gives an appreciation of the skill with which this type of patterning is used. Once again, variety of technique is important, given that an entire textile piece was often created using the medium of gold-work. The exception in such pieces are the faces and hands of figures which are often worked in silk split stitch, a standard embroidery stitch in which one stitch is made and then a second stitch comes up from the back of the work and pierces the middle of the first stitch, thereby softening the effect of the stitch and leaving virtually no visible piercing of the cloth. Split stitch is an ideal method for all-over embroidery in a small space as it can be highly fluid and creates excellent shading. Many liturgical embroideries feature figures with very delicately worked faces that from a distance look almost painted in their intricacy and expression. This iconographic effect is achieved through the masterly use of the split stitch.

While most Orthodox Christians today think of embroidery on velvet as being the finest type of embroidered textile available, the advent of velvet as the background fabric for liturgical embroideries is quite late, appearing in about the seventeenth century.[xvii] Prior to the use of velvet, various types of silk were employed, most commonly burgundy-red or blue in color. With even a cursory knowledge of embroidery, it is easy to see that a woven silk with its flat surface would be far more conducive to lavish embroidery work than the raised nap of velvet which presents certain challenges similar to working an embroidery on carpet.[12]

The general method in which a liturgical embroidery would be made is as follows: a silk background fabric was strengthened with interfacing, typically linen, and a design was then marked on the surface, usually by a special embroidery designer with a knowledge of iconography so that the pattern was in keeping with Orthodox aesthetic tradition. Next, the silk split-stitch work was most likely done first since the gold-work would cover any starts and stops of the split-stitch work. Then the largest task, the working of the gold couched threads, would be executed. After this time-consuming process was complete, the edges of the cloth would be finished with trimming and the entire piece would be lined. With its silk background, linen interfacing and heavy gold-work couching, a textile of this sort would last for many centuries since it was essentially a finely wrought piece of metal (in fact, at certain times in history these pieces were melted down for their gold content). The sheer weight and solidity created by such methods is the primary reason many of these pieces still survive. The sublime designs and marvelous craftsmanship of these liturgical textiles necessitates that they be valued and treated as the great historical treasures they are,

---

12. A return to silk background fabrics for Orthodox liturgical embroideries would not only be more in keeping with tradition, but would eliminate many of the technical difficulties attendant upon work on velvet.

one of the most beautiful links in the chain of traditional Orthodox Christian art forms.

Endnotes

i. Slobodan Curcic, ed. *Architecture as Icon: Perception and Representation of Architecture in Byzantine Art*, exhibition catalog (New Haven, CT: Yale University Press, 2010), 39.

ii. Jean Lassus, *The Early Christian and Byzantine World* (New York, NY: McGraw-Hill Book Company, 1967), 11.

iii. Robert Taft, "The Liturgy of the Great Church: An Initial Synthesis of Structure and Interpretation on the Eve of Iconoclasm." *Dumbarton Oaks Papers*, Vol. 34/35 (1980–1981): 74.

iv. Taft, 73.

v. Pauline Johnstone, *Byzantine Tradition in Church Embroidery* (London: Alec Tiranti, 1967), 24.

vi. Cyril Mango, *The Art of the Byzantine Empire 312–1453* (Toronto: University of Toronto Press, 1986), 88–89.

vii. Warren Woodfin, "Late Byzantine Liturgical Vestments and the Iconography of Sacerdotal Power," doctoral dissertation (Urbana, IL: University of Illinois at Urbana-Champaign, 1999), 50.

viii. Paul the Silentiary, *Descriptio Sanctae Sophiae,* excerpted in Cyril Mango, *The Art of the Byzantine Empire 312–1453* (Toronto: University of Toronto Press, 1986), 806.

ix. Johnstone, 35.

x. Slobodan Curcic, "Late Byzantine Loca Sancta? Some Questions Regarding the Form and Function of Epitaphioi," *Twilight of Byzantium* (Princeton, NJ: Princeton University, 1991), 251.

xi. Hans Belting, "An Image and Its Function in the Liturgy: The Man of Sorrows in Byzantium," *Dumbarton Oaks Papers*, Vol. 34/35 (1980–81): 1–16.

xii. Joseph Rahal, ed. *The Services of Great and Holy Week and Pascha* (Englewood, NJ: Antakya Press, 2006), 614.

xiii. Curcic, "Late Byzantine Loca Sancta," 260.

xiv. Johnstone, 22.

xv. Curcic, *Architecture as Icon*, 26.

xvi. Eleni Vlachopoulou-Karabina, *Holy Monastery of Iveron Gold Embroideries* (Mount Athos: Holy Monastery of Iveron, 1998), 13–14.

xvii. Johnstone, 65.

Chapter Five

A Meadow in Full Bloom

Who could recount the beauty of the columns and the marbles with which the church is adorned? One might imagine that one has chanced upon a meadow in full bloom. For one would surely marvel at the purple hue of some, the green of others, at those on which the crimson blooms, at those that flash with white, at those, too, which Nature, like a painter, has varied with the most contrasting colors. Whenever one goes to this church to pray, one understands immediately that this work has been fashioned not by human power or skill, but by the influence of God. And so the visitor's mind is lifted up to God and floats aloft, thinking that He cannot be far away, but must love to dwell in this place which He himself has chosen. . . .[i]

Procopios describing Agia Sophia, Constantinople, c. AD 537

Step into almost any Orthodox Christian Church today and those colors which Procopios praised in Agia Sophia still abound—rich burgundies, olive greens, deep blues, bright scarlets, with gold intertwining and outlining all. These hues form a veritable feast for the "queen of the senses," as the Byzantines called sight, and it is not uncommon to hear a first-time visitor remark, "it took my breath away." The most famous first-time visitors in Orthodox Christian history, the Slavic emissaries who visited Agia Sophia on behalf of Prince Vladimir in the tenth century, memorably exclaimed, "we knew not whether we were in heaven or on earth."[ii]

What makes these rich and beautiful colors an essential subject for the student of liturgical garments and textiles? The answer is to be found in an examination of how color has been perceived throughout history and how such perceptions were radically altered following scientific developments of the modern age. Remarkably, the ancient world's perception of color—an approach to color that spans over 3000 years—is still maintained within the traditions of color usage in the Orthodox Christian Church. Yet the modern understanding of color, based upon scientific discoveries of the last 300 years, is structured in a fundamentally different way. An awareness of these distinct ways of perceiving and utilizing color is not only crucial to a correct understanding of color usage within the Church, but is also vital to the ability of the Church to retain her historic color traditions in the face of countervailing cultural trends.

Color Perception: Modern vs. Ancient

Orthodox Christian services are a blaze of color: the holy table may be vested in a deep burgundy that gleams with metallic thread embroidery while the deacons and priests wear brocades ranging from golds to reds, blues, greens, blue-purples, and even black. The altar servers may be wearing yet other fabrics that might be gold, red, white or blue. To the unaccustomed eye it all looks rather disorganized, even startling, as if there were a merry dance going on in which no one is quite sure of the steps. But the choreography of this dance was determined thousands of years ago by how the ancient world approached color, a system of classification that is radically different from how we perceive color in the twenty-first century. To better understand the ancient method of delineating color it is helpful to first examine the modern method, a system so familiar to us we usually simply take it for granted.

In the modern world we are trained to define colors according to the divisions of the rainbow spectrum first delineated by Isaac Newton in AD 1672 as a part of his scientific inquiry into light wavelengths. As young children we are taught to organize colors according to Newton's rainbow of seven colors—red, orange, yellow, green, blue, indigo, and violet—and by adulthood we are completely entrenched in this system of classifying colors, using it to describe everything from the paint we use to decorate our houses to the clothes we wear, even the cars we drive. A brief glance through a clothing catalog introduces a fanciful smorgasbord of color names: eggplant, plum, celery, celadon, peach, ruby, coral, chartreuse, cayenne, ivy, olive. Even as we read these color names, however, in our mind's eye we are assigning them their correct position in the "ROY G. BIV" spectrum we learned in childhood. Those of us with more advanced color knowledge might even be aware of the relationships between so-called primary, secondary, and tertiary colors and why blue looks good with orange and what makes the red and green typically associated with Christmas decorations so pleasing, but this is as far as our inquiry usually takes us—never questioning the basic underpinnings of the Newtonian classification.

The delineation of the color spectrum envisioned by the ancient world was fundamentally different. Moreover, the use of color was no incidental matter to the ancients, because the sense of sight was considered the preeminent of the five senses. St John of Damascus tells us, "the first sense is sight and the organs of sight are the nerves of the brain and the eyes. Now sight is primarily the perception of color...."[iii] How the ancient world approached the classification of color was based upon various principles, some related to the natural world (some cultures assigned elemental properties to each color: white was "sky," red was "blood," etc.) while others had to do with certain philosophies of aesthetics (in which only four colors were allowed in exist in "good" art—though this was most likely a type of intellectual high ground, as over twenty-five distinct pigments have been discovered in the ruins of Pompeii). But regardless of its theoretical foundation, the historic spectrum began with white on one side and ended with black on the other. In this arrangement yellows came just after white, reds and greens were in the middle (in fact, due to this proximity, the terms for "red" and "green" were often used interchangeably in medieval texts) and blue was closest to black. Some scholars have even argued that the *brilliance* of a color, rather than its *hue*, was a more significant consideration and that the ancient spectrum was actually one of bright progressing to dark.[iv] As

Gervase Mathew observes, "It can clearly be only an assumption that the Byzantine saw exactly as we see. It is possible that their color sense . . . was more vivid and perhaps more subtle than our own."[v]

Not only what the Byzantine saw, but what any pre-modern man saw: the bright-to-dark spectrum existed long before the Byzantine Empire, beginning sometime in the pre-Christian era, continuing through ancient Greece and Rome to the Late Antique and Middle Ages, and even persisting after the Fall of Constantinople into the Renaissance. As Philip Ball explains, "The reliance of medieval scholars on classical Greek texts ensured that this color scale was perpetuated for centuries after the temples of Athens stood in ruins. In the tenth century AD the monk Heraclius still classified all colors as black, white, and 'intermediate.'"[vi] A conservative estimate puts the length of such perception at 3000 years—a very long time indeed.

When contrasted with the modern "ROY G. BIV" rainbow spectrum, the ancient spectrum is seen to be a broader and more flexible method for classifying color. There is room in it for all sorts of colors appearing in nature: the brown of rich soil, the silver of salmon skin, the gold of summer wheat, the brilliant, almost iridescent black of a crow's feather with its undertones of blue. Because the bright-to-dark spectrum was concerned with two qualities of color—*hue* and *brilliance*—it could form a kind of *x-y* coordinate plane with hue (bright-to-dark) on one axis and brilliance (brilliant-to-matte) on the other, which resulted in a fuller and more complex expression of the human experience of color. The modern Newtonian spectrum is arguably more limited—where does brown fit?—and more regimented in its description of color because it is concerned with the *scientific* classification of color, not the *natural* expression of color. Its primary concern is not what the human mind experiences when it encounters color, but rather the ability of color to become a symbol for scientific and intellectual ideals. As Philip Ball points out, "Newton saw fit to identify an arbitrary seven subdivisions of the prismatic spectrum purely to establish consonance with ideas about musical harmony. . . . And so the Newtonian rainbow acquired its indigo and violet where I defy anyone to see other than a blue deepening to purple."[vii] Forcing color into such rigid, scientific classifications is bound to leave significant gaps.

Remarkably, the ancient approach to color is still alive and well within the Orthodox Christian Church. The liturgical rubrics governing the colors of vestments used at certain seasons and services even use the ancient terminology of "bright" and "dark." Instead of the Newtonian cubbyholes of red, purple, blue and the like, there are only two distinct categories given for the use of color within the Orthodox Christian Church; for example, rubrics for the Feast of the Transfiguration would specify bright vestments whereas those for Great and Holy Friday would specify dark vestments.

To the modern mind's eye, dulled by the rigidly categorized Newtonian rainbow, these bright-to-dark rubrics can seem too simplistic and confusing: Where does red fit? Is green considered bright? Is gold mixed with burgundy bright or dark? But with the ancient bright-to-dark categories, it can be seen that the bright and dark rubrics, rather than *limiting* the colors that can be used, are actually *encompassing* the entire natural canon of color; instead of two small camps of color we have the two bookends of a wide spectrum. In lieu of a constricted, dualistic approach to color in which some days utilize only white and other days only purple (an occasional misinterpretation of the bright and dark rubrics), we find rather a joyous fullness of color, a complete embrace of *every* color from bright to dark.

It is exactly this bright-to-dark usage that gives Orthodox Christian services their brilliance and aesthetically pleasing sensibility and allows for the ample use of multiple colors within a single service, not to mention the entire liturgical year. There is a vibrant and multi-faceted character to the use of color within the Church that is the chromatic expression of the concept of aesthetic "layering" that was discussed in Chapter One. Bright is a very wide category that can include the following: pure white; white with gold accents; gold with white accents; gold on gold; white with gold and red accents; gold with red accents; ivory with gold and burgundy embroidery; ivory with blue, green, and gold embroidery; white with gold and silver embroidery; multicolored brocades with gold, silver, blue, green, coral, gold, and burgundy; white with silver accents; ivory or white with gold, green, and burgundy embroidery; blue with silver; blue with gold; white with blue; green with silver or gold; and white with green. At the other end of the ancient spectrum, the dark category is equally broad: deep red with gold accents; burgundy with gold accents; black with gold and red accents; black with burgundy accents; black embroidered with silver; black embroidered with gold; purple with gold accents; purple with black accents; pure black; burgundy; purple; deep red; red with gold embroidery; burgundy with gold embroidery; burgundy with gold and silver embroidery.

How the use of this ancient color spectrum plays out in actual liturgical services is quite fascinating and, at its heart, not only distinctly beautiful but also supremely practical. A newly ordained clergyman need only own two vestment sets—bright and dark—and he uses these alternately throughout the year according to the basic rubrics. As time goes on, a kindly parishioner may gift him a set of multi-colored brocade vestments, which he will use for Pascha and possibly the Feast of the Nativity, because they are his finest set, his most brilliant set, even though they contain green, silver, red, gold and blue.[1] As he adds to his collection of vestments over the years, he will follow some of the regional color traditions that have become part of the color usage of the Church over time, such as wearing blue for feasts of the Mother of God or green for Pentecost. When he visits a neighboring parish to concelebrate on their feast day he may wear his multi-colored brocade set while the *proistamenos* of the church wears gold with red and another visiting presbyter wears an ivory set of vestments embroidered with gold crosses and multi-colored grapevines.

In traditional Orthodox Christian practice, *quality* and *brilliance* are considered equally important to color, indeed more important. Wearing an old, dingy set of white vestments for Great and Holy Pascha simply to fulfill the arbitrary category of "white" is completely foreign to the traditional sensibility of the

---

1. One of the most stunning sets of vestments I have ever encountered was a remarkable hand-embroidered set from the famous monastery of Ormylia in Greece which had coral and brown embroidery upon an ivory ground—truly a bright set, but not falling into any simple color category of gold, red, green, blue, or purple.

Church. If a clergyman's finest set of vestments are gold with blue, then he would wear these for major feast days because they are not only bright, but also brilliant. In the color usage of Orthodox Christian liturgical vesture, the ancient concepts of brilliance and brightness remain far more significant than a modern affinity for a specific color hue.

Leukos: White or Brilliant?

The most common word used for a light, bright hue in historic Greek texts is *"leukos"* (λευκός, pronounced lef-KOS). When used in liturgical texts this word is typically rendered in English as "white" which is why Orthodox rubrics in English sometimes specify "white" where our preceding investigation might lead us to expect "bright." While the generally accepted definition of this word is the color perceived in the modern world as white, a glance at its entry in Liddell and Scott's *Greek-English Lexicon* proves suggestive of far greater complexity, especially when viewed in light of how color was perceived in the ancient world: "λευκός . . . *light, bright, brilliant*, of sun light . . . of metallic surfaces . . . of water, generally *bright, limpid* . . . of the skin, *white, fair. . . .*"[viii]

"Leukos" is used in all sorts of physical descriptions: "fair-cheeked," "white-armed," "bare-footed," "white-winged" (as of a ship), "white-ankled," "white-gleaming," "white-browed," "white rock," "white horses," and "white-robed." While some of these images are truly the color that the modern world perceives as white—white robes, white rocks, or white horses, for instance—others are not at all the color we associate with "white;" fair cheeks, arms, and bare feet are certainly not white but composed of various warm-toned skin pigments, and the natural color of the canvas of white-winged ships is a warm, almost wheat-like color. But, what all of these various things do have in common is brilliance—they are all bright. Even in our modern English usage, although we commonly refer to Caucasian skin as "white," we do not truly perceive it as such but rather would go on to describe its color more precisely or poetically as "flesh-toned," "roses and cream" or "fair-faced" in an effort to encompass its complexity.

The study of historic color perception is relatively new, so it is understandable that English translations of ancient Greek texts would use the familiar term "white" to render "*leukos*" instead of the word "brilliant," though the latter is arguably better aligned with ancient color perception. In addition, translating "*leukos*" as "white" seems far more comfortable to the modern mind given our contemporary conception of color identification as a linear expression with specific hues in regimented positions. We want translations to be as accurate as possible and assigning to ancient color terms what appears to be their modern-language equivalent is altogether understandable, though probably misleading. While further scholarly development is needed in this fascinating field it is important in the meantime to exercise caution in applying modern, scientific color categories to our interpretation of historic texts.

When St Symeon, the fifteenth-century Archbishop of Thessaloniki, asserts that, "The vestments are white [*leukos*] because of the purity and illumination of Grace. . . ." or that the priest, "is vested 'in the role of the angel' in white [*leukos*] epitrachelion and phelonion like the angel who also was dressed in 'a flashing white [*leukos*] garment'" (Mt 28.3, Mk 16.5),[ix] we can understand this "white" in the fuller context of "brilliant" and, in so doing, see a stronger link to the color usage traditions of the Orthodox Christian Church. Such traditional usage is grounded, as we have observed, in the bright-to-dark spectrum of the ancient world, a spectrum which almost certainly would have determined the way that St Symeon himself perceived and interpreted color. It is fairly safe to assume that it would not have occurred to any writer in the fifteenth century to attempt to scientifically identify a color by a highly specific color name or shade designation, given the inherent flexibility of the ancient color scale that still held sway at that time.

Once "*leukos*" is understood to have a fuller definition than simply the modern color "white," many texts gain a fuller, richer meaning. In the Gospel of John (Jn 4.35) when Christ exhorts his disciples that the fields are "white [*leukos*] unto harvest," we envisage a brilliant, bright wheat field that is not the color white, but rather a living, radiant, glowing gold. When St Mark describes the transfiguration in which Christ's "clothes became shining, exceedingly white [*leukos*], like snow, such as no launderer on earth can whiten them [make them brilliant]" (Mk 9.3), we envisage not merely a snow-colored robe, but rather a brilliant garment radiating light as snow reflects the blinding brilliance of the sun at noonday.

Evidence of the continuing influence of ancient color perception may be sought not only in texts but also in traditional Orthodox Christian iconography as it reflects an aesthetic tradition founded and formed within the ancient approach to color. In the earliest extant icon of the Transfiguration (which adorns the apse of the *katholikon* of St Catherine's Monastery, Sinai) Christ is robed not in pure white (as He is portrayed in many modern icons of the same event) but rather in an exquisite robe of bluish-white trimmed with gold that is certainly not white according to modern color classification, but is most emphatically brilliant. In Rublev's famous Icon of the Trinity, the garment of the angel who appears to represent the Lord (i.e., the one towards whom the other two angelic figures incline their heads) is made up of a variety of colors, blended together in a golden hue with various streaks of color shining through. It is often remarked to be an indescribable color and those who have seen the original do not easily forget its unique and arresting quality. Likewise it is interesting to note that halos in icons are gold, not white. The reason for this color convention becomes clear when we recall that the halo in an icon is not intended to depict a flat disc behind the head of a saint, but rather to portray the orb of uncreated light that emanates from the saint's visage. The golden halo is not meant to depict a two-dimensional crown, but rather a three-dimensional, spiritual reality.[2] When it is portrayed in Orthodox Christian iconography, this halo is not white, but a brilliant, gleaming gold that may also be classified as "*leukos*."

Some of the earliest vestments are thought to have been gold due to the mention of a golden vestment given by the

---

2. For these observations on the symbolic significance of the halo in iconography, as well as for drawing my attention to the garment colors in Rublev's Trinity icon, I am indebted to Frederica Mathewes-Green's article, "Rublev's Old Testament Trinity," <http://www.frederica.com/writings/rublevs-old-testament-trinity.html>, April 18, 2013 (originally published in *The Cresset*, April 2004).

Emperor Constantine to Makarios, Bishop of Jerusalem, in the fourth century.[x] It is highly probable that early vestments, especially those that were gifted by the imperial court or high-ranking nobility, were usually golden in hue as there were not only silks available at this time that were richly colored and woven with gold threads, but also textiles embellished with gold embroidery. Moreover, the Byzantines simply delighted in the brilliance of gold. As Gervase Mathew relates:

> The characteristic Byzantine conception of the relation between color and light, and the Byzantine delight in the color of gold, are already explicit in the first Ennead. 'All the loveliness of color and the light of the sun.' 'And how comes gold to be a beautiful thing? And lightning by night and stars, which are these so fair?' 'The beauty of color is also the outcome of unification; it derives from shape, from the conquest of darkness inherent in matter by the pouring in of light, the unembodied.'[xi]

The Color Dark

With an understanding of the historic concept of "brilliance" well in hand, we now must explore the other end of the ancient spectrum, that encompassed by the category "dark." While this category is just as flexible as that of "bright," and contains many varied shades, the use of "dark" can be especially confusing due to one modern custom in particular: the dedicated use of blue-purple during Great and Holy Lent. While the historic rubrics for Lent denote bright on Sundays in Lent (every Sunday being a celebration of the Resurrection) and dark for the weekday Lenten services due to their penitential character, it has become customary in many North American Orthodox parishes to use exclusively the blue-purple shade (commonly called "purple" in modern English) for both Sunday and mid-week Lenten services. The reason often given for Sunday usage is pastoral necessity: if mid-week services are poorly attended then a priest may deem it necessary to wear purple on Sundays so that the laity are aware of the liturgical season. While the setting aside of the traditional rubrics of bright for Sunday usage in Lent due to poor church attendance is itself a matter of concern, an even more disturbing departure from traditional practice is that one particular shade of purple, known to the ancient world as *"hyakinthos"* (blue-purple), has become intrinsically connected with Lent, rather than the broader, more historic practice of using any color in the dark category, which would have included deep red, burgundy, red-purple, blue-purple, and black as well as any combination of these colors. This change in practice might seem at first a minor point—after all, blue-purple does fulfill the rubric of dark—but it becomes a major concern when one specific modern hue displaces the traditional usage. While there are many local traditions associating certain colors with certain seasons (e.g., blue for feasts of the Theotokos or green for Palm Sunday), they do so only as a preference, not to the entire exclusion of all other colors; in other words, a priest could wear gold vestments for the Feast of the Dormition and still be deemed in conformance with the rubrics. The practice of one single color being assigned to one single liturgical season to the exclusion of all other colors is foreign to the ethos of the Orthodox Christian liturgical cycle.

Not only is this modernistic color influence creeping into Lenten liturgical practice a matter of serious concern on its own, more broadly the laying aside of the ancient category of "dark" during Great Lent in favor of the use of only one specific color—blue-purple—tends toward the creation of a slippery slope upon which the remainder of Orthodox Christian color usage could slide into a completely modernistic color practice wherein the various liturgical seasons are assigned specific, regimented colors. While such practice is common in the Western Christian communions (though even there it is a late development), embracing such a practice in the Orthodox Church would be a rejection of an ancient bright-dark color tradition in favor of an innovation only a few hundred years old.

Additionally, in Orthodox Christian aesthetics, there is often an underlying principle of practicality—it is understood that one beautiful altar cloth can be used for the entire liturgical year if that is the best the community has—and the bright-dark rubrics may be seen as the pinnacle of such practicality. If a priest does not own seven sets of vestments, he may still honorably serve the liturgical year with two. Once again, the focus is on quality and beauty rather than on rigid adherence to specific hue.

The exclusive use of blue-purple for Great Lent is a practice acquired during the twentieth century when Orthodox Christians in North American rarely had access to traditional brocades with their distinctive, Byzantine-influenced colorations, but had to rely instead upon the fabrics available through Western Christian liturgical goods suppliers. Many of the historic, multi-colored brocades utilized in Orthodox Christian practice were simply not available and, through many decades of reliance on American liturgical suppliers, Orthodox Christians became accustomed to Western color practices which tend toward the monochromatic in order to fit within the Newtonian-influenced, Western color canon.

Another reason that blue-purple has achieved and maintained such prominence is the mystery surrounding the historic color "purple," a color which has been the mark of emperors and kings, associated with honor and prestige, but the exact hue of which eluded scientists and scholars alike for centuries following the collapse of the historic purple dyestuff industry after the fall of Constantinople.

The Purple Paradox

Far back beyond the mists of history, ancient legend has it that Hercules was walking along the coast when his dog ate a sea snail, resulting in a deep red stain around the dog's mouth. While the story is mythical, it speaks of the undoubtedly accidental, initial discovery of a natural process that would have a profound and lasting impact on human history. Two species of the humble Mediterranean sea snail (*Murex brandaris* and *Murex trunculus*) when crushed, exude a clear liquid which, when properly prepared, will color wool or silk fibers with a brilliant, reddish-purple color that will not wash out. From this discovery came one of the most lucrative industries the world has ever known.

Credit for the original discovery of this remarkable dyestuff seems to belong to the Phoenicians whose very name was wrapped up in this color—the ancient Greeks called them "*Phoinikes*," which means "red-colored."[xii] Because the precious dyestuff was produced in Tyre in Phoenicia, it became known as "Tyrian purple," and eventually the knowledge of its production made its way to the Greeks.

Tyrian purple's rich, intense color ensured that it would be highly valued. But this was not the whole of its appeal—much of its value lay in the fact that it was also "fast," which meant the dye would not rinse out little by little in each washing as was the case with most ancient dyestuffs. Ancient reports of Tyrian purple's fastness are impressive: in one of his campaigns against the Persians, Alexander the Great took approximately 275,000 pounds of murex-dyed fabric as war booty from the city of Shushan. This fabric had been stored in the city's treasury rooms for almost 200 years and yet it retained its original "fresh and strong color."[xiii]

These two qualities—remarkable color and highly desirable permanency—along with a phenomenally time-consuming method of production requiring approximately 12,000 sea snails for every 1.4 grams of pure dye, combined to create one of human history's most fantastically expensive products. Dyestuffs commanded a wide range of prices in antiquity depending on how abundant they were in the natural world, how difficult they were to produce, and whether they were locally available or had to be transported from distant lands. The desire for color was a source of big business in earlier ages; even during the Renaissance painters would sign formal contracts with their patrons that specified which pigments were to be used and such contracts often contained clauses forbidding the artist from using cheaper substitutes.[xiv]

In the modern age we do not generally associate particular colors with luxury because the advent of synthetic dyestuffs in the late nineteenth century meant that all dyestuffs came to be similarly priced since they could be manufactured chemically. No longer are the scarcity of natural occurrence or the difficulty of production major factors in the cost of a particular color. In the ancient world, however, Tyrian purple reigned supreme as the most expensive dyestuff known to mankind. In Rome, coins were marked with an image of the murex shellfish, functioning as a type of ancient dollar sign.[xv] When St Luke tells of Lydia, "a seller of purple," in Acts 16.14, he is referring to a very wealthy woman. In our modern context it would be akin to saying "Lydia, the multi-millionaire," or "Lydia, the owner of a software company," as those who sold the purple dye dealt in a highly lucrative industry, one which most likely required large amounts of capital and gave the business owner access to the upper echelons of society.

By the time of the Byzantine Empire when the use of Tyrian purple was firmly established and was referred to as "murex purple" (Latin *"purpura"* or Greek *"porphyra"*) strict legislation was enacted governing its manufacture and distribution in order to

> protect an Imperial monopoly over certain murex dyed silks, and to make sure that murex dyers did not pass over trade secrets or sell certain murex dyes illegally. The special significance attached to the wearing of Imperial purple was jealously guarded right from the fourth to the twelfth centuries. The penalty for misappropriation of such purples or for their illegal manufacture and sale ranged from confiscation or loss of the right to manufacture, to loss of a limb or death.[xvi]

As this passage indicates, the Byzantines took their purple very seriously. Considering that it was classed with antiquity's greatest treasures, on a par with gold, silver, pearls and gems, it is no wonder that purple became the exclusive province of emperors and high-ranking nobility. The Byzantines used the beautiful dye not only for their own garments, but also to generate considerable revenues through exportation, to manipulate trade by limiting who had access to murex purple-dyed textiles, to set the tenor of diplomatic missions, to influence politics, and to maintain court privileges by the gifting of *purpura blatta* (i.e. purple silk, from the Latin *"blatta,"* meaning "moth").

Tyrian purple and the textiles it transformed became the quintessential hallmark of imperial privilege; it is no artistic whim that Justinian and Theodora are depicted in Tyrian-purple robes in the famous Ravenna mosaics, but rather a conscious use of color to symbolize power and prestige.[3] Certain Tyrian-purple-dyed silks were forbidden from leaving the confines of Constantinople and were relegated to the sole use of the Emperor and his court. While there has often been confusion in the academic world about who could wear Tyrian purple, with some scholars contending that only the Emperor himself could wear anything dyed with Tyrian purple, more recent research has suggested that the restriction of certain *purpura blatta* garments for the Emperor's sole use had to do with their color *and* their design, not simply that they were dyed with Tyrian purple. As Byzantine silk scholar Anna Muthesius states, "The regulations indicated not that the Imperial house had an exclusive right to wear Imperial purples of all types, but only that it had the exclusive right of wearing Imperial purple garments of special Imperial tailored 'cuts.'"[xvii]

Despite this long-standing regard for the imperial purple, which lasted almost 2000 years, the modern world knows little of this astonishing color. With the fall of Constantinople in 1453, the lucrative, yet highly technical, murex sea snail dye industry collapsed entirely and it was not until a handful of curious chemists began experimenting with murex sea snail extractions in the twentieth century that there came to be even a rudimentary knowledge of how this storied dye was produced. Not only was the method of its production shrouded in mystery, its actual shade or color—what it really *looked* like—was also unknown, creating great confusion for the modern mind that wanted a specific color hue assigned to the name "Tyrian purple," classifying it within the confines of Newton's rainbow.

---

3. Visiting Ravenna in 2012, I was fascinated to discover that rather than the blue-purple robes that are so often depicted in book reproductions of these famous mosaics, Justinian and Theodora are wearing robes that are almost burgundy in color, the same color as the porphyry marble that is seen in the churches of Ravenna, as well as the columns and the famous statue of the tetrarchs that adorn San Marco in Venice. After detailed examination of the mosaics in Ravenna, I discovered that blue-purple is nowhere to be found, only the red-purple color we generally call "burgundy." The fact that books often depict the garments in these mosaics as blue-purple (indeed my own guidebook did so) is due to the tonal limitations of modern printing methods.

It is precisely this modern need to classify all colors into specific hues that has contributed to such confusion regarding the use of purple within Great and Holy Lent. But as we have seen, clearly defined color terms are elusive in the ancient world as a few descriptions of Tyrian purple illustrate:

> Throughout the ancient and medieval world, *purpure* [Tyrian purple] could equally mean a shade of dark red or crimson, and indeed purple is steeped in associations with blood.[xviii]

> The color was "dark" with a reddish tinge.[xix]

> Writers of Hellenistic times understood "purple" to mean several colors: dull red, magenta, blue, and violet-purple. The most expensive dye was the Tyrian dull red.[xx]

> But it seems likely that at least by the 12th century the Imperial purple [Tyrian purple] was normally a dark red; Mesarites notes in his Ekphrasis that the Imperial Chrysobulls were signed in the colour of the blood of Christ.[xxi]

> It is possible to produce deep red, blue violet, and dark blue tones, depending on the technique.[xxii]

> There is a great range of purples ranging from the color of congealed blood to a light violet or blue and every shade in between depending on the precise species [of sea snail], the amount of dye used, and . . . the exposure to light which results in a blue color. . . .[xxiii]

In the descriptions given above we note a wide color range, rather puzzling at first, but comprehensible when several factors are taken into account: first, the different species of the murex mollusk yielded different shades of the dyestuff, some tending towards red-purple (*purpura* or *porphyra*) and others towards blue-purple (*hyakinthos*). The red-purple colors, which are closest to the color we today call "burgundy" or "wine," were the most prized. Pliny refers to this shade as being "the color of clotted blood, dark by reflected and brilliant by transmitted light."[xxiv] Secondly, exposure to light during production could change the dye and it had to be manufactured under specific light conditions to give the most desirable, reddish tone. Thirdly, since murex was such a precious dyestuff, dye baths were used multiple times, each successive dye lot being of a lighter shade until the bath was exhausted. This created initial dye lots of the highly desirable, intense *porphyra* color but went on to produce successive dye lots of pale mauves and blues that were less desirable and therefore less valuable.[xxv] As dye expert Gosta Sandberg explains:

> When we use the word purple in daily speech, we believe it stands for a quite well-defined and singular color designation. However, this is not the case. With a purple secretion as a starting material, it is possible to produce an entire range of color tones and nuances. The nature of the secretion, the mordant, and the dyeing method all play a decisive role in the appearance of the purple-dyed fiber.... It is also very clear that during antiquity there were special terms for the various colors that dyers could produce. The writer Marcus Vitruvius clearly distinguished between red Tyrian purple and blue hyacinthine purple, and in a decree the Emperor Diocletian mentions an additional number of different purple tones of varying coloristic appearance.[xxvi]

Given an understanding of the factors that would influence color variations from a single dyestuff material, we begin to see that, similar to the ancient color spectrum, we have in Tyrian purple a color *category* rather than a specific *hue*. This collection of a broad range of colors under one term was quite logical to the ancient mind, especially given the ancient approach to color and its inherent flexibility of classification.

Tyrian purple, however, is unique even in the ancient spectrum. Because the most-valuable *porphyra*, the color we now refer to as "burgundy," was "dark by reflected light and brilliant by transmitted light" as Pliny recounts, it inhabited the center of the ancient color spectrum, both in terms of its color, halfway between white and black (red was at the center of the ancient color spectrum), and having qualities both of darkness (by reflected light) and brilliance (by transmitted light). Placed in its proper position in the ancient color spectrum, Tyrian purple becomes a type of bridge color between light and dark; if the x-y coordinate plane of ancient color perception is brought to mind, Tyrian purple occupies a distinctive place at the conjunction of both axes.[4] While it is speculative, it is not inconceivable that the symbological significance of this color would not have been lost on the highly symbolically attuned Byzantines. Just as Christ is the bridge between God and man, so *porphyra* was the bridge between light and dark and therefore the symbolically appropriate color for the King of Heaven. Knowledge of the ancient world's perception of color along with an awareness of the affinity for symbolic "layering" within the Orthodox Church provides a better understanding of how a color like Tyrian purple could carry multiple symbological associations: *porphyra* as the center of all the colors, *porphyra* as the color of royalty, *porphyra* as the color of the royal robe placed upon Christ during His mockery and scourging becoming also, paradoxically, associated with His humiliation and suffering.

To the ancient Orthodox Christian mind, all of these ideas could have been at play at one and the same time when viewing this color—the only color that had these particular associations with both royalty and suffering, high regard and humiliation. Such symbology may very well be why purple is used in penitential seasons, recalling Christ's degradation while yet foreshadowing His triumph as the King of Heaven.

---

4. To extend the mathematical metaphor, Tyrian purple would be located at the point of origin (0,0).

Once it is understood that Tyrian purple, the red-purple that we call "burgundy," occupies such important symbological ground, certain ancient texts take on additional significance. One of the most notable examples is the recounting of the Annuncation of the Theotokos in the *Protoevangelion* of James. In this passage the high priest has the temple virgins cast lots for who are to weave the various colors needed for the veil of the temple:

> And the servants went and brought them [the virgins] into the temple of the Lord, and the high-priest said unto them "Cast lots before me now, who of you shall spin the golden thread, who the blue, who the scarlet, who the fine linen, and who the true [Tyrian] purple." Then the high-priest knew Mary, that she was of the tribe of David; and he called her, and the true purple fell to her lot to spin, and she went away to her own house. But from that time Zacharias the high-priest became dumb, and Samuel was placed in his room till Zacharias spoke again. But Mary took the true purple, and did spin it. And she took a pot, and went out to draw water, and heard a voice saying unto her, "Hail thou who art full of grace, the Lord is with thee; thou art blessed among women." And she looked around to the right and to the left (to see) whence that voice came, and then trembling went into her house, and laying down the water-pot she took the purple, and sat down in her seat to work it. And behold the angel of the Lord stood by her, and said, "Fear not, Mary, for thou hast found favour in the sight of God...."[xxvii]

To those living in an age of Tyrian purple and its ubiquitous associations with royalty and imperial privilege, the very color the girl Mary was weaving would have been highly significant in the recounting of the Annunciation. The Mother of God was spinning the color of imperial rank and honor, as well as that of blood and suffering, even as the King of Heaven was woven within her womb.

This "purple paradox," purple with its multi-faceted hues and layered symbology, is undoubtedly what has contributed to *porphyra* becoming the most commonly used color in the Orthodox Church besides gold. When it is understood that Tyrian purple, in its most highly regarded form, is not the blue-purple *hyakinthos,* but rather the color we call "burgundy," then it is easy to see why Orthodox Christian churches frequently have myriad altar furnishings in this shade—burgundy velvet Beautiful Gate curtains, burgundy altar cloths, burgundy banners, and burgundy velvet chalice veil sets. Tyrian purple, the color of both kings and penitents, is everywhere in an Orthodox Christian church, proclaiming both our joy in our King and our redemption through His suffering.

A Brief History of Natural Dyestuffs

While Tyrian purple certainly occupied a special position in the ancient world, the other colors of antiquity also serve as a testament to man's quest for the sublime and his desire to use the material world to glorify God. Many liturgical textiles made from fabrics produced in such historic textile centers as Egypt, India, Persia, Byzantium, Russia, Serbia, and Romania now reside in museum collections where they are prized for their complexity and beauty. Until the mid-1860s, natural dyestuffs were the only products available for textile coloration, thus the distinctive colors that they render have occupied a prominent place in the aesthetics of the Orthodox Christian Church for over 1800 years. The beauty everywhere on display in historic churches is due in no small part to the compelling shades and tonal qualities of natural dyestuffs, so it is worthwhile to take a brief tour through the history of their production.

When one conjures up the idea of naturally dyed fabric, it is easy to bring to mind an image of a peasant dipping cloth in a pot of water he has colored by stewing local plants and roots. However, the reality of historic dye production was quite different from this quaint scenario. Natural dyestuffs were complicated and time-consuming, and they required a high level of artistic skill to produce. They fall into one of three categories based on how they are transmitted to the fabric: first, direct dyes, in which fabric is soaked in a solution of the dye-producing material and thus absorbs the color; second, indirect dyes, in which fabric is treated with a mordant or fixative, such as alum, and then soaked in dye solution (the pre-soaking in a mordant allows the fabric to "take" the dye); third, vat dyes, in which a plant material is soaked in a vat until it begins to decompose and form a sediment at the bottom of the vat. This sediment is gathered, dried, and typically formed into a kind of cake or tablet that when later dissolved in an alkaline solution forms a dye bath into which cloth is dipped.[xxviii]

Yellows were often produced from saffron (from the Arabic "za'fran"), which is the dried stigmata of a crocus that grew in Greece and Asia Minor. It is one of the few naturally occurring direct dyes and Pliny mentions it as the best yellow dye known. Turmeric, another yellow dyestuff, is a small perennial plant and was used from classical times into modernity. It was especially prized to dye silk. Yellow's close cousin, orange, was made from annatto which is another direct dyestuff. Whatever their original intensity, yellow dyestuffs are not as permanent as other dyestuffs which is why so many historic textiles, such as tapestries on display in museums, look predominantly blue or red due to the fading of the yellow tones over time.[xxix]

Reds have been produced since the art of dyeing began due to their appealing intensity and the wide availability of the two predominant red dyestuff components, the madder plant and the kermes insect. Madder-based dye, one of the oldest and most frequently used throughout Europe, India, and the Middle East, comes from the *Rubiaceae* plant family and produces a wide range of colors from red to orange to yellowish-red to russet-red.[xxx] Madder is an indirect dye requiring a mordant, usually alum. This widely available dye was probably the most common ancient dyestuff, along with indigo. Kermes, another famous red dye of the ancient world, was not produced from a plant, but from a species of scale insect that lives on the scarlet oak tree growing in various regions around the northern periphery of the Mediterranean. The harvested insects were killed with vinegar and then dried in the sun. Once dry, they were crushed and packed ready for sale. Over 25,000 insects were needed to produce one pound of dyestuff.[xxxi]

After the fall of Constantinople and the subsequent collapse of the Tyrian purple industry, kermes dye took the place of Tyrian purple as the most prized of all dyestuffs due to its brilliant and saturated red tone. It was a very ancient dyestuff and had been used in pre-Christian times; according to author Philip Ball it

> was called kermes, from the Sanskrit word *kirmidja*, "derived from a worm." The Hebrew name for it was *tola' at shani*, "worm scarlet". . . . Kermes is the linguistic root of the English *crimson* and *carmine* and the French *cramoisie*. But because an encrustation of kermes insects on a branch resembles a cluster of berries, Greek writers such as Aristotle's pupil Theophrastus (*c.* 300 BC) refer to them as *kokkos*, meaning "berry." In Latin this becomes *coccus*, a word found in Pliny's writings on kermes dye. Yet Pliny also uses the term *granum* ("grain"), again alluding to the deceptively vegetative appearance of the insects. Grain thus became one of the perplexing names by which this crimson dye was known in medieval Europe. Chaucer refers to a cloth that is "dyed in grain," meaning dyed crimson. Because of the strong, lasting nature of this color, the phrase came simply to mean deeply or permanently dyed. From this comes the English word *ingrained*.[xxxii]

With the exploration of South America by the Spanish in the sixteenth century, another highly lucrative dyestuff entered the European market and contributed directly to the power and economic might of Spain: "By the late 1500s, cochineal had become the third most valuable export from the Spanish colonies, after gold and silver."[xxxiii] Similar to kermes, cochineal was a dye-producing insect that lived on cacti in South America and was harvested in much the same painstaking way as kermes insects, with one incredible difference: cochineal dye was ten times stronger. Cochineal produced a truly rich, saturated, red dye and quickly supplanted even kermes as a substitute for the lost Tyrian purple, the color of rank and status. Many Renaissance paintings feature this striking scarlet color as a symbol of the patron's wealth and power. In the eighteenth century it was used to dye the uniforms of British soldiers, hence giving them the moniker "Redcoats," and, as legend has it, also colored the cloth Betsy Ross used for the first flag of the United States.[xxxiv] Cochineal is one of the few natural dyestuffs still in wide use today, primarily used to color foodstuffs and cosmetics.

While Tyrian purple was the supreme color of antiquity, from pre-Christian times onwards there was also a thriving business in pseudo-purples, substitutes for those who could not afford, or were not allowed to wear, the true Tyrian shade. These colors were made by mixing indigo with either madder-dyed or kermes-dyed fibers through multiple dye baths which involved dyeing the fabric first in madder and then in indigo (or vice versa) or by weaving two differently dyed fibers together. The final shade produced could be endlessly adapted from the blue-purple scale of hyacinthine to the red-purple scale of Tyrian purple.

To create shades in the green range, dyestuffs were combined—either indigo with local yellow dyestuffs or, in some cases, yellow dyestuffs were treated with mordants in such a way as to obtain green tones. It is one of the great ironies of nature that even as we are surrounded by green trees and a multitude of green plant material, there are very few naturally occurring green dyestuffs.

Next to the red dyes, indigo was the most common ancient dye, used across the world from India to Byzantium to Europe. A perennial herb that has been harvested from antiquity to the present day, indigo contains the same coloring matter as its close cousin, woad, another blue dyestuff. Both indigo and woad are vat dyes and their tablet form made them easy to transport and sell in various markets. Each of these natural dyes could produce a wide range of colors based on factors such as the choice of mordant, length of dye bath, or its combination with other dyestuffs.

All of these beautiful natural dyes provided the textile craftsman of antiquity a rich and broad palette with which to work as is attested by the surviving Byzantine silks. As Byzantine silk scholar Anna Muthesius explains:

> To the naked eye, the extant Byzantine silks reveal that a wide color palette was in use by the 12th century. . . . For instance, a bright polychrome palette of reds, blues, greens, ochres, and off-white was in vogue in the 8th to 9th century. By the 10th and 11th centuries, side by side with a still comparatively brightly colored mixed palette, monochrome tones were in demand. Single-color golden yellow, purple-blue, olive green, or cherry red Byzantine silks . . . survive in quantity.[xxxv]

Viewing the faded remnants of such textiles in museums, one cannot help but wish that one had seen them in all their brilliant, multi-colored glory when they made the world resplendent so long ago.

The Advent of Synthetic Dyes

While the mythical discovery of Tyrian purple finds Hercules watching his dog munch a sea snail, the other end of this historical continuum introduces us to the singular figure of William Perkin, an 18-year-old chemistry student at work in his makeshift backyard laboratory in the spring of 1856, attempting to find a cure for malaria. While some advancement had been made in the treatment of this worldwide affliction, Perkin was hopeful that by heating coal tar he might be able to create synthetic quinine, an anti-malarial drug in great demand. Quinine is clear, so Perkin looked on in frustration as his coal tar turned into a red powder and he might have been inclined to toss it out and start over, as many chemists would have done. However, in a fleeting moment of frugality or intuition, he would change how humanity approaches color. By further experimenting with the disappointing red powder, he eventually found that one of the resultant compounds produced a bluish-purple dye that, when combined with alcohol, would not wash out of fabric.

William Perkin had created a synthetic dyestuff. What set his discovery apart from those of other chemists who had found similar synthetic coloring agents, was that he recognized the great potential for a chemical dyestuff and began to actively market it, something that had not occurred to other chemists. With his father and brother, he built a factory to produce the new dye he named "mauveine." Initially, this synthetic dye was a hard sell in a world accustomed to natural dyestuffs and, if not for the whims of fashion and the taste of an empress, Perkin would most likely have ended up a bankrupt nobody. But shortly after his discovery of mauveine, the Empress Eugenie, wife of Napoleon III and an important fashion trendsetter, began to wear mauve-colored garments. Queen Victoria, following Eugenie's lead, wore mauve to her daughter's wedding and sparked a mauve craze in the fashion world. This trend caused a major demand for the new mauveine dye which, by Perkin's methods, could be produced easily and quickly in a modern factory without all the fuss and bother of natural dyestuffs. Due to the incredible success of his new color Perkin was a millionaire by the age of twenty-two, and thus was born the modern industry of synthetic dyestuffs.[xxxvi]

Other chemical dyestuffs were discovered in rapid succession and the new industry flourished. German firms quickly dominated the market, producing eighty percent of the world's chemical dyes by 1914. From the consumer's point of view, synthetic dyes were a wonder—they were permanent and could be made in a dizzyingly endless range of new colors. For the manufacturer, synthetic dyes were cheap, consistent and yielded higher profits. No longer was the dyer at the mercy of the unpredictability of natural dyes with their varying yields and complicated methods of production.[xxxvii]

After three millennia or more of relying upon expensive dyestuffs that required specific, artistic know-how, now virtually anyone with a small factory and a few cheap chemicals could produce the colors of the rainbow. But there remained a nostalgia for the ancient colors, as Philip Ball points out:

> The tremendous worth of the ancient purple and its association with royalty and high office have become the stuff of legend. It is no coincidence

that when the first synthetic mauve dye appeared on the market in the mid-nineteenth century, it was sold under the canny (and wholly inaccurate) name of Tyrian purple.[xxxviii]

Initially, the amazing discovery of synthetic dyestuffs seemed like a miracle, but within barely a century, scholars and critics began to comment on how unlimited access to the colors of Newton's rainbow would alter mankind's perception of color:

> By the time of the founding of the Mediterranean civilizations, what we could consider the classical palette for natural dyes had already been established.... This classical palette was only challenged by the audacity of chemists, who created new molecules, and colors never seen before, from the mid-19th century on.[xxxix]

And,

> The first fruit of this new understanding was both to show that nature's chemistry could be equaled in the laboratory and to initiate the ascendancy of synthetic over natural dyestuffs. Once that happened, says art historian Manlio Brusatin, "there would be a different way of seeing and perceiving colors because there would be an entirely different way of producing them, with the birth of a modern industry of chemical colors on the horizon, looming over the back room of the old dyeshop with its rare, dyed garments and its antiquated trade in privilege."[xl]

The synthetic dyes were admittedly amazing and, through their inexpensive and reliable production methods, they made color available to all levels of society. No longer were certain shades the exclusive privilege of the wealthy or noble-born. But, alas, these chemical prodigies brought with them problems of their own: harsh, brash tones instead of the rich, saturated hues of natural dyes; an insatiable appetite on the part of the consumer for ever more and more new colors as evidenced by the home décor and fashion industries of today; and, most important to a discussion of the liturgical garment tradition of the Orthodox Christian Church, the virtual abandonment of the ancient way of perceiving color, in favor of the modern, chemical approach to color.

The very thing that made synthetic dyes so wondrous and compelling—their consistency—was to bring about a complete collapse of the ancient color spectrum (although awareness of it is retained in certain circles of academia and within the rubrics of the Orthodox Christian Church). Instead of embracing a color family referred to as "brilliant," the modern world wanted rigid, scientifically produced, specific shades. Where antiquity had "*leukos*," there were now "white," "off-white," "natural," "lace ivory," "antique ivory," "champagne" and the like. In exchange for the ancient color spectrum comprised of *qualities* of color, the world clamored for a set of Pantone color chips.

Until 1860, the variability of natural dyes was what made the ancient color spectrum so flexible and practical. When one dye vat could produce five different shades, it was simply impossible to classify colors absolutely. As historic dye scholar Dominique Cardon elucidates:

> The dawn of synthetic dyes opportunely corresponded with a time when industrialized societies were enthusiastically exploring the pathways opened by the exploitation of fossil resources: first coal, then petrol. The most emblematic of these dyes, manmade out of black tar from black coal or black petrol, was aniline black. One dye-bath, composed of a definite amount of one and the same molecule, could now produce a color that, in the past, had always required complex combinations of dyestuffs and mordants. Cheap and easy to apply, synthetic dyes and pigments have produced a major cultural revolution that has irreversibly changed the whole world. People everywhere are now accustomed to take colors for granted, to be surrounded by them in most

circumstances of their lives without necessarily paying conscious attention to them.[xli]

If we are to learn to be conscious of colors once again, a significant effort must be made within the Orthodox Christian Church to embrace and cherish the traditional rubrics with their broad, albeit occasionally confusing, designations of "bright" and "dark." It is essential that we relearn how to see and value colors as our forebears did, according to category rather than scientifically defined hue.

Color Usage Today

Even though the tremendous breadth of the historic "bright" and "dark" categories poses a challenge to the modern mind that feels compelled to analyze and quantify color within very limited confines, we must strive to maintain ancient color traditions within the Orthodox Christian Church. One of the best ways this can be accomplished is through the reintroduction of lavish, multi-colored brocades. Floral designs that incorporate a great variety of coloration have been employed to great effect in the Church's historical tradition as the Figure 1 below illustrates most vividly.

Figure 1. Finnish tri-brocade phelonion (*From Chaos to a Collection: The Orthodox Church Museum of Finland*, p. 24).

It is safe to say that a phelonion similar to that shown above would be virtually impossible to find in any current church inventory in North America. Neither would analogues to the Russian vestments—dated to 1890 and gifted to the City Art Museum of St. Louis in 1949, described as "suggesting a strong Oriental influence ... of salmon-colored silk with brocade blue, green, gold, and silver floral decoration"—be readily found in any modern collection of vestments.[xlii]

Salmon-colored, indeed! That all-too-often-repeated question "What color is it?", that bane of all historically minded ecclesiastical tailors, should no longer be allowed to fall from our lips; rather we should strive to classify our liturgical garments and textiles solely within the traditionally based categories of "bright" and "dark." This might mean using a bright, multi-colored floral brocade for Pascha instead of the limited (and rather dull) white and silver combination so commonly observed in churches in North America, or perhaps vesting in a white, gold, and blue brocade as an "every Sunday" set of vestments in a church dedicated to the Theotokos. The flexibility inherent in the traditional rubrics of the Church is nearly endless and provides a practically limitless range of colors to be utilized and enjoyed.

Once a particular vestment is placed in the appropriate "bright" or "dark" category, a clergyman then needs only further follow local or regional traditions, which vary widely throughout the Orthodox Christian world. While the rubrics specify only bright and dark, there are some longstanding color associations within the Church's usage: the most notable of these is blue for feasts of the Mother of God. In Greece blue is also used for Feast of Theophany, due to its association with water, whereas other locales use white or gold for Theophany. For Palm Sunday, the Island of Patmos uses green (a nod to the green palms that characterize this feast) while most parishes in North America will use gold vestments for the celebration of the entrance of Christ into Jerusalem.

Another means of embracing traditional color usage is to focus on harmonizing the colors in a particular service or church interior design scheme rather than attempting to have all vestments and paraments be identical in fabric and finishings. It should be typical in any Orthodox Christian service with multiple clergy to see a variety of fabrics and colors: on a Sunday morning one priest might be clothed in ivory vestments embroidered with gold and burgundy, while another is vested in a rich gold metallic brocade, while yet a third dons liturgical garments emblazoned with green leaves and red grapes along with gold and silver crosses. In the description of Procopios which opens this chapter we see the Byzantines combining a wide range of colors of marble within the church—purple, green, crimson, and white—and it is important to note that, given the vast resources of the Byzantine Empire, these columns could easily have been made identical if sameness was truly the desired end. Likewise, we should feel comfortable using a variety of textiles and colors within our own churches as long as we are adhering to the general rubrics. This same principle of harmonizing colors rather than identically matching them is typically viewed in iconography: it is far more common in iconography to see groups of saintly bishops arrayed in a variety of fabrics, designs, and colors rather than portrayed in exactly matching vestments.

For the category "dark," a much wider range of colors than the prevailing blue-purple should be encouraged, including deep red, burgundy, and even black, all of which clearly fit within the "dark" classification. Instead of a priest vesting in a blue-purple set of vestments which he may only use during Great Lent, he could vest in burgundy vestments which he would be able to use not only during the Great Fast but also for the numerous other days assigned "dark" in the rubrics (e.g. commemorations of martyrs, the Exaltation of the Holy Cross, Nativity Fast).

Finally, in addition to color itself, we must also consider the matter of appearance versus substance. During the period of discovery of new painters' pigments in the Renaissance, artists would trade secrets and techniques of how to make yellow pigments—historically the cheapest and easiest to obtain—appear to be gold.[xliii] This kind of visual trickery began a new way of thinking that placed a higher value on the appearance of a thing—simply what it *looks* like—rather than its substance, *the value of that from which it is made*. This mindset was further entrenched during the shift to synthetic dyes, which had the virtual appearance of the old dyes, but not the substance of the precious, natural dyestuff.

In traditional Orthodox Christian color practice, quality and substance were just as important as adherence to the rubrics. As was discussed in Chapter One, Orthodox Christian theology confirms that matter, or substance, is vitally important. Our churches do not simply appear to be the Kingdom of Heaven on earth like some kind of grand and showy stage production with people going about in glitzy costumes; rather, our churches are truly the materialization of the Kingdom of Heaven, populated by the saints and servants of the Heavenly King wearing the garments of salvation. Our modern world has traded substance for appearance, a real jewel for a fantasy, and this change in outlook is precisely what leads many to believe that vestments need have only an outward pretense of glamour rather than a true and lasting substance of beauty. Looking showy is not the same thing as being beautiful and inferior-quality vestments are not appropriate for attendance at the banquet of Christ.

By following the guidance of ancient color perception with its broader, fuller, and ultimately, more joyous and heavenly expression of color, as well as giving thoughtful attention to the quality of the fabrics and brocades these colors enliven, we will continue to follow an ancient tradition and once again have our visitors remark, in concert with St. Vladimir's emissaries:

> Then we went on to Greece, and the Greeks led us to the edifices where they worship their God, and we knew not whether we were in heaven or on earth. For on earth there is no such splendour or such beauty, and we are at a loss how to describe it. We know only that God dwells there among men, and their service is fairer than the ceremonies of other nations. For we cannot forget that beauty. Every man, after tasting something sweet, is afterward unwilling to accept that which is bitter, and therefore we cannot dwell longer here.[xliv]

May we too aim to be "at a loss to describe" the wonder and beauty of our faith as expressed in the adornment of our churches. Such sweetness will be a balm to our weary souls and keep us ever in mind of our eternal home.

Endnotes

i. Cyril Mango, *The Art of the Byzantine Empire 312-1453* (Toronto: University of Toronto Press, 1986), 76.

ii. Samuel Hazzard Cross and Olgerd P. Sherbowitz-Wetzor, trans., *The Russian Primary Chronicle*, Laurentian Text (Cambridge, MA: The Mediaeval Academy of America, 1953), 10.

iii. Gervase Mathew, *Byzantine Aesthetics* (London: John Murray, 1963), 118.

iv. Philip Ball, *Bright Earth* (New York: Farrar, Straus and Giroux, 2001), 17.

v. Mathew, 35.

vi. Ball, 15.

vii. Ball, 25.

viii. Liddell and Scott, *Greek–English Lexicon* (Oxford: Oxford University Press, 1989), 470.

ix. Patrick O'Grady and Michel Najim, *The Liturgical Books of the Holy Orthodox-Catholic Church, Vol. 1, The Scriptural Books* (publication forthcoming).

x. Janet Mayo, *A History of Ecclesiastical Dress* (London: B.T. Batsford Ltd, 1984), 15.

xi. Mathew, 19.

xii. Thomas Bechtold and Rita Mussak, eds., *Handbook of Natural Colorants* (Hoboken, NJ: John Wiley & Sons, 2009), 3.

xiii. Gosta Sandberg, Edith M Matteson, trans, *The Red Dyes: Cochineal, Madder, and Murex Purple: A World Tour of Textile Techniques* (Asheville, NC: Lark Books, 1997), 21.

xiv. Ball, 119.

xv. Faber, G.A., "Dyeing and Tanning in Classical Antiquity," Society of Chemical Industry in Basle (1938), 292.

xvi. Anna Muthesius, *Byzantine Silk Weaving: AD 400 to AD 1200* (Vienna: Fassbaender, 1997), 27.

xvii. Muthesius, 25.

xviii. Ball, 197–8.

xix. Lloyd B. Jensen, "Royal Purple of Tyre" *Journal of Near Eastern Studies*, Vol. 22, No. 2 (April 1963): 108.

xx. Jensen, 113.
xxi. Mathew, 147.
xxii. Sandberg, 26.
xxiii. John Edmonds, *The Mystery of Imperial Purple Dye*, Historic Dye Series No. 7 (2000), 24–5.
xxiv. Ball, 197–8.
xxv. Bechtold and Mussak, 22.
xxvi. Sandberg, 37.
xxvii. *The Protoevangelion of James* (London: William Hone, 1820), 29.
xxviii. Ruth G. Kassinger, *Sea Snails to Synthetics* (Minneapolis: The Millbrook Press, 2003), 30.
xxix. Bechtold and Mussak, 15.
xxx. Sandberg, 75.
xxxi. Sandberg, 60.
xxxii. Ball, 60.
xxxiii. Kassinger, 53.
xxxiv. Kassinger, 54.
xxxv. Anna Muthesius, *Studies in Silk in Byzantium* (London: Pindar Press, 2004), 49.
xxxvi. Kassinger, 62–4.
xxxvii. Kassinger, 67.
xxxviii. Ball, 59.
xxxix. Bechtold and Mussak, 3–4.
xl. Ball, 218–9.
xli. Bechtold and Mussak, 25.
xlii. Catherine Filsinger, "A Gift of Russian Vestments," *Bulletin of the City Art Museum of St. Louis*, Vol. 34, No. 4 (Fall 1949): 54–59.
xliii. Ball, 100.
xliv. Cross and Sherbowitz-Wetzor, 10.

Chapter Six

Woven unto Life

Divine worship is the heart of the monastic life, just as the katholikon is the centre of the monastery complex; and in a great imperial and patriarchal monastery such as that of Iveron, whose tradition acknowledges how much it respects ecclesiastical order and loves the comeliness of the House of God, it is natural that care is taken over the priestly vestments of worship, the drapings below the holy icons, the covers of the sacred vessels and the other decorative veils. All these things, divinely ornamented, together weave the raiment of the Church and evoke the beauty and grace of the worship of God and particularly of the Divine Liturgy, as the sacrament which sums up the mystery of the Church and of the salvation of the whole world, in which Christ, God and Man, through His sacrifice upon the cross 'clothed Himself with majesty', and in which the priest, 'arrayed in the grace of priesthood' is deemed worthy to celebrate the awful mysteries. And this unseen grace of priesthood which the priest receives at his ordination is rendered visible by the wearing of the sacred vestments. It will, therefore, be readily understood with how much love for beauty and how much awe, the tasteful spirit of the Monastery will have adorned the gold embroidered vestments for Him who 'is clothed with light as with a garment'.

Archimandrite Vasileios, Abbot of Iveron Monastery[i]

While the covering of his nakedness betokened the beginning of man's shame after the Fall, paradoxically the development of textiles has become over time one of mankind's most stunning technological and artistic achievements. Taking a chief place among the finest examples of the textile arts are the vibrant, complex, and intricate fabrics that have been employed for liturgical garments and furnishings for almost two millennia in the Orthodox Christian Church. These beautiful brocades and embroideries have made churches glorious, amazed men, and—along with architecture, iconography, and music—been rightly acclaimed as being among the foremost arts of the Orthodox Christian world. As Byzantine scholar Gervase Mathew explains: "The textile arts ... are never 'minor',"[ii] for, "It seems likely that textiles were judged by the same standards as mosaics, marble paneling, ivory-work and carved capitals."[iii] When we begin to explore the textiles that constitute this venerable tradition of adornment within the Orthodox Christian Church, we are continually reminded of this truth. Woven of the most precious fibers, adorned with gold threads, and featuring designs and symbols that hearken to the earliest days of the Church's history, these textiles take their rightful place among the major arts and continue to be treasured in churches and museums to this day.

A Brief History of Textiles

Before taking a closer look at the textiles used specifically for liturgical items it is first necessary to discuss textiles in general. There are four distinct fibers occurring in nature—wool, flax, silk, and cotton—and two basic tools—the loom and the needle—used for transforming them into textiles.

The loom has been used from ancient times to produce woven fabrics. A loom is a device that allows threads to be wrapped around it in a vertical orientation (known as "warp" threads) which are then pulled taut. A weaver then takes additional threads and, by means of a shuttle or similar apparatus, feeds these threads (known as "weft" threads) horizontally over and under the warp threads to create a fabric grid, tamping the weft threads every row to tighten them together and create a dense fabric. The most basic woven fabric is created using a single strand of thread with a "one-under, one-over" pattern which yields a monochromatic, plain-weave fabric.

The loom itself started out as a very simple structure—just two sticks set a distance apart with the necessary tension being achieved by either wrapping a harness attached to one stick around the weaver (as in the back strap loom still used in South America) or hanging the sticks horizontally and allowing gravity to provide tension as in the warp-weighted loom. Both of these basic types of loom can be dated to the earliest periods of human civilization.

The deceptively simple, binary concept of weaving can be expanded to create exceptionally sophisticated patterns with complex coloration depending on such factors as the fiber of the warp and weft threads, the colors of the warp and weft threads, and the intricacy of the design. The first major technological advance in weaving was tapestry weaving, in which threads of various colors were interwoven in small sections that completely obscured the warp threads. Early tapestry woven pieces were often made as bands or squares that would then be attached to garments as a form of ornamentation. This type of weaving has a very dense quality which tends to make it quite durable. Many excellent examples of ancient woven tapestry work have been preserved in Egypt where the low-humidity conditions are conducive to textile preservation.

As the complexity of weaving techniques progressed, fibers, colors, and patterns were adapted to create new and more elaborate textiles. Yet simply changing thread colors and decorative patterns was eventually not enough to satisfy the desire for innovation; the technology of the loom had to be modified as well. The development of drawloom technology sometime in the early Christian period had lasting repercussions, as textile expert Adele Weibel relates:

> A fundamental change in the method of pattern weaving took place in the early centuries of the Christian era. Until then all elaborate patterns had been produced by the technique of tapestry weaving. Now the desire to weave such patterns in mechanical repetition led to the most important

improvement of the loom, the invention of the drawloom. Only one other invention equals that of the drawloom in revolutionary economic importance: the invention of the printing press a thousand years later.[iv]

The introduction of the drawloom represents a tremendous step forward in the production of textiles. Its complex arrangement of warp threads being placed, or "drawn" (hence the name), through a board drilled with a specific hole for each thread gives the weaver far better control over each thread and this allowed for the creation of more fantastical designs, in a faster and more regular fashion. In fact much of the weaving produced in Constantinople over a thousand years ago is so sophisticated that, even with the technological knowledge of our own age, it is still not fully understood how it was created.

Embroidered textiles take woven fabric one step further: the woven fabric serves as a "ground" fabric (typically reinforced with a linen backing to provide strength) which is then marked with a design and stretched taut on some kind of frame to provide uniform tension. The design is covered with a variety of stitches worked with a needle pulling through either silk floss or "metal" threads (which are comprised of a core of silk wrapped with paper-thin sheets of gold or silver), or a combination of the two, through the woven fabric. The amazing creativity and artistry of the historic embroiderer knew almost no bounds and has been discussed more fully in Chapter Four. Due to their significant metal content, many historic embroideries have stood the test of time well and excellent examples may be found in the collections of many museums.

By approximately the third or fourth century AD, woven and embroidered textiles had come to comprise the two distinct groups of fabrics used for Orthodox Christian liturgical garments and furnishings. Throughout the history of the Church, woven fabrics have been by far the predominant type of textile. Embroidered textiles have tended to be reserved for smaller pieces that were given as gifts or awards, such as the *epigonation* and *epimanikia*, or items that were used as the focus of major liturgical rites, such as the *epitaphios* of Great and Holy Friday. Although embroidered vestments may still be seen today, historically they have been the exception rather than the rule. While some scholars have argued that embroidery served as a less expensive substitute for complex woven fabrics until its ascendency in the twelfth century,[v] the existence of gold-embroidery guilds from the time of Imperial Rome and throughout the Byzantine era, as well as the descriptions of particular altar cloths (most notably the panegyric of Paul the Silentiary that is quoted at length in Chapter Four) call such a theory into question. It is more probable that embroideries co-existed with woven fabrics, but were confined to items of a more specific use such as altar cloths and award pieces, much as they still are today.

Whether woven or embroidered, the fibers used to create textiles were of paramount importance in the ancient world. Nature had given mankind just four basic fiber building blocks and from these he had to clothe himself, assign honor and prestige, adorn his dwellings, and beautify his places of worship. The raw materials of sheep's wool, silk strands from the silkworm, and plant fibers, had to be painstakingly transformed into something useful and beautiful, and this endeavor had all the characteristics and value of similarly complex arts such as carving and metalwork. To create textiles required tremendous skill, artistic ability, specific technical knowledge, and, in some cases, access to the most expensive raw materials the ancient world knew. A piece of fabric laboriously and carefully woven, whether in a domestic setting or in the commercial, imperial workshops of Constantinople, would be valued to the last thread, because each and every one of those threads had to be worked by hand. These valuable fabrics would be used and treasured for many years and when they eventually began to wear out, they would be re-cut and re-fashioned to further embellish garments and hangings, even if only as a small border or decorative patch.

In ancient Rome, wool was the fiber of choice for most garments because the Roman landscape was well-suited to the raising of sheep. Wool is a highly versatile fiber and has many excellent properties: it is water-resistant and fire-resistant, it retains its insulating properties even when wet, protects against cold, is breathable in hot weather, and is even antibacterial to some measure. Wool takes dyes very well and is a readily renewable resource. Togas and tunics alike were made from hand-woven wool, in a variety of grades, weights, and colors. Tunics were often further ornamented with multi-colored tapestry-woven bands and decorations which could be removed and re-sewn to a new tunic once the original began to wear out. Togas were finished with bands of specific colors that denoted status. Cloaks and wraps were also made of wool, lighter for warm weather and heavier for cold or wet weather. Today wool is often perceived as a heavy, coarse fabric due to our frequent use of wool for outerwear, but in ancient usage there were also light, fine wools, some of which could rival even the fineness of silk.

Far from the Roman hills with their grazing sheep, across the Mediterranean Sea, lay the great land of Egypt sweltering in the sun. With its wide, open fields and hot climate, Egypt's landscape was ideal for growing flax, the raw material necessary to create the preeminent fabric of Egypt, linen. Whereas wool was ideally suited for garments worn in the temperate climate of ancient Rome, linen was the fiber of choice in Egypt's hot environment. Linen is exceptionally breathable and comfortable, resists moths and dirt, and is a very strong fabric with great durability, one of the few natural fibers that is stronger when wet than when dry. In the heat of Egypt, linen kept its wearer comfortable and it is easy to see how the garment designs of ancient Egypt were molded by its distinctive properties. If a Roman toga, with its multiple folds and draping, had been made from linen it would have been a wrinkly mess, but the more tailored Egyptian *kalasiris* made from linen was a garment of great beauty in line and form.

There was robust commerce in the ancient Mediterranean world and therefore linen was imported from Egypt to Greece and Rome, but due to its appearance—even at its best, linen is not a showy fabric—it was most often reserved for under-tunics and, in the Byzantine era was used for lining certain silk garments; in fact, our English terms "lingerie" and "lining" both come from the word "linen." While the Egyptians frequently wore linen garments, the Romans did not embrace them until quite late and even then relegated this fiber, when used for outer garments, exclusively to women.[vi] Wool remained the predominant fiber of ancient Rome.

In the very earliest days of the Church the garments used in liturgical settings were likely most often made from wool, given that these early vestments were adapted from standard Roman and Greek garments. However, this was not necessarily a coarse, rough, "simple" fabric as is sometimes sentimentally imagined. In a time and place that viewed textiles as both a valuable commodity and a status symbol, the early garments of the Church would most likely have been of the best quality that the wearer or community could afford.[1] Early iconography depicting the apostles and other saints in full-length tunics and togas does so in order to illustrate their revered position as "philosophers," i.e., "lovers of Wisdom" ("Wisdom" being Christ in this context) and such garments in the ancient world would have been made from beautiful and finely woven wool.

In addition to linen and wool, the ancient world was also acquainted with silk, though it was long reserved for the use of the wealthy and powerful due to the exorbitant cost of importing it from the Orient. This vivid and gleaming textile of luxury and privilege began to be coveted in Rome around the first century BC, mostly for women's attire. The Roman Senate at first tried to curtail its use due to its high cost as well as the perception that it could foster immorality due to its transparency.

Despite the Senate's edicts the lure of silk took hold. Once seen and held in the hand, it is easy to see why: silk has an ethereal drape, a compelling brilliance when dyed, and a unique, lustrous sheen. These particular qualities are not found in any other natural fiber. In addition to its beautiful appearance, it is also exceptionally durable, having been used throughout history to fashion such diverse products as the coronation robes of many Western European houses and the parachutes of World War II. The wealthy and privileged of Eastern Roman society

---

1. Despite the fact that no direct evidence survives, it is likely that early *phelonia* were made from wool, given the ubiquitous use of wool in Roman world and the conversely limited use of linen. Wool is an ideal textile for the cut and fit of the *paenula*, the outer cloak that was the direct precursor to the *phelonion*.

demanded silk as their rightful adornment, woven into hangings for their homes, fashioned into beautiful garments, and sanctified to the glory of God through its use for vestments and paraments.

Silk was here to stay.

A Heritage of Silk: The Byzantine Silk Industry

Within two centuries of the birth of Christ, the use of silk was firmly entrenched in the Roman Empire and the unique economic, social, and liturgical power it wielded would continue for another twelve hundred years until the fall of Constantinople. Even after the destruction of the famed imperial silk workshops, silk continued to reign supreme among textiles until the development of synthetic textiles in the late nineteenth century, just a little over a hundred years ago. The history of the Orthodox Christian Church is literally interwoven with silk and if one is to have a fully informed understanding of the traditional aesthetic sensibilities of the Church, a familiarity with the importance of silk in the Byzantine world is absolutely vital.

By the time of Constantine the Great the weaving of silk had already reached a high level of sophistication in the Roman world. The use of gold threads interwoven with silk was not uncommon, as is attested by the famous account of a golden vestment given to Bishop Makarios of Jerusalem by Constantine.[vii] While silk thread was dyed and woven in Constantinople, the raw silk fibers themselves had to be imported from the Orient, the ancient cultures of which carefully guarded the secrets of sericulture (i.e., silk harvesting), much to their economic benefit. However by the time of Justinian, the Byzantine Empire had grown weary of the heavy costs of importing raw silk (the value of which was on a par with gold),[viii] and this ambitious emperor was greatly motivated to establish a domestic supply of raw silk in order to meet the growing demand for the luxury textile and procure additional revenue for his empire. A well-known tale relates that two monks traveled to the Far East at Justinian's behest in order to discover the secrets of the valuable silkworm. In the manner of modern-day industrial spies they returned to Constantinople with silkworm cocoons hidden in their hollow walking sticks and so began the storied sericulture industry of Byzantium.

Raising silkworms is a complicated process that requires very exacting conditions, the most notable of which is an ample supply of mulberry leaves, the exclusive diet of the silkworm. In addition to raising the worms in the proper environment on the mulberry leaf diet, obtaining the valuable silk thread is no mean feat, as textile historian Adele Weibel describes:

> The silkworm ... although a voracious eater, is so lazy that during the month of its growth it must daily be lifted onto its new supply of chopped mulberry leaves. But on the thirty-second day *Bombys mori* starts working and for sixty hours ceaselessly spins one long fine thread, round and round, with pendulous motion of the head and figure-of-eight movements of the fore part of the body. The spinning glands exhausted, he rests in his cocoon, and after 2–3 weeks the chrysalis breaks the wall of the cocoon and emerges as a moth. . . . the cocoon is then immersed in a hot bath, to loosen the gelatinous binder. Then four or five of the four-hundred- to a thousand-yard-long threads from as many cocoons are reeled off simultaneously and twisted into one strong thread.[ix]

The thread that this arduous process produces is then ready to be dyed and woven into myriad designs, suitable for both secular and liturgical use.

The time involved in silk production alone was enough to warrant a very high price for the finished fabric. Yet in addition to the intrinsic worth of silk, Justinian further raised its value by instituting a unique set of laws that may be described as "hierarchy through clothing" in which the use of particular garments was restricted by social position. While the idea of specific garments being reserved for certain social positions dated back to Imperial Rome with its variety of purple-edged togas worn only in particular settings and by specific persons, Justinian took the idea of "hierarchy through clothing" and applied it to the supply of silk, effectively managing all levels of Byzantine society. Certain designs, colors, and garments were restricted to imperial usage while others were allocated for various levels of state officialdom or specific state occasions. Designated state officials even made sure that no one was buying or wearing silk to which they were not entitled.[x] In the social structure of the Byzantine Empire, you were what you wore.

Beyond its value as a mark of social status, silk also functioned as a very important commodity in the Byzantine economy. It was considered wise for noblemen to keep some of their wealth as bolts of silk since they were easy to sell in an emergency. Silks were light and easily transportable, making them a common form of currency among travelers and tradesmen.[xi] Not only the Byzantine economy, but also Byzantine diplomacy was dependent upon silk. Silks were given as gifts on diplomatic missions and, in certain instances, their exportation was utilized to affect political relationships within a given region by either allowing or limiting access to silks.

While the finest-grade silks were the most desirable for both secular and liturgical use, their high cost prohibited their exclusive use and necessitated a more economical substitute. In situations in which first-grade silk could not be procured, "half-silks" would be used. These textiles were made by weaving silk with another fiber, typically linen, wool, cotton or hemp, to reduce their cost while still retaining some silk content.[2]

Silk in all its forms was a way of life for those residing in the Byzantine Empire and directly or indirectly affected almost all aspects of Byzantine life from social status to worship and even politics. This is a far cry from our approach to textiles as a status symbol in the present age: while we do retain a decided infatuation with fashion, we do so primarily based upon brand development and marketing. We generally wear what we are told is high fashion with very little ability to evaluate such clothing

---

2. A personal favorite from among all the cassocks I have designed was made from a silk and wool blend fabric. This blend made an impression on me as it seemed to have all of the positive attributes of each fiber, without any negative ones: it was light, breathable, and had a particularly lovely, understated sheen from the silk fibers.

or textiles upon their actual merits or intrinsic value. The same medium-grade wool might be used to manufacture a $20 dress bought at a low-end department store or a $200 dress purchased at a high-end boutique and most of us would not know the difference. Only the manufacturer's tag sewn into the garment would tell us whether we were buying status or not. Today we buy brands without any awareness of the actual value of the item we purchase, which is yet another instance of the modern preference for appearance over substance. But in Byzantium substance mattered and much of the economy and social structure was based upon either manufacturing or acquiring prized textiles. As medieval economics scholar Robert Sabatino Lopez explains:

> The Byzantine Emperors or Basileis of the early Middle Ages controlled the supply of silk, purple, and gold embroidery. These precious textiles were among the paramount articles of international trade, since most countries were practically self-sufficient in regard to most of the basic necessities in the way of essential foodstuffs, woolen cloth, metals and earthenware. By releasing silk, purple, and gold embroidery for export, the Basileis could secure a considerable revenue from customs duties, and stimulate a flow of foreign gold into their states. But precious cloth was not just another commodity. It possessed special significance. It was the attire of the Emperor and the aristocracy, an indispensable symbol of political authority, and a prime requirement for ecclesiastical ceremonies. Control of precious cloth, therefore, was almost as powerful a weapon in the hands of the Byzantine Emperor as the possession of such key strategic materials as oil, coal, and iron is in the hands of the American or British government.[xii]

The production of Byzantine silk was a sophisticated industry, built upon a specialized workforce, a complex system of regulation, and a system of imperial and private guilds, all operating under the close scrutiny of state officials. This highly organized system of manufacture allowed the Byzantine silk industry to flourish for over eight centuries, truly a remarkable achievement. The backbone of this impressive industrial infrastructure was the guild system. In Constantinople there were two main types of guilds: the imperial guilds, whose workshops were housed next to the royal palaces and which produced the most valuable, imperial silks; and the private guilds, with members producing their lesser-valued goods in various workshops scattered throughout the city.

The imperial guilds descended directly from the guild system of ancient Rome and consisted of three distinct groups: the clothiers and tailors, the purple-dyers, and the gold embroiderers.[xiii] Membership in an imperial guild was restricted to descendants or relatives of guild members and was tightly controlled. Both men and women worked in the imperial factories in various capacities from spinning to weaving, dyeing, and embroidering. As Robert Sabatino Lopez recounts:

> By that time [the tenth century] the imperial workers evidently had become a sort of aristocracy of labor. A special place on formal court processions was reserved for them. They well deserved it. Many of them were artists, not unworthy brothers of the artisans who built and decorated Saint Sophia, illustrated the manuscripts of the Byzantine libraries, or carved the ivories gracing so many European museums.[xiv]

While the imperial guilds supplied the emperor and his family and friends with the finest silks, the private guilds supplied the majority of Byzantine society with silks that were available for purchase to anyone who could afford to pay. As Lopez goes on to explain:

> Any nobleman and any citizen of Constantinople was allowed to buy in the market precious garments of whatever price, quality, and size. The noblemen ... had the special right of having

their garments made in their own *gynaecia* [workshop]. But all residents in the capital could purchase similar fabrics from the city guilds in unlimited quantity. That is why Constantinople, showplace of the nation, impressed the foreigners with an unforgettable vision of wealth.[xv]

These private guilds comprised five sectors of the silk industry: the merchants of raw silk, the silk spinners, the clothiers and dyers (who manufactured, dyed, and sold cloth), the merchants of domestic garments, and the merchants of foreign (imported) silk fabrics.[xvi] Unlike the imperial guilds, the members of private guilds were not state employees, but rather independent merchants and artisans.

The system of imperial and private guilds, along with strict state regulation, is one of the primary reasons the Byzantine silk industry endured for such a considerable period of time. Just as the aesthetic tradition of the Orthodox Christian Church places a high value on stability and constancy, so the structure of the guilds similarly emphasized stability and adherence to received patterns. As we have seen before, what the Byzantine mind desired was tradition rather than innovation. The guild system, with its centuries-long management of the silk industry, was not only an important component of the economic backbone of Byzantium, but also helped to safeguard and perpetuate the aesthetic traditions of the Church.

The high value placed upon silks within Byzantine society and their ready availability demanded that they also be used liturgically. In a city such as Constantinople, where men went about attired in finely woven, gleaming silks, it would have been inconceivable that such adornment would be confined solely to secular use. Constantinople was, above all, the city of churches and its populace sought to adorn and beautify those churches magnificently. To do so necessitated the use of silk within the church for every type of adornment.

Historically the silks devoted to Church use would have come from both kinds of workshop. In the case of gifts from the emperor or his retinue the silks would have been imperial silks, produced near the palace, of the finest quality materials, dyed with the imperial purple (Tyrian purple), and embellished with gold threads, either woven or embroidered. Gifts of silk from donors outside the imperial circle would have been purchased from the private guild workshops, and their design and quality would have been dependent on the donor's means and the workshop's capabilities and could have ranged from high-grade, pure silks to half-silks. So while silk was the predominant fabric used for liturgical garments and furnishings, there would have been various grades, designs, and qualities used depending on the size of the church, the wealth of the donor, and the guild from which the donor could purchase cloth. Because they had a high value to begin with and were then further imbued with symbolic significance, silks used for liturgical purposes would have been more carefully handled and preserved than those used in normal daily life. Once a liturgical silk was beginning to show wear, it would have been cut down and remade into smaller pieces or become a form of ornament, such as a border for a new vestment or parament. A number of such silks can be seen in their faded, yet still resplendent, glory in museums throughout the world.

During the long period of silk production in Byzantium, the residents of Constantinople were not the only people who desired beautiful silk brocades. There was a steady stream of visitors to the imperial city who, after witnessing the splendor of Constantinopolitan dress, also wanted to possess these lovely fabrics. Diplomats and important visitors were given gifts of silks and they took these back to their homelands where the lustrous beauty of these textiles created a sensation. Other cities with textile production centers wanted to learn to make the Byzantine-styled silks, but production methods were held tightly as state secrets of the highest order.

Everyone wanted Byzantine silk, but its high value and the massive amounts of revenue it produced insured that the Byzantines kept the knowledge of its manufacture undisclosed. Textile artisans in other European lands began to unravel the simpler methods of its fabrication, but knowledge of the finer, higher-quality silk techniques was a closely guarded secret until well past the tenth century. The Byzantines knew the value of what they possessed, so much so that one Byzantine emperor wrote to warn his son against "giving barbarians imperial cloth, imperial crowns, and the technique of Greek fire."[xvii] Eventually, though, other cities in Europe began to solve the puzzle of how to create the higher-grade silks, with the various city-states of Italy leading the way sometime around the mid-twelfth century.[xviii] This is not surprising when one considers the regular commercial interchange between Italy and Byzantium. The Crusaders' sack of Constantinople in 1204 was most likely a significant turning point, as scholar David Jacoby explains:

> Venice became the second major manufacturer of silks in the Christian West. The chronological conjunction of the collapse of silk manufacture in Constantinople in the wake of the Latin conquest of the city in 1204 and the launching of high-grade silk production in Venice around that time does not appear to have been coincidental. Venetian merchants previously acquainted with Byzantine silk centers must have been instrumental in the creation of the required industrial infrastructure in their own city and in the recruitment of the required workforce. It is not impossible that silk artisans from Constantinople arrived spontaneously or were brought to Venice.[xix]

Silk continued to be in high demand from this period forward and, after the fall of Constantinople in 1453, the center of manufacture moved to the Italian city-states as well as certain other cities in Western Europe. Many of the brocade designs used in the Orthodox Christian Church today are assigned the stylistic description "Venetian" and are highly valued due to their quality and their unique large motif designs that are reminiscent of historic Byzantine silk designs. Brocade manufacturing centers were subsequently established in France and Germany during the late Medieval and early Renaissance periods and a number of metallic brocades used for vestments today come from French or German looms.

The use of high-grade silk and half-silk brocades continued in the Church until the advent of synthetic textiles which began to be developed in the late nineteenth century. Wood-based fibers, such as rayon and acetate were first utilized for "artificial" fabrics (technically not "synthetic" since the wood pulp used as the base for these fabrics is naturally occurring). The use of petroleum-based polyester for textile manufacture began in earnest in the late 1950s and within a few decades had overtaken the majority of the liturgical brocade market. While the glory days of Byzantine-silk-style vestments are not entirely over—a small quantity of hand-loomed, silk brocades are still made for liturgical use—polyester, with its advantages of durability and high color retention, is now the fiber of choice for the majority of liturgical brocades used in the Orthodox Christian Church.

While technological advances such as polyester fibers have dramatically changed the liturgical brocade market, some of the fibers used since ancient times are still preferred for vestment construction due to their unrivaled properties. Cotton canvas remains one of the best interfacings for providing stability and structure to vestment pieces due to its tight weave and remarkable durability. Silk broadcloth is still sometimes used for priest's *sticharia* due to its subtle beauty and unsurpassed breathability, an important concern for someone wearing up to ten extra pounds of clothing for hours at a time. Cassocks continue to be made from fine-grade wool, the drape and elegance of which cannot be equaled by synthetics, and also from true silk crepe (as opposed to "artificial silk," a common term for polyester or rayon silk substitutes), which is arguably the finest fabric from which a cassock can be tailored.

While hand-embroidered pieces continue to be made, their use remains largely limited to award pieces or the Holy Friday *epitaphios*. Hand-embroidered vestments are available, but rarely seen due to their high cost. The use of machine embroidery has become so widespread that it now constitutes a specific category of vestment fabric used for so-called "lightweight" or "summer" vestments. This type of fabric is comprised of an extra-wide ground fabric which is machine-embroidered with various traditional designs such as floral sprays or grapevines alternated with crosses in a grid pattern. The comfort of these machine-embroidered fabrics (when made into vestments, they weigh almost half the amount of a comparable brocade vestment set) as well as their beauty and durability, make these fabrics quite popular in the Church today.

Regardless of the fibers utilized, whether hand-loomed silk or modern polyester, the ancient designs of Byzantium still characterize Orthodox Christian liturgical fabrics and make them unique in the world of modern textiles. It is to the rich and sublime symbology of these designs that we shall turn next.

The Designs of Liturgical Textiles

A visit to an ecclesiastical tailoring shop in Athens or Thessaloniki is undeniably a heady experience. Everywhere one looks lie bolts of brocades in an abundance of rich, saturated colors: deep golds shot with red, brilliant whites married with silver, mellow burgundies interwoven with brighter reds and golds, vivid blues, and vibrant, multi-colored brocades in unusual and arresting color combinations—gold mixed with blue, purple, green and red, or silver mixed with green and coral. Yet when one looks closer or perhaps asks for a bolt to be brought down and laid out on the cutting table, the wonder of the colors is superseded by the complexity and beauty of the designs they enliven.

To examine a selection of liturgical brocades used for Orthodox Christian vestments and altar furnishings is to take a walk through history. Here are the ancient knots and vines of the pre-Christian era, the vegetative and floral motifs of Mesopotamia, the urns of ancient Greece and Rome, and myriad variations upon that epitome of Christian symbols, the cross. No two designs are alike, though they share similar motifs and design structure. Just as the use of color within the Church maintains continuity with the ancient perception of the color spectrum, so too the designs used to ornament liturgical fabrics are marked with the most universal and lasting symbols known to humanity.

Mankind has always delighted in decorative embellishment. The history of art, and more specifically textiles, attests to this. Soon after discovering how to weave, man went on to display great ingenuity and creativity in adapting this technology for ornamentation. Some of the earliest-surviving textile fragments are not simple, plain-weave, monochromatic fabrics, but rather sophisticated checker-work designs, similar to modern-day plaids. As opposed to working with a single color in a rote fashion, the production of ornamented textiles demands great focus, time, knowledge, and skill of the artisan, all of which add to the value of the textiles produced. From the artisan's perspective, it is far more pleasurable to see a design come alive under one's fingers than to view a monotonous, monochromatic expanse.

To better understand the origins of liturgical textile designs, the environment in which such designs were first created and fostered, that of ancient Greece and Rome, must be considered. The people who lived in these ancient societies placed a high value on symbols and used them lavishly. In a world with many unknowns and frequent instability due to natural disasters, war, and political upheaval, symbols comforted and protected. Most of the symbols used in the ancient world can be categorized under two broad headings. The first group, referred to as "apotropaic" (from the Greek "to ward off") is made up of symbols intended to deflect evils and protect the owner. The second group, "provisionary," is comprised of symbols believed to ensure plenty. Both apotropaic and provisionary symbols were believed to be invested with supernatural powers. These images were found virtually everywhere from door lintels to domestic household goods, but especially on textiles and similar artwork such as pottery and metalwork. A tapestry-woven panel, emblazoned with provisionary animals and birds, was hung in a doorway to keep out draughts but was also considered to bring plenty to the occupant. A tunic finished with an apotropaic, knot-work border was believed to keep sickness at bay. In a time and place in which literacy was marginal, symbols functioned as a sort of supernatural shorthand and daily life was replete with them.

With the coming of Christ, there was a major shift in the understanding of these ancient symbols. No longer was man subject to the whims of unknown and frightening deities; instead, through grace, he was now under the loving and merciful care of the one, true God. The symbols that pervaded and informed daily life were seen in a new light and were redeemed to serve a new purpose, that of bringing the spiritual world ever to mind as one went about the duties and activities of the material world. The warding off of evil began to be understood as the warding off of the passions and demonic powers, whereas the desire for plenty was broadened to include not only earthly bounty and the staving off of hunger, but also the desire for spiritual riches and blessings.

This concept of the intertwining of the spiritual and material worlds was incorporated into Christian art from the earliest period but found its greatest flowering in Byzantine aesthetics. We observe this interchange of the earthly and heavenly first and foremost in iconography, but it also permeates all other art forms such as textiles, carving, and metalwork. The idea of a cosmic interchange between the spiritual and material worlds is characteristic of a fundamentally Eastern mindset; the modern mind, influenced by Western European culture over the last 500 years, prefers a more one-dimensional reality rooted in logic and reason. But the uniquely Eastern Christian worldview deeply affected early Christian art. As Byzantine scholar Slobodan Curcic states:

> The crucial point is that the Byzantine conception of aesthetics in art is not at all related to the Western one. For Westerners, art was a means of representing reality and at times even bettering it, while for Byzantines, art was never an end in itself, but a facilitator of access to the spiritual world, the indescribable, non-containable universe of the divine spirit.[xx]

Textiles—along with the other creative works of the Church such as iconography, architecture, chant, metalwork, stone and marble work, and woodcarving—formed a connection with the spiritual realm and opened to the viewer a new, heavenly vista. While supplemental factors, such as a mathematical approach to beauty, a respect for earlier classical works, and a preoccupation with color, shaped and informed Byzantine art,[xxi] the revolutionary foundation of this new, Christ-centered art was the conviction that the material is intertwined with the spiritual, the external with the internal, the earth with heaven. This was the overarching concept in Byzantine art that informed every artistic endeavor.

It may seem disconcerting to the modern mind that so-called "secular" textiles were repurposed for religious use. But, when understood according to the ancient mindset in which substance was far more important than mere appearance, if the finest silks were those produced for the secular market then those were precisely the silks that would be deemed most suitable for a liturgical setting. Just as it would be inconceivable to the Christian of Byzantium that one would use within the church a cheap brocade marked with crosses instead of a sumptuous silk covered with flowers and vinework, even so the modern mind must lay aside the assumption that only fabrics covered in crosses can be used for religious ends. This is why an exploration of the development of secular textiles is essential to a discussion of liturgical vestments—sometimes these were the only textiles available and often they were superior in quality to all else. Additionally, due to the fragility of textiles through the ages, there is an overwhelmingly larger number of "secular" silks extant and these are the ones with which we must content ourselves when studying the history of textiles devoted to liturgical use.

The earliest and most common design structure for Byzantine textiles, was the all-over design, typically laid out in a grid. Figure 1 illustrates this with a diagonal lozenge pattern that has, worked inside the lozenges, alternating designs of two birds nesting in a tree and two peacocks flanking a tree. The vinework that forms the division of the lozenges is lively and intricate and at the intersections of the lines is a cross design made of hearts. The birds and the lush vinework serve together as symbols of abundance and evoke the image of Paradise. The high contrast of the coloration makes the design exceptionally clear and crisp.

Figure 1. Silk twill, Egypt, 6–7th century (Adele Coulin Weibel, *Two Thousand Years of Textiles*, Pantheon Books, Plate 52).

While Byzantine aesthetics were underpinned with the theology of the Orthodox Christian Church, art of the early Byzantine period was not immune to the influence of other cultural currents, especially those of neighboring empires, most notably Sassanid Persia. The early period of Byzantine art relied heavily on the roundel design, the use of which in textiles is thought to have originated in Persia. As can be observed in Figure 2, the roundel, or circle, was a geometric design, but rather than shapes that alternated every row, as with the diagonal lozenge pattern of Figure 1, roundels were stacked in neat rows both vertically and horizontally. Circles were associated with eternity, which may have been part of the appeal of this design, but it must also have been its sheer boldness and visual interest that kept it a favored design motif throughout the entire period of Byzantine silk manufacture. The center of the roundel provided an excellent canvas to display the weaver's skill and various motifs, both secular and religious, were employed to great effect. Hunters, animals (both real and imaginary), as well as scenes such as the Annunciation pictured in Figure 3, were intricately portrayed. The border of the roundel formed a design feature in its own right and could be comprised of either simple "pearls" as in Figure 2 or complex floral work as in Figure 3. An orderly array of roundels also created a superb opportunity for secondary ornamentation in the diamond-shaped space formed between the grid of roundels, and in these interstices we see further sophisticated designs.

Figure 2. Silk twill, Byzantine, 12th century (Adele Coulin Weibel, *Two Thousand Years of Textiles*, Pantheon Books, Plate 64).

Figure 3. Annunciation silk, Egypt, 6th cent, Rome, Vatican, Museo Cristiano (Ernst Flemming, *Encyclopedia of Textiles*, Federick A. Praeger, Inc., 14).

In addition to the secondary spaces of the roundel design and their elaborate motifs, the Annunciation silk in Figure 3 displays yet another characteristic feature of Byzantine textile design: the interlocking, knotwork borders that form the roundels. In recent years, art historical scholarship has begun to explore the possibility that such borders had their origins in mosaic tile work. Regardless of their provenance, however, we know that knotwork was an especially important design element in the ancient world, as Byzantine scholar Henry Maguire recounts:

> Among the most frequent motifs on textiles, especially the earlier ones, of the third to sixth centuries, are knots and interlaces.... The power of such designs in the supernatural realm was conveyed by the Greek language itself, for the verb "katadeo" meant both to bind physically and to bind by spells, or to enchant. Knots and interlaces were not confined to the decoration of textiles, but they appeared in several other media, especially floor mosaics.[xxii]

As Maguire explains and other scholars have suggested, there was a dynamic interchange of designs among artisans in various fields that would have been facilitated by the easy transportation of small artifacts such as ceramics, metalwork, and even sketches and manuscripts so that a craftsman in one field, such as goldsmithing or woodcarving, would have been aware of new textile designs and vice versa.[xxiii] It would have been normal for these various ornamental designs to flow back and forth among craftsmen and influence everything from textiles to mosaic work and ceramics. Basic lozenge patterns as well as the knotwork described above are all found frequently in mosaics of the Byzantine era and it has even been shown that the vaults in the Mausoleum of Galla Placidia in Ravenna, Italy (which contain some of the finest examples of early Byzantine mosaics still extant) took their overall design from woven silks.[xxiv] Figure 4 demonstrates how the more rigid composition of mosaic floor patterns could have been adapted to the border of textile designs: what begins in (a) as a rigid structure becomes subsequently embellished in (b), given more negative space in (c) and reaches its final sophistication in the circles-within-circles design of (d):

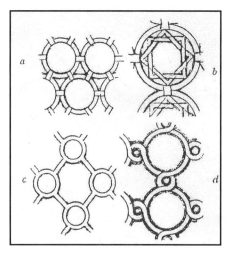

Figure 4. Sketch showing mosaic to textile development (R.W. Lethaby, "Byzantine Silks in London Museums," *The Burlington Magazine for Connoisseurs*, Vol. 24, 140).

Many permutations of this interlaced border were devised because it worked well on the drawloom of the Byzantine silk industry and was highly appealing with its primary and secondary motifs forming a visual back-and-forth energy combined with a restful intricacy. A further adaptation of this design can be seen in Figure 5 below:

Figure 5. Silk, Italy, 13th century (Adele Coulin Weibel, *Two Thousand Years of Textiles*, Pantheon Books, Plate 168).

This adaptation in Figure 5 shows a quatrefoil medallion taking the place of the roundels and a palmette border with a very fine double outline. It is a graceful and sublime design and echoes of it can be seen in the modern liturgical brocade of Figure 6.

Figure 6. Large Normandy brocade (courtesy of LaLame, Inc.).

In Figure 7, a new variation of the design is shown, in which the borders now take up the entire secondary space, forming undulating waves as well as the illusion of a monochrome background against which the now-oval medallions are set:

Figure 7. Silk twill, Turkey, 16–17th century (Adele Coulin Weibel, *Two Thousand Years of Textiles*, Pantheon Books, Plate 155).

Viewing two samples of Venetian brocades in Figures 8 and 9, we see the border now becoming almost the primary design element with the medallions seeming to recede, and the secondary spaces now the same size as the medallions and either containing the same design motif or providing an alternate design motif:

Figures 8. & 9. Silk brocades, Venice, 15th century (Ernst Flemming, *Encyclopedia of Textiles*, Frederick A. Praeger, Inc., 77).

From this beginning roundel design and its variations as shown in the above figures, there may be observed in Byzantine silks and their close cousins, the Italian, French, and Turkish brocades that followed, a basic design structure of three elements: first, some kind of primary medallion, either roundel, oval, or quatrefoil; second, the border around the primary medallion; and third, the secondary motifs that fill the spaces between the primary medallions, or in the case of the later development, become the same as the primary medallion. This basic design structure was to undergo a further development in which the primary medallions became significantly larger and even more oval in shape and the borders stretched and widened to become elaborate vine and floral work intertwining the primary motif rather than strictly confining it. An example of a French silk from the seventeenth century in Figure 10 demonstrates this development:

Figure 10. Silk brocade, France, 17th century (Ernst Flemming, *Encyclopedia of Textiles*, Frederick A. Praeger, Inc., 162).

The primary medallion can still be seen, but its borders have been "exploded" into a riot of vines and floral work. While the example shown above is French, this type of design was often manufactured in Venice and other parts of Italy and is occasionally referred to in modern parlance as a "Venetian" design. These brocade designs are still used today for some of the highest-quality vestments due to their superior level of quality, their metal thread content, and their complex coloration. Photos from the monasteries of Mount Athos frequently depict the most ascetic of monastics in these rich and heavy brocades worn for special feast days and important processions. One of the reasons these Venetian brocades have enjoyed such favor in Orthodox Christian usage is due to the fact that the Venetian silk industry followed the historic Byzantine designs more closely and for a much longer period of time than did other European centers of textile production.[xxv]

A consideration of the history of brocade design as it pertains to Orthodox Christian liturgical usage would not be complete without a mention of the quest for realism in art that began in the Renaissance, a search that was not limited solely to the art of painting, but also eventually influenced textile design as well as evinced by Figure 11. The realism portrayed in this brocade, with its lifelike fronds and lush, overblown flowers, is nearly photographic, and it is most likely due to the naturalistic aesthetic sensibility, so foreign to the Byzantine preference for symbols and multiple layers of meaning, that this type of brocade never became popular in Orthodox Christian vestment usage.

Figure 11. Satin brocade, Venice, early 18th century (Adele Weibel, *Two Thousand Years of Textiles*, Pantheon Books, Plate 255).

Ornamented brocades such as those we have examined were the predominant textiles used for historic Orthodox Christian vestments and continue to make up the largest category of textiles used today in Orthodox Christian churches; however, there is another textile design worthy of mention, the famous *polystavros* design depicted in icons such as the "Three Holy Hierarchs" in Figure 12. The *polystavros* was introduced into ecclesiastical use sometime in the eleventh or twelfth century. Its use was, at first, apparently restricted to patriarchs and metropolitans, but in time it came to be used by the episcopate in general and much later by presbyters and deacons.[xxvi]

Figure 12. Icon of the Three Holy Hierarchs (Hagiographer: Monk Michael, courtesy of Asperges & Co., www.asperges.com).

While the *polystavros* design can appear to the uninitiated as nothing more than a dizzying geometric puzzle of squares within squares, its design actually references the command given in Exodus 28.4 that the Old Testament high priest wear a tunic of "checkerwork" (i.e., a "net-like" design, LXX χιτῶνα κοσυμβωτόν), a reference that surely would not have been lost on the more educated citizens of Constantinople, steeped in knowledge of the Scriptures as they were. The *polystavros* is not only a design imbued with spiritual significance on account of the portrayal of so many crosses, it is also a continuation one of the most ancient weaving patterns known to mankind. Throughout the history of textiles, checkerwork designs, from the *polystavros* all the way back to the earliest-known textile fragments with their plaid-like designs, may be seen to be universal, appearing in nearly every ancient culture in one form or another. In true Eastern fashion, this imbues yet another layer of meaning, that of the Orthodox Christian priest being clothed in the ancient, universal garments of humanity.

Galloon

Virtually all Orthodox Christian liturgical garments (and most paraments) are finished with galloon, a metallic banding that is woven with patterns and colors designed to coordinate with the fabric it frames. Because galloon is necessary to finish the raw edges of the brocade and lining, it is integral to the proper finishing of vestments and forms an intrinsic part of the overall aesthetic of Orthodox Christian liturgical dress. A well-chosen galloon is harmonious with the brocade and, while some galloons have minimal motifs such as a monochrome, geometric pattern, others can be replete with a wide variety of symbols as is shown in Figure 13.

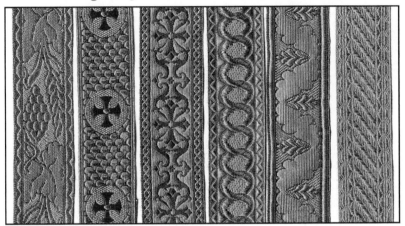

Figure 13. A sampling of galloons: the one on the far right is considered an "outline" galloon while the others are considered "contrast" galloons.

While the combinations of galloons and brocades can be almost endless, there tend to be two general aesthetic categories: those that simply *outline* the brocade in an aesthetically neutral fashion by "framing" the fabric (these galloons have simple geometric patterns such as diagonal lines or tiny checkerwork patterns), and those that *contrast* with the brocade either by their elaborate pattern or their contrasting color. The first category is fairly straightforward and would encompass such combinations as a red brocade finished with an all-gold geometric galloon (seen on the far right of Figure 13), but the second category is much broader and, for ultimate effect, should be selected by a tailor with a good knowledge of the available brocade designs and galloon symbols in order to achieve the desired contrast while still maintaining a harmonious whole. The small sampling of galloons in Figure 13 shows a variety of symbol patterns used in galloons—grapes and leaves, crosses in circles on a "net" of fish scales (an early Byzantine motif), interlocking crosses with miniscule knotwork borders (a border within a border), interlaced circles inside zigzag borders, a wavy leaf pattern alternating with floral sprays, and a simple diagonal geometric.

The importance of the proper galloon in finishing Orthodox Christian textiles cannot be overstated. Almost thirty yards of galloon are used on a set of priest's or deacon's vestments and this seemingly inconsequential finishing detail provides a large portion of the overall aesthetic effect of the finished vestments. Proper galloon selection truly "makes or breaks" a set of vestments. Suitably combining the pattern of a galloon with the overall design of a brocade requires a knowledge of available designs of each, an awareness of complementary symbol patterns (e.g., it would be jarring to pair an early-Byzantine, fish-scale galloon with a Venetian brocade), and expertise at mixing the various colors of brocades and galloons so that the final combination does not clash, but achieves the desired, harmonious blend.

When properly selected and applied, an intricate, symbolically rich galloon takes even a rather simple brocade and raises it to new heights. This distinctive feature of bordering Orthodox Christian vesture with another layer of symbols brings to mind the earliest types of decoration known to mankind and provides yet more evidence of the multi-faceted quality that is an essential element of Orthodox Christian adornment.

Liturgical Textile Symbols

Now that we have explored the overall design structure of the types of brocades used for Orthodox Christian liturgical purposes, it remains for us to discuss specific symbolic motifs used within such textiles. Textile symbols have been employed across a wide range of history and cultures, so the overview presented here represents only a portion of the myriad motifs used throughout the Church's history.

Knotwork

As seen above, knotwork and interlacing are used abundantly in liturgical textiles, outlining certain designs and providing the main decorative scheme of others. These are possibly the most ancient of all symbols and were first used in ancient Mesopotamian art. Through frequent use on textiles, the knot design motif spread rapidly through many cultures from Persia to ancient Greece and Rome, Egypt, and even as far afield as the Celts. Byzantine art features a profusion of beautiful interlacings which can be seen on everything from manuscripts and chalices to the borders of floor and ceiling mosaics. These complex arrangements of unending knots, cables, and ropes grace many textiles, lending fluidity, visual movement, and intricacy.

Cross

The cross, the quintessential symbol of Christendom, is so familiar and expected on liturgical textiles that one almost need not mention it. The cross is combined with virtually every other Christian symbol to create a vast number of designs. Crosses used in vestment fabrics range in style from very geometric, early Byzantine versions, to more augmented styles of the mid- to late-Byzantine periods, progressing to far more elaborate, Italianate varieties.

The power of the cross was, and still is, evoked to keep evil forces at bay and put the wearer or viewer ever in remembrance of the suffering of Christ. It is the symbol of redemption par excellence in that the implement of a humiliating and horrendous form of execution has been transformed by Christ's death and resurrection into the greatest sign of victory and triumph known to Christianity.

Monograms

As many manuscripts, stone carvings, and metal objects amply demonstrate, the Byzantines loved monograms and they used these symbolic arrangements of letters in textiles as well. A variety of Christological monograms have been used for many centuries such as the ChiRho (the first two letters of "Christ" in Greek), the Iota Chi (the first letters of "Jesus Christ"), the Alpha and Omega, and the "IC XC NIKA" ("Jesus Christ conquers") as well as various combinations of these such as the Iota Chi with the Alpha and Omega or the Chi Rho with the Alpha and Omega.

Figure 14. Stone carving designs from Sant' Appolinare in Ravenna, Italy with monogram designs (Arne Dehli, *Treasury of Byzantine Ornament: 255 Motifs from St. Mark's and Ravenna*, Dover Publications, 77).

Monograms provide literary overtones to a brocade design and are often worked in rather ingenuous ways, sprouting from urns of flowers, forming the center design of the meeting point of borders, and even serving as the central medallion in some roundel designs.

Figure 15. Polyester brocade, Greece, 2012, showing close-up of woven monogram.

Floral Designs—Carnations, Palmettes, Roses/Hearts, Lilies, Trees, Lotus, etc.

Intermixed with all of the above symbols and forming a consistent backdrop to them is an amazing array of various floral patterns. Floral designs have their origins in the abundance symbols of the ancient world but have taken on deeper, more spiritual significance with their incorporation into Orthodox Christian liturgical textiles. Flower designs such as the carnation, palmette, roses (occasionally referred to as hearts—see below), laurels, acanthus leaves, lilies, and even trees, have all been featured to bring to mind the flowering of Christianity, the abundance of God's mercy, and the natural beauty of the world as a foreshadowing of the surpassing beauty of Heaven. These elements bring to mind Paradise and man's communion with God before the Fall, how the Mother of God is the "flower of humanity," and how our spirits blossom in the light of God's loving grace. It was inevitable that floral patterns, capable of bearing so much symbolic freight, should take a prominent place among the venerable symbols of the Church. A distinctive feature of the Orthodox Christian aesthetic tradition is its ability to embrace floral patterns from various cultures and locales and harmoniously interweave them. It is not uncommon to see a laurel leaf border, the pre-eminent sign of victory in ancient Rome, side-by-side with the palmette spray of ancient Egypt or the rose favored in Byzantium. Traditional Orthodox Christian culture has never been uncomfortable with mixing disparate elements into a harmonious whole.

The rose motif is one of the most fascinating of floral patterns with an interesting debate surrounding its proper identification. This motif is best seen in Figure 6 in the primary medallion: in the floral sprays that fill the quatrefoil medallion, the roses are the portion of the flower that is cupped between the two leaves (these four floral sprays when taken together form the arms of a floral "cross"). The base portion of this flower looks very similar to the heart motif that is found on an ordinary pack of playing cards. While Byzantine art scholar, O. M. Dalton in his classic tome *Byzantine Art and Archaeology* propounds that such floral motifs originated from the top of the palmette,[xxvii] another scholar of design,

W.R. Lethaby, the first Professor of Design at the Royal College of Art in London, gives an alternate explanation of the origin of this motif:

> The roses in this kind of border have been called hearts, or degraded palmettes, but if several examples are compared it becomes plain that they are really roses. . . . The roses in profile are represented like a single heart-shaped petal, but the leaves, the colour, and the association with the full roses make the intention certain. These rose patterns are specially characteristic of late Hellenistic and early Coptic art.[xxviii]

Whether deriving from a palmette top or the roses that most likely grew abundantly in the warm, Mediterranean climate, the rose motif is frequently used due to its great adaptability and strong line. In some instances it is used without any surrounding leaves, and then it becomes another type of geometric border.

Intertwining and filling many textile designs are the acanthus leaf and the palmette. Their basic shape can be seen in Figures 16 and 17:

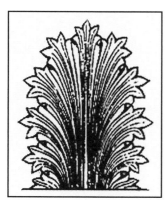

Figure 16. Acanthus leaf (Arne Dehli, *Treasury of Byzantine Ornament: 255 Motifs from St. Mark's and Ravenna*, Dover Publications, 48).

Figure 17. Palmette (Natascha Kubisch and Pia Anna Seger, *Ornaments: Patterns for Interior Decoration*, Konemann, 49).

These remarkably flexible motifs are lavishly used in textile designs across many cultures and artistic periods. As can be viewed in the above figures, there is similarity of overall structure between these two motifs and Dalton asserts that, "the acanthus developed out of the palmette, the palmette being first 'acanthized' and the complete acanthus following later...."[xxix] Because the acanthus and palmette form the backdrop of so many textiles, their presence is easy to miss, but when one scrutinizes various liturgical textiles, their vining patterns can be frequently seen, as is the case in Figure 6 which displays a tiny acanthus leaf pattern inside the border of the quatrefoil medallion. Both of these designs became the stuff of high art when utilized by the ever-creative Byzantines, as the manuscript borders of Figures 18 and 19 show. Due to their continual presence in liturgical textiles, it is understood that the acanthus and palmette must have been one of the most common of "cross-over" motifs amongst the variety of the Byzantine arts.

Figure 18. Acanthus leaf border (T. Vaboulis, *Byzantine Decorative Art*, Papadimitriou Publications, 66).

Figure 19. Byzantine manuscript with confronted palmette motif (T. Vaboulis, *Byzantine Decorative Art*, Papadimitriou Publications, 58).

Similar to these vining leaves and flowers, trees and other plants were commonly used in textile design. While sometimes ascribed to a Persian origin, this type of motif is often found on Coptic linens embellished with tapestry-weaving, and silks of the early Christian period.[xxx]

Birds and Animals

While bird and animal motifs had their origin in the abundance symbols of the ancient world, they came to be highly prized symbols, not only showcasing the weaver's skill but anchoring a design by their complexity and visual interest. Yet such symbols were not purely decorative fillers. For instance, the pelican that is often used in Orthodox Christian liturgical designs carried strong Christological and Eucharistic associations due to the wide-spread belief (attributed to Aristotle) that the mother pelican pierces her own breast to draw blood with which to feed her young.

Birds, with their gift of flight, were associated with the heavenly realm and frequently used as symbols of Paradise. This explains why it is common to see liturgical designs featuring an urn or fountain with confronted birds. Peacocks, with their remarkable coloring, were a favored symbol of immortality. The stonecarving in Figure 14 shows an elegant use of confronted peacocks on either side of a ChiRho and Alpha and Omega monogram, a complex, but utterly sublime mixture of the various motifs used within the Orthodox Christian Church.

The use of bird motifs in liturgical brocades today tends to be limited to either the lightweight, machine-embroidered type of vestments (which can feature peacocks or pelicans in roundels alternating with cross motifs as well as an arrangement very similar to the peacocks in Figure 14, confronted on either side of a cross) or a very small handful of metallic brocades based upon early Byzantine roundel designs which feature either peacocks or pelicans in the roundel.

Vegetative Motifs

While vegetative symbols might most precisely be encompassed within the category of floral motifs, there are some distinctive symbols contained within this cornucopia. The pineapple, often situated in an urn, was an ancient symbol of hospitality, so its adaptation as a Christian symbol is easy to understand. Urns were an essential decorative element of Classical art and, because of this pedigree, were a treasured element within the canon of Byzantine symbols as well.

The ultimate vegetative design within Christianity is the grapevine. Winding its beautiful way through stunning textiles, golden chalices, intricate jewelry, glimmering mosaics, and virtually all types of art made in Byzantium and every Christian country and culture since, the grapevine is second only to the cross and abounds with a multiplicity of symbological associations.

First and foremost, the grapevine symbolizes the Holy Mysteries and the transformation of wine into the Blood of Christ. Still other meanings are found within the Scriptures. In the Gospel of John (15.5) Christ tells his disciples, "I am the vine, you are the branches. He who abides in Me, and I in him, bears much fruit; for without Me you can do nothing." Christ's words serve as a reminder not only of man's place in the universe, a branch dependant on the loving mercy of Christ the vine, but also as an admonition that in the Christian life we are called to bear spiritual fruit, as described in St Paul's Epistle to the Galatians (5.22–23): "But the fruit of the Spirit is love, joy, peace, longsuffering, kindness, goodness, faithfulness, gentleness, self-control." The grapevine is arguably the most multifaceted of Christian symbols, both in its symbological connotations and in its ornamental representations. In this capacity it also serves as the premier visual expression of the concept of multi-layered symbology found within the aesthetic tradition of the Orthodox Christian Church.

The Legacy of Orthodox Christian Textiles

While many historic brocade designs and textile symbols have continued in use from the fall of Constantinople to the present day, the collapse of the great center of silk and dye manufacturing has had lasting repercussions on the availability of textiles for use within the Orthodox Christian Church and has left the Church somewhat open to various Western aesthetic influences.

Happily though, the great legacy of Orthodox Christian textile art has prevailed and it is delightful to see the wide variety of textiles and symbols that still flourish in Orthodox churches today. This continuity seems rather improbable, given the complete collapse of silk manufacturing following the fall of Constantinople, but a passage from the *Cambridge Medieval History of Byzantium* provides illumination:

> It is somewhat surprising to see that Byzantium was still capable of inspiring an artistic movement destined to exert a lasting influence among peoples so different, and in the face of the rapid progress of western experiments in art. This success is no doubt partly accounted for by the large numbers of craftsmen in the great city on the Bosphorus, unrivalled by those of any other town or region of eastern Europe at that time. But the main reason is to be found in its position as the Centre of Orthodoxy which it always retained; this gave it a prestige which was reflected in all it produced, especially in its religious art. The great work of the Palaeologian period [AD 1259 to 1453] is almost exclusively ecclesiastical, and for this reason, quite apart from any aesthetic considerations, it was welcomed with open arms in all countries looking to Constantinople as the

capital of their faith. Yet it was not a uniform art which thus radiated outwards from Byzantium: it was continually subjected to local influences and acquired in varying degrees a specialized and localized character. Thus, in the thirteenth century the development of autonomous schools began, not only in Serbia and Bulgaria but also at Mistra and perhaps in Macedonia, that is to say in both Slav and Greek countries. The capitals of little principalities and the palaces of their rulers, of differing races but united by their Orthodox faith, became for a time centres of a flourishing religious art which, within the general Palaeologian framework, showed distinct variations—local dialects rather than separate languages. This regrouping of creative artistic forces widened the Byzantine outlook in a way unknown in the previous period.[xxxi]

The liturgical textile traditions of the Orthodox Christian Church are alive and well as can be seen in the small sampling of brocades in current use as seen in Figures 20 through 23 and the remarkable continuum of both designs and symbols as well as their affinity with the ancient brocades:

Figure 20 Polyester brocade, Greece, "Ravenna" design.

Figure 21 Polyester brocade, Greece, "Alexandria" design.

Figure 22 Polyester brocade, Greece, "Paschal" design.

Figure 23 Metallic brocade, Greece, "Jerusalem" design.

Such continuity, an artistic chain forged for the glory of God and unbroken for two millennia, is a cause for great rejoicing. Just as in Constantinople so long ago, it continues to be true that we Orthodox Christians "are what we wear" and we are thus justified in treasuring and revering our liturgical vestments and textiles as our true garments of salvation. May we continue to reap the glorious spiritual fruits of this heavenly heritage!

Endnotes

i. Eleni Vlachopoulou-Karabina, *Holy Monastery of Iveron Gold Embroideries* (Mount Athos: Holy Monastery of Iveron, 1998), 9.

ii. Gervase Mathew, *Byzantine Aesthetics* (London: John Murray, 1963), 11.

iii. Mathew, 87.

iv. Adele Weibel, *Two Thousand Years of Textiles* (New York NY: Pantheon Books, 1952), 16.

v. Pauline Johnstone, *Byzantine Tradition in Church Embroidery* (London: Alec Tiranti, 1967), 10.

vi. G. A. Farber, *Notes on Dyeing and Tanning in Classical Antiquity* (CIBA Review 1937), 296.

vii. Janet Mayo, *A History of Ecclesiastical Dress* (London: Batsford, 1984), 15.

viii. Farber, 297.

ix. Weibel, 5.

x. Robert Sabatino Lopez, "Silk Industry in the Byzantine Empire," *Speculum*, Vol. 20, No. 1 (January 1945): 20.

xi. David Jacoby, "Silk Economics and Cross-Cultural Artistic Interaction: Byzantium, the Muslin World, and the Christian West," *Dumbarton Oaks Papers*, Vol. 58 (2004): 215.

xii. Lopez, 1.

xiii. Lopez, 4.

xiv. Lopez, 5.

xv. Lopez, 22.

xvi. Lopez, 8-9.

xvii. Lopez, 41.

xviii. Jacoby, 228.

xix. Jacoby, 229.

xx. Slobodan Curcic, ed. *Architecture as Icon: Perception and Representation of Architecture in Byzantine Art,* exhibition catalog (New Haven, CT: Yale University Press, 2010), 7.

xxi. Mathew, 1.

xxii. Henry Maguire, "Garments Pleasing to God: The Significance of Domestic Textile Designs in the Early Byzantine Period," *Dumbarton Oaks Papers*, Vol. 44 (1990): 216.

xxiii. Jacoby, 222.

xxiv. Anna Gonosova, "The Formation and Sources of Early Byzantine Floral Semis and Floral Diaper Patterns Reexamined," *Dumbarton Oaks Papers*, Vol. 41 (1987): 230.

xxv. Jacoby, 230.

xxvi. Warren Woodfin, "On Late Byzantine Liturgical Vestments and the Iconography of Sacerdotal Power," doctoral dissertation (Urbana, IL: University of Illinois at Urbana-Champaign, 1999), 226–8.

xxvii. O. M. Dalton, *Byzantine Art and Archaeology* (Mineola, NY: Dover Publications), 690.

xxviii. W.R. Lethaby, "Byzantine Silks in London Museums," *The Burlington Magazine for Connoisseurs*, Vol. 24, No. 129 (1913): 143.

xxix. Dalton, 688–9.

xxx. Lethaby, 146.

xxxi. J.M. Hussey, ed., *The Cambridge Medieval History, Vol. IV: The Byzantine Empire, Part II: Government, Church and Civilisation* (Cambridge, MA: Cambridge University Press, 1967), 348.

Afterword

While we do see a truly remarkable historical continuum in the vestments and paraments of the Orthodox Christian Church, along with the textiles and symbols used for their manufacture and adornment, as a professional ecclesiastical tailor, I believe that we stand at a crossroads in the aesthetic history of the Orthodox Christian Church. This belief is rooted in the almost twenty years I have spent working with deacons, priests, bishops, and laity throughout North America. During this time, I have witnessed a promising shift toward the use of more traditional brocade designs and colors as well as a desire on the part of both the laity and the clergy to become more educated about our glorious vestment tradition. Giving lectures at the various Orthodox seminaries as well as some parish settings brings me great joy as I see the faithful hearken after the historic "look" of the Church, even if they are initially ignorant about how to achieve the particulars.

Yet, despite these happy occurrences which make my work such a blessing, I still deal with such frustrating situations as a parish community that has spent millions in building a new church only to request the least expensive fabrics or galloons to outfit their altar ("whatever you have that's cheap" is the common request), or the church school coordinator who calls me wanting samples of the "six liturgical colors," or the photos I see that depict a church with astounding iconography on an elaborately carved iconostasis only to show the priest in the poorest-quality vestments made from Western textile designs.

I take heart from the resurgent interest in traditional Orthodox Christian textiles and vestments, but at the same time I am gravely aware that if this interest does not become a universal return to the reverence for vestments and altar furnishings previous generations knew and valued, we are in danger of losing this precious legacy.

By far and away, the most pernicious influence on our vestment tradition today is the creeping assumption that vestments just aren't that important. Churches spend millions on architecture and iconography and yet I can count on one hand the number of communities I have worked with who have beautification committees devoted to the adornment of the church through vestments and altar furnishings.

Meanwhile, we have reached an all-time historical low in the casualness of our daily secular dress and this change in popular culture, in which a woman can be considered at the height of fashion by wearing the right brand of jeans to church, has negatively influenced not only our society, but more to the point, our liturgical traditions. When I began as a tailor, it was the norm for priests to wear some kind of collared shirt underneath their cassocks; after all, most professional men were still wearing shirts, ties, and jackets. But over the last two decades, I have witnessed a shockingly swift change in expectations of professional dress, including that of the clergy (needless to say, I am not a fan of "Casual Fridays"). Now, I struggle to educate my clientele that their cassock really will fit better and look more seemly if they wear a collared shirt underneath, but I know that I have failed once again when I hear the oft-repeated phrase "Oh, I'll just wear a T-shirt underneath"; after all, a growing number of my clientele has never even owned a collared shirt.

In an age where more formal dress was expected and respected, people knew their textiles. A man knew how to buy a good-quality wool suit and a woman knew the difference between rayon and real silk. Clothes were designed to last and fashions changed at a much slower pace. While a parish then might not have been able to afford a hand-embroidered, real metal thread epitaphios, they knew that it was higher-quality, and therefore, *better*, than the machine-embroidered version their budget necessitated they purchase.

Along with the move towards more casual dress has come the advent of lightning-fast changes in the secular fashion industry and a "throwaway" clothing culture has emerged, virtually gutting the supply of high-quality fabrics available to the small workshop that produces Orthodox Christian vestments. Interfacings are just one small example of this phenomenon—most are now designed with a maximum two-year intended lifespan, which means that when they are used in liturgical vestments they will begin to disintegrate in just twelve months, drastically shortening the lifespan of the vestments and causing unnecessary waste and expense.

But of far more dire consequence to the Church's liturgical garment tradition is the absurdly high value the secular fashion scene places on appearance over substance. As long as it looks OK, it is OK, the thinking goes and the resulting theory that quality no longer matters has been the single most discouraging assumption I have encountered in my time as a church tailor. All too often, I see clergy and laity approach the procurement of vestments and paraments in the same manner they would purchase their own clothes at the local discount store and this proves to be quite problematic, both practically and spiritually. In the first case, it results in poor-quality items that degrade far too quickly, and in the second, it puts adorning the Church, the very Kingdom of Heaven on earth in which the angels and saints are present, on a par with buying a sweatshirt. The caricatures of vestments so obtained, looking like a loan from the wardrobe department of an epic movie of the 1960s, lead to poor liturgizing and a lost opportunity for making Paradise real to each soul that walks through the doors of the church.

Cheap clothes we have everywhere, the Kingdom of heaven we do not.

And, so while an overview of historical textiles and liturgical garments is supremely edifying—after all, our priests still wear the same liturgical garments that St John Chrysostom or St John of Damascus did—we must labor untiringly to preserve this tradition and protect it from the weak fiber of the modern world in which we live. To do so is a holy work and one that brings great blessing, as I can personally attest. As the priest says at the end of every Divine Liturgy "Sanctify those who love the beauty of Your house."

May it be blessed!

Khouria Krista West

Appendix A

Care and Laundering of Orthodox Liturgical Vestments and Paraments[1]

Proper Cleaning of Vestments and Paraments

In general or when in doubt, all vestments should be dry-cleaned. This includes deacons', priests', and bishops' vestments as well as altar servers' robes and all paraments (altar cloths and fabric hangings). However, some vestments are machine-washable (e.g., "woven" vestments and pre-washed poly-cotton poplin priests' sticharia) and in these cases the items should be washed with cold water on the delicate or hand-wash cycle and then hung to dry (never put in a heated dryer). The best care for washable vestments is to wash them by hand in a large tub with cool water and a soap-based cleanser rather than a detergent. Detergent is harsher on fabrics and will cause dye bleeding, making the vestments degrade faster over time. Vestments that are dry-cleaned should never be stored in the dry-cleaner's plastic wraps as the off-gassing of the plastic can cause the brocade to discolor.

Vestments that are worn frequently, such as bright vestments used nearly every Sunday, should be cleaned once or twice a year; vestments used less frequently can be cleaned every year or two. Altar cloths require only infrequent dry-cleaning—once every three or four years usually suffices—though they should

---

1. These instructions apply only to modern vestments in current use. The care of antique and historic vestments should always be entrusted to a conservation expert.

be brushed regularly (a brass-bristle tailor's brush works best) to remove dust.

Cleaning Velvet

To clean velvet on a regular basis, simply use a lint roller to pick up dust or debris or a soft brush and a vacuum. Dry-clean periodically as needed.

Removing Wax on Vestments

Lay the stained area out on an ironing board. Place a paper towel under the wax stain and a paper towel on top of the wax stain, "sandwiching" the stain. Using a warm iron without steam, gently rub the tip of the iron back and forth over the stain. The paper towel will begin to absorb the wax. Reposition the paper towel frequently until it is no longer absorbing wax. Have item dry-cleaned as soon as possible to remove the residue from the wax stain. This technique can also be used on *zostika* and *exorasa*.

Proper Care of Communion Cloths

Note that only a priest or deacon is permitted to handle and launder used communion cloths. Place a mesh laundry bag in the sacristy where it will receive plenty of air circulation (it can be mounted on the wall with cup hooks). After the use of a communion cloth, place it unfolded in the mesh bag until the time of laundering. This prevents the consecrated wine from permanently staining the fabric. Wash the cloths by hand and make sure all water used is reverently drained into the ground (not a sewer). For communion cloths that are already badly stained, first rinse in the proper manner, then soak the cloths in a solution of one gallon of warm water mixed with one cup of non-chlorine bleach powder (Biz brand works well) for up to three days. Proceed to launder the cloths as usual.

Rotating Vestments

One of the best ways to prolong the life of vestments is to regularly rotate them. This means using several different sets of bright vestments for Sundays so that a single set is not used excessively. This might, for instance, mean wearing a blue or green set occasionally for Sunday use in order to give a heavily used gold/white set a rest. It might also mean budgeting for a second bright/every-Sunday set before acquiring additional colors of vestments.

Storage of Vestments and Paraments

The proper storage of vestments and paraments is as important as their proper cleaning in order to ensure maximum longevity.

Vestments that are in frequent use can be hung on wide hangers (either large hangers designed for suits or wide, padded hangers) in the church sacristy. Vestments used infrequently should be folded in the "off-season" and stored on hangers only when in use (e.g., dark vestments for Great Lent can be folded for most of the year, then hung on hangers during Great Lent). The reason for folding vestments used infrequently is that the brocade and lining fabrics will stretch slightly over time, although not necessarily at the same rate, which means a vestment such as a phelonion or deacon's sticharion hung on a hanger without being regularly worn may eventually have its lining stretch enough to fall below the brocade. This situation is mitigated in the case of vestments frequently worn because regular wear allows the fabrics to be shaped by the body and keeps the brocade and lining in better overall alignment over time.

Paraments should be either stored on hangers or folded and kept in drawers.

Pest Protection

It is wise to keep some kind of pest protection in the same space where the vestments and paraments are stored. The best option is muslin bags containing cedar chips, herbal mixes, or lavender. Note that most pests that destroy fabric actually feed on the perspiration, dirt and debris in the fabric, not the fabric itself, so regular cleaning is the best way to insure that vestment pieces remain pest-free.

Storing *Epitaphoi*

Since the *epitaphios* is used only during Holy Week and the Paschal season, it is imperative that it be stored in an appropriate manner, both to show due reverence and ensure maximum longevity. If an *epitaphios* is to be hung it must have a very sturdy casing sewn to the back along the entire top length. It can then be either hung on a dowel or drapery rod, or stored in a shadow-box-type frame. If the piece is hung on display throughout the year, care should be taken that the weight of the piece is evenly distributed along the top edge (hooks should not be used solely at the corners). It is traditional to hang the *epitaphios* on the west wall of the nave above the main doors.

Long-Term Storage of Vestments

For vestments that need to be stored long-term, choose acid-free boxes and store in a well-ventilated, dry area using acid-free tissue paper inside the garments. Do not store in cedar chests, wood boxes, or non-acid-free boxes (such as a regular cardboard box) as some woods and wood fibers can off-gas VOCs (volatile organic compounds) into their environment which will weaken fabric fibers over time, damaging the dyes, fibers, and metal threads.

Insuring Vestments

It is important to verify that vestments and paraments are covered under the parish's insurance policy at their full replacement value. A special rider may need to be included on the policy. It is best to take photographs as well. Insurance agents can provide further details.

Proper Cleaning and Care of Cassocks

Cassocks should to be cleaned according to their fiber content. Most polyester fabrics, hemp, and poly-cotton blends can be machine-washed, but wool, wool blends, and silks need to be dry-cleaned.

To machine-wash a cassock, use cold or cool water and the delicate or hand-wash cycle and wash the garment by itself (not with other laundry). Hang dry for maximum longevity and to avoid shrinkage. For the initial wash after purchasing the garment, add one cup of white vinegar without soap to the wash to help set the dye. If needed, a low-heat iron can be used to put the pressed creases in the sleeves and along the center back, but it is best to test the iron on an inside portion of the hem to make sure the fabric can tolerate the heat. A cassock may also be hand-washed in a large tub or sink.

For cassocks that are dry-cleaned, instruct the dry-cleaner to put in pressed creases in the sleeves (pressed inside-out) and along the center back from collar to hem (pressed right side out); these creases help facilitate proper folding of the garments.

The required frequency of cassock cleaning will vary significantly, depending on how often the garment is worn and what fiber it is made from. Wool and hemp are naturally anti-bacterial and will not retain odors; polyester and polyester-blends are not and so may need to be cleaned more frequently.

To Remove Dirt from *Exorasa* Hems

Frequently after the committal at a cemetery, there will be mud or dirt stains on the hem of an *exorason*. Hang the garment for a day until the dirt has fully dried, then take a stiff brush (preferably a brass-bristle tailor's brush) and brush off as much dirt as possible. Following this treatment, have the garment dry-cleaned.

Disposal of Vestments

When vestments or paraments have reached the end of their life, they must be disposed of by either being buried (less desirable) or burned. Because many newer vestments contain synthetic materials, burning should always take place out of doors, never in an enclosed space. Typically, a set of vestments can be burned until only ashes and metal parts such as buttons and cuffs remain; these ashes may then be buried.

Cassocks may be disposed of in the same manner.

Appendix B

Liturgical Color Guidelines

This Liturgical Color Guide was originally compiled by His Grace, Bishop Basil, and is used with his permission. I have adapted his original and made note of specific color usages as they are commonly employed within the various Orthodox Christian jurisdictions of North America.

Color According to Liturgical Date

Date	Bright/Dark	Specific Color*
Sept 1, Indiction of the Liturgical Year	Bright	Gold**
Sept 2-7	Bright	***
Sept 8-12, Nativity of Theotokos through Leavetaking (TL)	Bright	Blue, Gold
Sept 13, Dedication of the Church of the Resurrection	Bright	Gold
Sept 14-21, Elevation of the Cross TL	Dark	Burgundy, Red
Sept 22-Nov 14	Bright	***
Nov 15-20, Nativity Fast	Dark	Burgundy, Red
Nov 21-25, Presentation of the Theotokos TL	Bright	Blue, Gold
Nov 26-Dec 24, Nativity Fast	Dark	Burgundy, Red
Dec 25-Jan 5, Nativity of the Lord	Bright	Gold, Red, White
Jan 6-14, Theophany TL	Bright	Gold, Blue, White
Jan 15-Feb 1	Bright	***
Feb 2-9, Meeting of the Lord in the Temple TL	Bright	Blue, Gold
Feb 10 through Cheesefare Sunday	Bright	***
Mar 25, Annunciation	Bright	Blue, Gold

Date	Bright/Dark	Specific Color*
Great Fast and the Great and Holy Week		
Forgiveness Vespers	Bright	Gold
Changed during Prokeimenon to	Dark	Purple, Burgundy, Black
Weekdays of the Great Fast	Dark	Purple, Burgundy, Black
Little Compline with Akathist Hymn	Bright	Blue, Gold
Saturdays and Sundays	Bright	Gold, Bright Purple
Some use	Dark	Purple
Sunday of the Cross and the week following	Dark	Red, Burgundy
Some use	Dark	Purple
Saturday of the Akathist Hymn	Bright	Blue, Gold
Lazarus Saturday and Palm Sunday	Bright	Gold, Green, Red
Palm Sunday pm through Wednesday pm	Dark	Black, Purple, Burgundy
Great Thursday Vesperal Divine Liturgy	Dark	Red, Burgundy
Great Thursday pm through Friday pm	Dark	Black, Purple, Burgundy
Great Saturday Vesperal Divine Liturgy	Dark	Black, Purple, Burgundy
Changed during "Arise, O God" to	Bright	White, Gold
Great & Holy Pascha Resurrection Service	Bright	White, Gold, Red
Paschaltide (Agape Vespers through 40 days of Pascha)	Bright	White, Gold, Red
Pentecost through Jun 28	Bright	Green, Gold, White
Jun 29-30 (Ss Peter and Paul)	Dark	Burgundy, Red
Jul 1-31	Bright	Green, Gold
Aug 1-15, Dormition Fast	Dark	Blue, Burgundy
Aug 6, Transfiguration of the Lord	Bright	Gold, White
Aug 7-12, Dormition Fast	Dark	Blue, Burgundy
Aug 13, Leavetaking of Transfiguration	Bright	Gold, White
Aug 14, Dormition Fast	Dark	Blue, Burgundy
Aug 15-23, Dormition TL	Bright	Blue, Gold
Aug 24-28	Bright	***

Date	Bright/Dark	Specific Color*
Aug 29, Beheading of the Forerunner	Dark	Burgundy, Red
Aug 30-31	Bright	***

In addition to categorizing color by specific liturgical date, color usage may also be organized by either the general category of feast or season as follows:

Color According to Category of Commemoration

Date	Bright/Dark
Feasts of the Lord	Bright
Feasts of the Theotokos	Bright
Commemorations of the Cross	Dark
Commemorations of the Forerunner, Apostles & Martyrs	Dark
Commemorations of other Saints & Events	Bright

Color According to Season

Date	Bright/Dark
Pascha through the Saturday before Pentecost	Bright
Pentecost through Jul 31	Bright
Aug 1-23	Dark and Bright (see above)
Aug 24 through Nov 14	Bright
Nov 15 through Dec 24	Dark
Dec 25 through Jan 14	Bright
Jan 15 through Cheesefare Sunday	Bright
The Great Fast	Dark
Great and Holy Week	Dark

*Please note that these color recommendations, while based upon widely accepted usage, are not necessarily utilized by the entire Orthodox Christian community worldwide. As explained in Chapter 5, there is a great variety of color usage within the Church that is an accepted and laudable aspect of liturgical practice.

**A note about gold: It is a common misperception that when rubrics state "gold," the brocade used must be entirely gold, without admixture of any other color. This, however, is not the case in practice within the Orthodox Christian Church. "Gold" can mean any of the following color combinations: gold with white, white with gold, gold with red, gold with white and red, gold with white and other accent color (such as when a white/gold/blue brocade is used on general Sundays in a church dedicated to the Theotokos or when a white/gold/green brocade is used on general Sundays in a church dedicated to the Holy Spirit) or any multi-colored or floral brocade. For further information please see Chapter Five.

***As was explained in Chapter Five, specific colors within the "bright" category may include, but are not limited to: pure white; white with gold accents; gold with white accents; gold on gold; white with gold and red accents; gold with red accents; ivory with gold and burgundy embroidery; ivory with blue, green, and gold embroidery; white with gold and silver embroidery; multi-colored brocades with gold, silver, blue, green, coral, gold, and burgundy; white with silver accents; ivory or white with gold, green, and burgundy embroidery; blue with silver; blue with gold; white with blue; green with silver or gold; and white with green.

Appendix C

Vesting Prayers[i]

Of the Deacon

The deacon brings his sticharion, orarion and epimanikia to the priest. Facing east, the deacon makes three metanias, saying each time:

Deacon: O God, be gracious unto me the sinner.

He then says to the priest:

Deacon: Bless, master, the sticharion with the orarion.

The priest blesses them, saying:

Priest: Blessed is our God, always, now and ever, and unto ages of ages.

The deacon kisses the right hand of the priest and says Amen. The deacon then kisses the sticharion and puts it on, saying:

Deacon: Let us pray to the Lord. Lord, have mercy.

My soul shall rejoice in the Lord, for he hath clothed me with the garment of salvation, and with the robe of gladness hath he encompassed me. As a bridegroom he hath set a crown upon me, and as a bride hath he adorned me with ornament, always, now and ever, and unto ages of ages. Amen.

While kissing the orarion and putting it on his left shoulder, he may say:

Deacon: Holy, holy, holy, Lord of Sabaoth; heaven and earth are full of thy glory.

Kissing the right epimanikion, he puts it on, saying:

Deacon: Let us pray to the Lord. Lord have mercy.

Thy right hand, O Lord, is glorified in strength; they right hand, O Lord, hath shattered thine enemies, and in the multitude of thy glory hast thou crushed thine adversaries, always, now and ever, and unto ages of ages. Amen.

Kissing the left epimanikion, he puts it on, saying:

Deacon: Let us pray to the Lord. Lord, have mercy.

Thy hands have made and fashioned me; give me understanding and I will learn thy commandments, always, now and ever, and unto ages of ages. Amen.

The deacon then proceeds to the prosthesis and prepares the chalice, diskos, star, spear, cruets of water and wine, the prosphora, the aer, the chalice and diskos covers and the censer for the Proskomedia. After all has been prepared, the deacon joins the priest to wash their hands while the priest says, "I will wash my hands in innocence. . . ."

Of the Priest

Taking his sticharion in his left hand, the priest makes three metanias toward the east, saying each time:

Priest: O God, be gracious unto me the sinner.

Then he blesses the sticharion with his right hand and kisses it, saying:

Priest: Blessed is our God, always, now and ever, and unto ages of ages. Amen.

Putting it on, he says:

Priest: Let us pray to the Lord. Lord, have mercy.

My soul shall rejoice in the Lord, for he hath clothed me with the garment of salvation, and with the robe of gladness hath he encompassed me. As a bridegroom he hath set a crown upon me, and as a bride hath he adorned me with ornament, always, now and ever, and unto ages of ages. Amen.

Blessing the epitrachelion and kissing it, he puts it on, saying:

Priest: Let us pray to the Lord. Lord, have mercy.

Blessed is God, who poureth out his grace upon his priests, as oil of myrrh upon the head, which runneth down upon the beard, upon the beard of Aaron, which runneth down to the fringe of his raiment, always, now and ever, and unto ages of ages. Amen.

Blessing the zone and kissing it, he puts it on, saying:

Priest: Let us pray to the Lord. Lord, have mercy.

Blessed is God, who girdeth me with power and hath made my path blameless, always, now and ever, and unto ages of ages. Amen.

Kissing the right epimanikion, he puts it on, saying:

Priest: Let us pray to the Lord. Lord have mercy.

Thy right hand, O Lord, is glorified in strength; they right hand, O Lord, hath shattered thine enemies, and in the multitude of thy glory hast thou crushed thine adversaries, always, now and ever, and unto ages of ages. Amen.

Kissing the left epimanikion, he puts it on, saying:

Priest: Let us pray to the Lord. Lord, have mercy.

Thy hands have made and fashioned me; give me understanding and I will learn thy commandments, always, now and ever, and unto ages of ages. Amen.

If he has the dignity of the epigonation, he blesses and kisses it, and puts it on, saying:

Priest: Let us pray to the Lord. Lord, have mercy.

Gird thy sword upon thy thigh, O Mighty One, in they comeliness and thy beauty, and proceed prosperously, and be king because of truth and meekness and righteousness; and thy right hand shall guide thee wondrously, always, now and ever, and unto ages of ages. Amen.

Taking the phelonion, the priest blesses it (if there is an icon of Christ on the back of the phelonion, the priest does not bless it but simply kisses it), and puts it on, saying:

Priest: Let us pray to the Lord. Lord, have mercy.

Thy priests, O Lord, shall be clothed with righteousness, and thy holy ones shall rejoice with joy, always, now and ever, and unto ages of ages. Amen.

If he has the dignity of the pectoral cross, he kisses it and puts it on, saying:

Priest: Let us pray to the Lord. Lord, have mercy.

Whosoever will come after me, let him deny himself and take up his cross and follow me, always, now and ever, and unto ages of ages. Amen.

Before performing the Proskomedia the priest, joined by the deacon, washes his hands, saying:

Priest: I will wash my hands in innocence and I will compass thine altar, O Lord, that I may hear the voice of thy praise and tell of all thy wondrous works. O Lord, I have loved the beauty of thy house, and the place where thy glory dwelleth. Destroy not my soul with the ungodly, nor my life with the men of blood, in whose hands are iniquities; their right hand is full of bribes. But as for me, in mine innocence have I walked; redeem me, O Lord, and have mercy on me. My foot hath stood in uprightness; in the congregations will I will bless thee, O Lord.

The priest then proceeds to the prosthesis, where all has been made ready by the deacon.

Of the Bishop

Taking the sticharion, the first deacon says to the bishop:

1st Deacon: Bless, master, the holy sticharion. Let us pray to the Lord. Lord, have mercy.

The bishop blesses the sticharion and kisses it, as the deacons put it on him, saying:

1st Deacon: Thy soul shall rejoice in the Lord, for he hath clothed thee with the garment of salvation, and with the robe of gladness hath he encompassed thee. As a bridegroom he hath set a crown upon thee, and as a bride hath he adorned thee with ornament.

2nd Deacon: Always, now and ever, and unto ages of ages. Amen.

Taking the epitrachelion, the first deacon says to the bishop:

1st Deacon: Bless, master, the holy epitrachelion. Let us pray to the Lord. Lord, have mercy.

The bishop blesses the epitrachelion and kisses it, as the deacon puts it on him saying:

1st Deacon: Blessed is God, who poureth out his grace upon his high priests, as oil of myrrh upon the head,

	which runneth down upon the beard, upon the beard of Aaron, which runneth down to the fringe of his raiment.
2ⁿᵈ Deacon:	Always, now and ever, and unto ages of ages. Amen.

Taking the zone, the first deacon says to the bishop:

1ˢᵗ Deacon:	Bless, master, the holy zone. Let us pray to the Lord. Lord, have mercy.

The bishop blesses the zone and kisses it, as the deacons put it on him, saying:

1ˢᵗ Deacon:	Blessed is God, who girdeth thee with power and hath made thy path blameless.
2ⁿᵈ Deacon:	Always, now and ever, and unto ages of ages. Amen.

Taking the right epimanikion, the first deacon says to the bishop:

1ˢᵗ Deacon:	Bless, master, the holy epimanikion. Let us pray to the Lord. Lord, have mercy.

The bishop blesses the epimanikion and kisses it, as the deacons put it on him, saying:

1ˢᵗ Deacon:	Thy right hand, O Lord, is glorified in strength; thy right hand, O Lord, hath shattered thine enemies, and in the multitude of thy glory hast thou crushed thine adversaries.
2ⁿᵈ Deacon:	Always, now and ever, and unto ages of ages. Amen.

Taking the left epimanikion, the first deacon says to the bishop:

1ˢᵗ Deacon:	Bless, master, the holy epimanikion. Let us pray to the Lord. Lord, have mercy.

The bishop blesses the epimanikion and kisses it, as the deacons put it on him, saying:

1st Deacon: His hands have made and fashioned thee; may he give thee understanding and mayest thou learn his commandments.

2nd Deacon: Always, now and ever, and unto ages of ages. Amen.

Taking the epigonation, the first deacon says to the bishop:

1st Deacon: Bless, master, the holy epigonation. Let us pray to the Lord. Lord, have mercy.

The bishop blesses the epigonation and kisses it, as the deacons put it on him, saying:

1st Deacon: Gird thy sword upon thy thigh, O Mighty One, in thy comeliness and they beauty, and proceed prosperously, and be king because of truth and meekness and righteousness; and they right hand shall guide thee wondrously.

2nd Deacon: Always, now and ever, and unto ages of ages. Amen.

Taking the sakkos, the first deacon says to the bishop:

1st Deacon: Bless, master, the holy sakkos. Let us pray to the Lord. Lord, have mercy.

The bishop blesses the sakkos and kisses it, as the deacon puts it on him, saying:

1st Deacon: Thy high priests, O Lord, shall be clothed with righteousness, and thy holy ones shall rejoice with joy.

2nd Deacon: Always, now and ever, and unto ages of ages. Amen.

Taking the omophorion, the first deacon says to the bishop:

1st Deacon: Bless, master, the holy omophorion. Let us pray to the Lord. Lord, have mercy.

The bishop blesses the omophorion and kisses it, as the deacons put it on him, saying:

1st Deacon: When thou didst take upon thy shoulders human nature which had gone astray, O Christ, thou didst bear it to heaven unto thy God and Father.

2nd Deacon: Always, now and ever, and unto ages of ages. Amen.

Taking the pectoral cross, the first deacon says to the bishop:

1st Deacon: Let us pray to the Lord. Lord, have mercy.

The bishop kisses the pectoral cross, and the deacons put it on him, saying:

1st Deacon: Whosoever will come after me, let him deny himself and take up his cross and follow me.

2nd Deacon: Always, now and ever, and unto ages of ages. Amen.

Taking the engolpion, the first deacon says to the bishop:

1st Deacon: Let us pray to the Lord. Lord, have mercy.

The bishop kisses the engolpion, and the deacons put it on him, saying:

1st Deacon: May God create in thee a clean heart, and renew a right spirit within thee.

2nd Deacon: Always, now and ever, and unto ages of ages. Amen.

If the bishop has the dignity of a second engolpion, the first deacon takes the second engolpion and says to the bishop:

1ˢᵗ Deacon: Let us pray to the Lord. Lord, have mercy.

The bishop kisses the second engolpion, and the deacons put it on him, saying:

1ˢᵗ Deacon: Thy heart hath poured forth a good word; thou wilt speak of thy works to the King; thy tongue is the pen of a swiftly writing scribe.

2ⁿᵈ Deacon: Always, now and ever, and unto ages of ages. Amen.

Taking the mitre, the first deacon says to the bishop:

1ˢᵗ Deacon: Let us pray to the Lord. Lord, have mercy.

The bishop kisses the mitre, and the deacons put it on him, saying:

1ˢᵗ Deacon: He has set upon thine head a crown of precious stones; thou didst ask life of him, and he gave thee length of days.

2ⁿᵈ Deacon: Always, now and ever, and unto ages of ages. Amen.

Handing the pateritsa to the bishop and kissing his hand, the first deacon says:

1ˢᵗ Deacon: Let us pray to the Lord. Lord, have mercy.

A scepter of power shall the Lord send thee out of Sion; rule thou in the midst of thine enemies.

2ⁿᵈ Deacon: Always, now and ever, and unto ages of ages. Amen.

The first deacon takes up the trikirion and the second takes up the dikirion. As they stand facing the bishop, the first deacon on his right and the second deacon on his left, the first deacon says:

1ˢᵗ Deacon: Let us pray to the Lord. Lord, have mercy.

The bishop blesses the deacons, and the deacons say:

1st Deacon: Let thy light so shine before men, that they may see thy good works and give glory to thy Father who is in heaven.

2nd Deacon: Always, now and ever, and unto ages of ages. Amen.

The first deacon, followed by the second deacon, kisses the right hand of the bishop.

Endnotes

i. Bishop Basil (Essey), trans., *The Liturgikon* (Englewood, NJ: Antakya Press, 1989), 230–239. Reprinted by permission from Antakya Press.

Appendix D

Glossary

Aer – large liturgical veil that covers the Holy Gifts after their preparation on the prosthesis, is carried in procession at the Great Entrance, and then again covers the Holy Gifts on the Holy Table from the conclusion of the Great Entrance until the recitation of the Symbol of Faith ("Creed")

Analavos – garment which is bestowed upon monastics when they are tonsured to the great schema, adorned with an image of the Holy Cross and symbols of the Passion of Christ

Antimension – rectangular piece of cloth which historically served as a portable Holy Table; in current usage it is unfolded on the Holy Table under the chalice and diskos during the Divine Liturgy and represents the bishop's blessing for the Divine Liturgy to be celebrated on a particular Holy Table

Baptismal robe – floor-length tunic bestowed upon an Orthodox Christian at his baptism

Beautiful Gate (Holy Door) curtain – an embellished curtain which hangs in the Beautiful Gate and is opened and closed according to rubrical directions

Brocade – a fabric woven with an elaborate, decorative design

Chalice veils (potirokalymmata and diskokalymmata; kalymmata set) – liturgical veils that cover the chalice and diskos from the time of their preparation in the *Proskomedia* until they are placed upon the Holy Table at the conclusion of the Great Entrance of the Divine Liturgy

Chlamys (himation) – cloak used in ancient Greece

Clavi – ornamental bands on a *sticharion* or *toga*

Colobium – form of the tunic in which the garment was made from heavier fabric with shortened sleeves; the court dress of Byzantine emperors and empresses

Couching – specific embroidery stitch in which a heavy thread is affixed to the ground cloth by the means of small stitches of thin silk floss; typically the smaller stitches create a distinctive pattern

Dalmatic – form of tunic thought to have been worn by the inhabitants of ancient Dalmatia; currently used as the name for the Western diaconal tunic

Deacon's Door curtains – curtains which adorn the north and south side (deacon's) doors of the iconostasis

Deacon's sticharion – *sticharion* worn by deacon, more ornamented than a basic *sticharion*

Dikerotrikera – collective term for the two-candle and three-candle candelabra which a bishop uses to bestow blessings

Eiliton – historically a linen cloth that was placed under the diskos and chalice on a consecrated Holy Table; presently used to refer to a silk or satin protective cloth that wraps the folded *antimension* and is laid under the *antimension* when unfolded, or a white linen cloth, approximately the same size as the top of the Holy Table, that covers and protects the *endytei*

Endytei (altar cloth) – cloth that covers and adorns the Holy Table

Epanokalymmafchion – Monastic veil worn over a Greek-style *kalymmafchion*

Epigonation (palitsa) – lozenge-shaped vestment piece worn by bishops and some presbyters above the right knee

Epimanikia – cuffs worn upon the wrists by bishops, presbyters and deacons

Epitaphios – embroidered textile that portrays the lifeless body of Christ and is used for Great and Holy Friday and remains on the Holy Table for the 40 days of Pascha; historically derived from the *aer*

Epitaphios Sindon – *epitaphios* with a single figure of the lifeless body of Christ

Epitaphios Threnos – *epitaphios* with a figure of the lifeless body of Christ surrounded by mourning figures

Epitrachelion – scarf of office of the priesthood (worn by both presbyters and bishops); a long, narrow strip of fabric worn around the neck with both ends hanging down the front of the body

Exorason (epanorason, mandorason; Russian: ryasa) – outer cassock worn by bishops, priests, deacons, monastics and chanters

Galloon – decorative banding sewn to the perimeter of most vestments and paraments; also used as additional ornamentation on liturgical garments

Gospel cover – cloth that covers the Gospel on the Holy Table; removed during services

Himation (chlamys) – cloak used in ancient Greece

Kalymmafchion (Russian: kamilavka) – formal hat of Orthodox Christian monastics and clergy

Katasarkion – linen cloth placed upon a Holy Table at its consecration, never after removed; it is the first layer of covering upon the Table, completely overlaid by the *endytei*

Katholikon – principal church of a monastery

Klobuk – Monastic veil worn over a Russian-style *kalymmafchion (kamilavka)*

Kontoraki – shortened form of *exorason* worn by female monastics in combination with a full skirt

Kontorason – abbreviated form of the *exorason*; either in the form of a short coat or a clergy vest

Koukoulion – peaked cowl worn upon the head which descends into lappets, adorned with images of the seraphim, that drape over the shoulders; worn by great-schema monastics in the Russian tradition

Mandyas – sleeveless cloak worn by monastics and bishops

Nabedrennik – award piece for presbyters, restricted to Russian usage; a rectangle of fabric worn upon the right hip

Omophorion – scarf of office of the episcopate; a long strip of fabric worn elaborately draped about the neck and shoulders

Opelchye – embroidered fabric or velvet that is inserted in the top section of a Russian-style, high-back phelonion to provide further ornamentation

Orarion – scarf of office of the diaconate; a long, narrow strip of fabric worn upon the left shoulder and in some cases elaborated by wrapping about the torso

Paenula – a cloak of semi-circular shape used as an outer garment in the ancient world

Pallium – a long rectangular cloak or wrap used in the ancient world

Paramandyas – a fabric square decorated with an image of the Holy Cross that is worn by monastics over the inner cassock and under the outer garment with cords that tie around the body

Paterissa – bishop's pastoral staff

Phelonion – voluminous, cape-like outer garment of the presbyter and, historically, of the bishop

Podea – decorative veil for a particular icon or for an icon stand

Polystavrion – cord with many small crosses plaited into it that is wrapped about the arms and the body as a sort of yoke worn by monastics

Polystavros – checkerwork fabric design featuring a repeated motif of many crosses

Proskynitarion – stand on which to display icons

Proksynitarion cloth – decorative veil that covers a *proskynitarion*

Prothesis table – table on which the bread and wine are prepared for the Divine Liturgy

Sakkos – ornate, short tunic worn as outer garment of the bishop

Skoufaki – diminutive term for a small *skufos*

Skufos (Russian: skufia) – informal hat of Orthodox Christian monastics and clergy

Sticharion – long-sleeved, floor-length tunic which represents the baptismal robe, the most basic of all vestments

Tablion – an embellished textile award piece that was a part of Byzantine male court dress

Tetrapodion – four-legged table used for services on the ambon

Toga – large, elaborate, cloak-like garment worn by citizens of ancient Rome

Toga contabulatum – the form of the *toga picta* in which the toga was folded so that only the eight-inch decorative band (*clavi*) was visible; worn by Roman consuls

Toga picta – ceremonial *toga* which remained in use until at least the 2nd century AD; worn by Roman consuls

Tunic/Tunica/Chiton – see *sticharion*

Tunica talaris – the narrow-sleeved, undergarment version of the tunic

Zone – liturgical belt; worn by bishops and presbyters

Zostikon (anteri, esorason; Russian: podryasnik) – inner cassock, worn by bishops, priests, deacons, monastics and minor clerics

Appendix E

Sketches of Fully Vested Clergy

These images are used with the permission of Fr Maximos of Simonopetra (Nicholas Constas) based upon his original sketches that first appeared in *The Ierotelestikion: A Handbook of Rubrics* by Fr Alkiviadis C. Calivas, Holy Cross Greek Orthodox School of Theology, Brookline, Massachusetts 1984.

Figure 1. Fully vested deacon.

Figure 2. Fully vested priest.

Figure 3. Fully vested bishop.

Bibliography

Anchor Manual of Needlework. Loveland, CO: Interweave Press, 1990.

Ball, Philip. *Bright Earth: Art and the Invention of Color.* New York: Farrar, Straus and Giroux, 2001.

Baynes, N.H., and H. St. L.B. Moss. *Byzantium: An Introduction to East Roman Civilization.* Oxford: Clarendon Press, 1961.

Bechtold, Thomas, and Rita Mussak, editors. *Handbook of Natural Colorants.* Hoboken, NJ: John Wiley & Sons, 2009.

Beckwith, John. *Early Christian and Byzantine Art.* New Haven, CT: Yale University Press, 1986.

Belting, Hans. "An Image and Its Function in the Liturgy: The Man of Sorrows in Byzantium." *Dumbarton Oaks Papers* 34/35 (1980/1981): 1-16.

Braun, Joseph. *Die Liturgische Gewandung im Occident und Orient nach Ursprung und Entwicklung, Verwendung und Symbolik* (*Liturgical Dress in East and West According to Origin and Development, Use and Symbolism*). Freiburg im Breisgau, Germany: Herder, 1907.

Browning, Robert. *Justinian and Theodora.* Santa Barbara, CA: Praeger Publishers, 1971.

Butler Greenfield, Amy. *A Perfect Red.* New York: Harper Perennial, 2006.

Campbell-Harding, Valerie, Jane Lemon, and Kit Pyman. *Goldwork.* Tunbridge Wells, Kent: Search Press, 1995.

Cardon, Dominique. *Natural Dyes*. Paris: Archetype Publications, 2007.

Cavarnos, Constantine. *Byzantine Sacred Art*. Belmont, MA: Institute for Byzantine and Modern Greek Studies, 1985.

———. *Byzantine Thought and Art*. Belmont, MA: Institute for Byzantine and Modern Greek Studies, 2000.

———. *Fine Arts and Tradition*. Belmont, MA: Institute for Byzantine and Modern Greek Studies, 2004.

———. *Plato's Theory of Fine Art*. Belmont, MA: Institute for Byzantine and Modern Greek Studies, 1998.

———. *Spiritual Beauty*. Belmont, MA: Institute for Byzantine and Modern Greek Studies, 2000.

Chenciner, Robert. *Madder Red: A History of Luxury and Trade: Plant Dyes and Pigments in the World of Commerce and Art*. Richmond, UK: Curzon, 2000.

Christie, Archibald. *Pattern Design*. Mineola, NY: Dover Publications, 2011.

Chrysostomos, Archimandrite. *Orthodox Ecclesiastical Dress*. Brookline, MA: Holy Cross Orthodox Press, 1981

Cross, Samuel Hazzard, and Olgerd P. Sherbowitz-Wetzor, translators and editors. *The Russian Primary Chronicle, Laurentian Text*. Cambridge, MA: The Mediaeval Academy of America, 1953.

Curcic, Slobodan, ed. *Architecture as Icon: Perception and Representation of Architecture in Byzantine Art*. New Haven, CT: Yale University Press, 2010. Exhibition catalog.

———. "Late Byzantine Loca Sancta? Some Questions Regarding the Form and Function of Epitaphioi." *The Twilight of Byzantium*. Princeton: Princeton University Press, 1991.

Dalton, O.M. *Byzantine Art and Archaeology*. Mineola, NY: Dover Publications, 1961.

———. *East Christian Art: A Survey of the Monuments*. New York: Hacker Art Books, 1975.

Dearmer, Percy. *The Ornaments of the Ministers*. London: A.R. Mowbray & Co, 1901.

Dehli, Arne. *Treasury of Byzantine Ornament: 255 Motifs from St. Mark's and Ravenna*. Mineola, NY: Dover Publications, 2005.

Dostoevsky, Fyodor, *The Idiot*, Richard Pevear, trans. New York: Vintage, 2003.

Drandakis, N.V. *Ecclesiastical Embroidery at the Monastery of Arkadi*. Kloster Arkadi, Greece: Holy Monastery of Arkadi, 2000.

Duchesne, Louis. McClure, M.L., trans. *Christian Worship: Its Origins and Evolutions*. London: SPCK, 1904. <http://play.google.com/books/reader?id=1oYa63ObuyUC&printsec=frontcover&output=reader&authuser=0&hl=en>, May 25, 2012.

Edmonds, John. *The Mystery of Imperial Purple Dye*. Historic Dye Series No. 7. 2000.

(Essey), Bishop Basil, trans. *The Liturgikon*. Englewood, NJ: Antakaya Press, 1989.

Evans, Helen C., and William D. Wixom, eds. *The Glory of Byzantium: Art and Culture of the Middle Byzantine Era AD 843–1261*. New York: Metropolitan Museum of Art, 1997. Exhibition catalog.

Evdokimov, Paul. *The Art of the Icon*. Redondo Beach, CA: Oakwood Publications, 1990.

Faber, G.A. *Dyeing and Tanning in Classical Antiquity*. Basle, Switzerland: Society of Chemical Industry in Basle, 1938.

Filsinger, Catherine. "A Gift of Russian Vestments." *Bulletin of the City Art Museum of St. Louis* 34.4 (Fall 1949): 54-59.

Flanagan, J.F. "The Origin of the Drawloom Used in the Making of Early Byzantine Silks." *The Burlington Magazine for Connoisseurs* 35.199 (Oct 1919): 167–172.

Flemming, Ernst. *Encyclopedia of Textiles*. New York: Frederick A. Praeger, 1957.

Folk Russian Costume. Moscow: Sovetskaya Rossiya Publishers, 1989.

St Germanos. *On the Divine Liturgy*. Crestwood, NY: St Vladimir's Seminary Press, 1985.

Gonosova, Anna. "The Formation and Sources of Early Byzantine Floral Semis and Floral Diaper Patterns Reexamined." *Dumbarton Oaks Papers* 41 (1987): 227–237.

Harris, Christie, and Moira Johnston. *Figleafing through History: The Dynamics of Dress*. New York: Atheneum, 1971.

Hecht, Ann. *The Art of the Loom: Weaving, Spinning and Dyeing across the World*. New York: Rizzoli, 1989.

Herrin, Judith. *Byzantium: The Surprising Life of a Medieval Empire*. Princeton: Princeton University Press, 2009.

———. *Women in Purple*. Princeton: Princeton University Press, 2004.

Hoefnk de Graaff, Judith H. *The Colorful Past, Origins, Chemistry, and Identification of Natural Dyestuffs*. London: Archetype Publications, 2004.

Houston, Mary G. *Greek, Roman, and Byzantine Costume*. Mineola, NY: Dover Publications, 2011.

Hussey, J.M., ed. *The Cambridge Medieval History, Vol. IV, The Byzantine Empire, Part II: Government, Church and Civilisation*. Cambridge: Cambridge University Press, 1967.

Jacoby, David. "Silk Economics and Cross-Cultural Artistic Interaction: Byzantium, the Muslin World, and the Christian West." *Dumbarton Oaks Papers* 58 (2004): 197–240.

Jensen, Lloyd B. "Royal Purple of Tyre." *Journal of Near Eastern Studies* 22.2 (April 1963): 104–118.

Johnstone, Pauline. *Byzantine Tradition in Church Embroidery*. London: Alec Tiranti, 1967.

———. *A Guide to Greek Island Embroidery*. London: Victoria and Albert Museum, 1972.

Karydis, Christos. *The Orthodox Christian Sakkos: Ecclesiastical Garments Dating from the 15th to the 20th Centuries from the Holy Mountain of Athos*. London: BAR International Series 2172, 2010.

Kassinger, Ruth G. *Sea Snails to Synthetics*. Minneapolis, MN: The Millbrook Press, 2003.

Kitzinger, Ernst. *Byzantine Art in the Making: Main Lines of Stylistic Development in Mediterranean Art, 3rd–7th Centuries*. Cambridge, MA: Harvard University Press, 1977.

Kohler, Carl. *A History of Costume*. Mineola, NY: Dover Publications, 1963.

Kubisch, Natascha, and Pia Anna Seger. *Ornaments: Patterns for Interior Decoration*. Cologne, Germany: Konemann, 2001.

Lassus, Jean. *The Early Christian and Byzantine World*. New York: McGraw-Hill, 1967.

Legg, J.W. *Church Ornaments and Their Civil Antecedents*. San Antonio, TX: Pranava Books, 2009.

———. "Notes on the History of the Liturgical Colors," a paper read before the S. Paul's ecclesiological society. <http://books.google.com/books?id=M74CAAAAQAAJ&dq=j+w+legg+history+of+liturgical+colors&source=gbs_navlinks_s>.

Lethaby, W.R. "Byzantine Silks in London Museums." *The Burlington Magazine for Connoisseurs* 24.129 (Dec 1913): 138–146.

Liddell & Scott. *Greek–English Lexicon*. Oxford: Oxford University Press, 1989.

Lomny, Antonia. *The Art and Craft of Goldwork*. Cameray, Australia: Simon and Schuster Australia, 2004.

Lopez, Robert Sabatino. "Silk Industry in the Byzantine Empire." *Speculum* 20.1 (January 1945): 1–42.

Macalister, R.A.S. *Ecclesiastical Vestments: Their Development and History*. London: Elliot Stock, 1896.

Maguire, E.D., H.P. Maguire, and M.J. Duncan-Flowers, *Art and Holy Powers in the Early Christian House*. Urbana, IL: Krannert Art Museum, 1989. Exhibition catalog.

Maguire, Eunice D. *Weavings from Roman, Byzantine, and Islamic Egypt: The Rich Life and the Dance*. Urbana, IL: Krannert Art Museum, 1999.

Maguire, Henry. "Garments Pleasing to God: The Significance of Domestic Textile Designs in the Early Byzantine Period." *Dumbarton Oaks Papers* 44 (1990): 215–224.

———. *The Icons of Their Bodies: Saints and Their Images in Byzantium*. Princeton: Princeton University Press, 1996.

Maguire, Henry, ed. *Byzantine Court Culture from 829 to 1204*. Cambridge, MA: Harvard University Press, 1997.

Majeska, George P. "Notes on the Archeology of St. Sophia at Constantinople: The Green Marble Bands on the Floor." *Dumbarton Oaks Papers* 32 (1978): 299–308.

Mango, Cyril. *The Art of the Byzantine Empire 312–1453*. Toronto: University of Toronto Press, 1986.

———. *The Oxford History of Byzantium*. Oxford: Oxford University Press, 2002.

Marchese, Ronald T., and Marlene R. Breu. *Splendor and Pageantry: Textile Treasures from the Armenian Orthodox Churches of Istanbul*. Eden, SC: Nettleberry Publications, 2010.

Marriott, Rev. Wharton. *Vestiarium Christianum, The Origin and Gradual Development of the Dress of the Holy Ministry in the Church*. London: Rivingtons, 1868.

Mathew, Gervase. *Byzantine Aesthetics*. London: John Murray, 1963.

Mathewes-Green, Frederica. "Rublev's Old Testament Trinity." <http://www.frederica.com/writings/rublevs-old-testament-trinity.html>, April 18, 2013.

Mayo, Janet. *A History of Ecclesiastical Dress*. London: B.T. Batsford, Ltd, 1984.

Medieval Pictorial Embroidery: Byzantium, Balkans, Russia. Moscow: Catalogue of the Exhibition XVIIIth International Congress of Byzantinists, 1991.

Millet, Gabriel. *Broderies religieuses de style Byzantin*. Paris, 1939.

Muthesius, Anna. "The Byzantine Silk Industry: Lopez and Beyond." *Journal of Medieval History* 19 (1993): 1–67.

———. *Byzantine Silk Weaving: AD 400 to AD 1200*. Vienna: Fassbaender, 1997.

———. *Studies in Byzantine, Islamic and Near Eastern Silk Weaving*. London: Pindar Press, 2008.

———. *Studies in Silk in Byzantium*. London: Pindar Press, 2004.

Nelson, Robert S., and Kristen M. Collins. *Holy Image, Hallowed Ground: Icons from Sinai*. Los Angeles: Getty Publications, 2006.

Norris, Herbert. *Church Vestments: Their Origins and Development*. New York: Dutton & Co, 1950.

O'Grady, Patrick, and Michel Najim. *The Liturgical Books of the Holy Orthodox-Catholic Church*. Vol. 1, The Scriptural Books. Publication forthcoming.

Papas, Tano. *Studien zur Geschichte der Meßgewänder im byzantinischen Ritus* (*Studies on the History of Liturgical Dress in the Byzantine Rite*). Munich: Institut für Byzantinistik und Neugriechische Philologie, 1965.

Paul the Silentiary. *Descriptio Sanctae Sophiae*. Excerpted in Cyril Mango. *The Art of the Byzantine Empire 312–1453*. Toronto: University of Toronto Press, 1986.

Peirce, Hayford, and Royall Tyler. "The Prague Rider-Silk and the Persian-Byzantine Problem." *The Burlington Magazine for Connoisseurs* 68.398 (May 1936): 213–224.

Piltz, Elisabeth. *From Constantine the Great to Kandinsky: Studies in Byzantine and Post-Byzantine Art and Architecture.* Oxford: Archaeopress, 2007.

The Protoevangelion of James. London: William Hone, 1820.

Rahal, Joseph, ed. *The Services of Great and Holy Week and Pascha.* Englewood, NJ: Antakya Press, 2006.

Rice, David Talbot. *Art of the Byzantine Era.* New York: Frederick A. Praeger, 1963.

Riefstahl, Rudolf M. "Greek Orthodox Vestments and Ecclesiastical Fabrics." *The Art Bulletin* 14.4 (Dec 1932): 359–373.

Robinson, N.F. *Monasticism in the Orthodox Churches.* London: Cope and Fenwick, 1916.

Romanoff, H.C. *Rites and Customs of the Greco-Russian Church.* London: Rivingtons, 1869.

Runciman, Steven. *Byzantine Civilization.* London: E. Arnold, 1966.

Sandberg, Gosta. Edith M. Matteson, trans. *The Red Dyes: Cochineal, Madder, and Murex Purple: A World Tour of Textile Techniques.* Asheville, NC: Lark Books, 1997.

Schnabel, Nikodemus C. *Die liturgischen Gewänder und Insignien des Diakons, Presbyters und Bischofs in den Kirchen des Byzantinischen Ritus* (*Liturgical Dress and Insignia of the Deacon, Priest and Bishop in the Churches of the Byzantine Rite*). Würzburg: Echter Verlag, 2008.

Sophocles, E.A. *Greek Lexicon of the Roman and Byzantine Periods.* New York: Charles Scribner's Sons, 1900.

Stephenson, Paul, ed. *The Byzantine World.* Oxford: Routledge, 2010.

Sturm, Paivi, ed. *From Chaos to a Collection: The Orthodox Church Museum of Finland.* Kuopio, Finland: Suomen Ortodoksinen Kirkkomuseo, 2008.

Sucrow, Alexandra. *Griechische und Russische Goldstickereien des Ikonen-Museums Recklinghausen* (*Greek and Russian Gold Embroideries of the Icon Museum of Recklinghausen*). Recklinghausen: Museen der Stadt Recklinghausen, 1995.

Taft, Robert. *The Great Entrance: A History of the Transfer of Gifts and other Pre-anaphoral Rites of the Liturgy of St. John Chrysostom*. Rome: Pontificium Institutum Studiorum Orientalium, 1978.

———. "The Liturgy of the Great Church: An Initial Synthesis of Structure and Interpretation on the Eve of Iconoclasm." *Dumbarton Oaks Papers* 34/35 (1980/1981): 45–75.

Theocharis, Maria. *Ekklesiastika Chrysokenteta* (Ecclesiastical gold embroideries). Athens: Apostolike Diakonia tes Ekklesias tes Hellados, 1986.

Townsend, Gertrude. "Some Greek Liturgical Embroideries." *Bulletin of the Museum of Fine Arts* 42.250 (Dec. 1944): 73–81

Trenkle, Elisabeth. *Liturgische Geräte und Gewänder der Ostkirche* (*Liturgical Implements and Vestments of the Eastern Church*). Munich: Slavisches Institut, 1962.

Trilling, James. *The Roman Heritage: Textiles from Egypt and the Eastern Mediterranean 300 to 600 AD*. Washington, DC: The Textile Museum, 1982.

Tyack, George S. *Historical Dress of the Clergy*. San Antonio, TX: Pranava Books, 2008.

Underhill, Gertrude. "An Eleventh-Century Mesopotamian Embroidery." *The Bulletin of the Cleveland Museum of Art* 26.1 (Jan 1939): 4–5.

———. "A Tenth-Century Byzantine Silk from Antioch." *The Bulletin of the Cleveland Museum of Art* 29.1 (Jan 1942): 6–7.

Vaboulis, T. *Byzantine Decorative Art*. Athens: Astir Publishing Company, 1992.

Velimirovic, St Nikolai, *The Prologue of Ohrid*. Alhambra, CA: Serbian Orthodox Diocese of Western America, 2002.

Vlachopoulou-Karabina, Eleni. *Holy Monastery of Iveron Gold Embroideries*. Mount Athos: Holy Monastery of Iveron, 1998.

Von Simson, Otto G. *Sacred Fortress: Byzantine Art and Statecraft in Ravenna*. Princeton: Princeton University Press, 1987.

Walter, Christopher. *Art and Ritual of the Byzantine Church*. London: Variorum Publications Ltd, 1982.

Weibel, Adele. *Two Thousand Years of Textiles*. New York: Pantheon Books, 1952.

Woodin, Warren. "Late Byzantine Embroidered Vestments and the Iconography of Sacerdotal Power." Doctoral dissertation. Urbana, IL: *University of Illinois at Urbana-Champaign*, April 2002.

———. *The Embodied Icon: Liturgical Vestments and Sacramental Power in Byzantium*. Oxford: Oxford University Press, 2012.

Xinru, Liu. "Silks and Religions in Eurasia, c. AD 600–1200." *Journal of World History* 6.1 (Spring 1995): 25–48.

Index

Aer, 128, 135, 145-149, 258, 267-268
Agia Sophia, 25, 129-130, 138, 140, 165
Altar server's robe, 85-86, 247
Analavos, 94, 122-124, 267
Antimension, 128, 135-136, 143-144, 148, 150, 267-268

Baptismal robe, 81-83, 87, 92, 267, 271
Bishops' vestments (also bishop's vestments, vestments of the bishop), 75, 103, 107
Byzantine emperors, 52, 209, 268
Byzantine Empire, 33, 69, 78, 88, 130, 164, 168, 178, 194, 196, 206, 208, 240-241, 280-283
Byzantine silk industry, 16, 206, 210-211, 222, 283

Candle ribbons, 107
Chiton, 48, 60, 110, 138, 271
Clamys, 49
Clavi (sing. *clavus*), 50-51, 53-56, 61-62, 268, 271
Colobium, 48, 52-55, 61, 63, 76, 87, 104, 268
Communion cloth, 147, 248
Constantine, 16-17, 40, 56-57, 60, 68, 73, 174, 206, 278, 284
Cuffs, 72-73, 85, 87, 90, 92-93, 113, 251, 268; see also *epimanikia*

Dalmatic, 52, 54, 268
Deacon's vestments, 90-91, 229
Decorative veils, 128, 133, 152-153, 199
Dura Europos, 128-130, 137

Eiliton, 128, 135, 143-144, 268
Endytei, 134, 137, 143-144, 268-269
Epanokalymmafchion, 121, 268

Epigonation (pl. *epigonatia*), 73-75, 100-101, 103, 108, 125, 149, 202, 260, 263, 268

Epimanikia, 72-73, 75-76, 90, 92-93, 95, 100-101, 103, 108, 125, 149, 202, 257, 268; see also *cuffs*

Epitaphios (pl. *epitaphioi*), 128, 135-136, 145, 148-152, 161, 203, 214, 244, 250, 268-269

Epitaphios sindon, 149, 269

Epitaphios threnos, 136, 149, 269

Epitrachelion (pl. *epitrachelia*), 64, 67-68, 75-76, 92, 94-96, 100-103, 105, 108-109, 125, 172, 259, 261, 269

Exorason, 15, 92, 101-102, 110, 114-119, 122, 251, 269

Gold-work, 149, 151, 161-163
Gospel cover, 135, 144, 269
Great omophorion, 70, 76, 105-106, 108
Himation, 49-50, 52, 267, 269

Iconostasion (*iconostasis*), 121, 134, 153, 156, 158, 243, 268
Isaac Newton, 166

Justinian, 56-57, 59-61, 69, 73, 77, 130, 179, 206-207, 277

Kalymmafchion, 119-122, 268-269
Kamilavka, 120-121, 269
Katasarkion, 134-135, 137, 141, 143, 269
Klobuk, 120, 269
Kontorason, 111, 117-119, 269
Koukoulion, 123, 269

Leukos, 171-173, 191
Liturgical veils, 128, 145, 152, 267

Mandorason, 110, 115, 269
Mandyas, 107-109, 112, 115, 122, 270

Nabedrennik, 74, 100-101, 103, 125, 270

Omophorion, 62-64, 68, 70-71, 73, 75-76, 104-106, 108-109, 125, 264, 270
Opelchye, 97, 270
Orarion (pl. *oraria*), 60, 64-67, 84-86, 88-90, 92, 105, 114, 125, 257-258, 270

Paenula, 52-55, 62, 67, 96, 205, 270
Pallium, 52, 54-55, 64-70, 73, 270
Paludamentum, 73
Paramandyas, 122-123, 270
Paterissa, 107-108, 270
Phelonion (pl. *phelonia*), 60, 62-64, 75-76, 92, 96-102, 108, 113-114, 125, 172, 192-193, 205, 249, 260, 270
Podea, 128, 153-155, 157, 270
Podryasnik, 109-113, 115, 118, 271
Polystavrion, 122-123, 270
Polystavros, 75, 96, 226-227, 270
Porphyra, 178, 181-182, 184
Priest's vestments, 146
Proskynitarion, 133, 270

Ravenna, 4, 25, 42, 47, 55, 60, 78, 140, 179, 221, 231, 233, 238, 279, 286
Ryasa, 110, 114-116, 119, 269

Sakkos (pl. *sakkoi*), 48, 52, 61, 63, 75-76, 103-105, 108, 125, 263, 271, 281
San Vitale, 42, 47, 55, 60, 63, 73, 140
Sant' Apollinare in Classe, 42, 60, 62-63, 66, 73
Sant' Apollinare nuovo, 55
Scarf of office, 64-65, 67, 88, 94, 269-270
Schema, 26, 94, 123, 267, 269
Skoufaki, 120, 271
Skufos, 119-122, 271
Small omophorion, 70, 76, 105, 108-109
Sponge, 136, 148
St Athanasius the Great, 28
St Erasmus, 35-36
St Germanos, 27, 40, 72, 78, 107, 132, 280
St John Chrysostom, 32-33, 58, 60, 67, 245
St John of Damascus, 27, 30, 32, 36, 39-40, 167, 245
St Symeon of Thessaloniki, 75
Sticharion, 43, 47, 52, 60-65, 75-76, 79, 81, 83-85, 87-88, 90, 92-95, 100-101, 103-104, 108, 114, 125, 249, 257-258, 261, 268, 271

Tablion (pl. *tablia*), 74, 108, 271
Theodosian Code, 59, 61, 67, 70
Theosis, 23, 36
Toga, 50-55, 64, 68-71, 105-106, 204, 268, 271

Toga candida, 51
Toga contabulata, 53, 69, 71, 105-106
Tunic (also *tunica*), 43-45, 47-50, 52-55, 60-61, 72-73, 81, 83, 87, 104, 111-112, 204, 216, 227, 267-268, 271
Tunica talaris, 54, 61, 73, 81, 111, 271
Tyrian purple, 139, 177-184, 186-188, 190, 212

Venice, 179, 213, 224-226
Vinework, 74, 95, 100, 150-151, 218

William Perkin, 188-189

Zone, 72, 75, 92-93, 95-96, 100-101, 103, 108, 125, 259, 262, 271
Zostikon, 109-115, 117-119, 271